Beyond Abolition

Inventions Black Philosophy, Politics, Aesthetics

Edited by David Marriott

Beyond Abolition

"Self-Lynching" and Its Afterlife

Linette Eunjoo Park

Stanford University Press
Stanford, California

Stanford University Press
Stanford, California

Library of Congress Cataloging-in-Publication Data
Names: Park, Linette Eunjoo author
Title: Beyond abolition : "self-lynching" and its afterlife / Linette Eunjoo Park.
Other titles: Inventions (Series)
Description: Stanford, California : Stanford University Press, 2026. | Series: Inventions: black philosophy, politics, aesthetics | Includes bibliographical references and index.
Identifiers: LCCN 2026019182 (print) | LCCN 2026019183 (ebook) | ISBN 9781503630543 cloth | ISBN 9781503648357 paperback | ISBN 9781503648364 ebook
Subjects: LCSH: African Americans—Legal status, laws, etc. | Lynching—Law and legislation—United States | Anti-lynching movements—United States | Racism in law enforcement—United States | Racism against Black people—Philosophy | Critical race theory
Classification: LCC KF4757 .P37 2026 (print) | LCC KF4757 (ebook)
LC record available at https://lccn.loc.gov/2026019182
LC ebook record available at https://lccn.loc.gov/2026019183

Cover design: Bob Aufuldish / Aufuldish & Warinner

Cover art: Melvin Edwards (American, 1937–2026), *Takawira - J*, 1989; welded steel, 14 × 10 × 9 in; Brooklyn Museum, gift of Edward A. Bragaline, by exchange, 1990.104; © 2026 Melvin Edwards / Artists Rights Society (ARS), New York; photograph: Brooklyn Museum

The authorized representative in the EU for product safety and compliance is: Mare Nostrum Group B.V. | Doelen 72 | 4831 GR Breda | The Netherlands | Email address: gpsr@mare-nostrum.co.uk | KVK chamber of commerce number: 96249943

Printed and bound by CPI Group (UK) Ltd, Croydon, CR0 4YY

For Michael Cho

Contents

Acknowledgments

This book is the culmination of many hands, beginning with Erica Wetter and Caroline McKusick at Stanford University Press. I am deeply indebted to their patience and enthusiasm, which sustained me throughout the writing process.

I owe a singular debt of gratitude to David Marriott. His critical guidance, defining scholarship, and the work of his Invention Series have been a distinguished intellectual force. All served as the essential catalyst of my thinking, writing, and self-reflexive critique, ensuring the life of this project. Beyond this, David consistently modeled the highest level of rigor and precision—an inimitable quality through the critical unraveling that stems from philosophy and poetry, writing and reading. As he once told me, finding one's own voice on the page can initially feel quite harrowing, "as if running with one's eyes closed," yet can be uniquely liberating, in ways one cannot even imagine. This dialectical, often paradoxical relationship between an unsparing critical standard and poetic sensibility—between the absolute demands of writing and the infinite—remains the enduring signature of his profound influence.

I reserve a special measure of thanks for Kate Marshall, who first introduced me to the Press and believed in this project's initial vision. Without her, this book would not have found its critical home.

Chapters 3 and 5 represent a significant departure from preliminary inquiries and materials that appeared in *Theory & Event* (2019) and *Diacritics* (2021). Those initial explorations have been substantially reimagined and conceptually reframed for this book, emerging here as distinct works that respond to the manuscript's broader theoretical arc and arrive at a final form that constitutes new work.

The two anonymous readers' reports were essential in the final developments of this manuscript. The project could have not reached its final form without their insightful and critical conversations.

This project received support from several fellowships and grants over the years (in no particular order): the University of California-New Center for Psychoanalysis Interdisciplinary Hayman Fellowship; the Psychoanalytic Fellowship with the Psychoanalytic Center of Philadelphia; the Scholarly Writing and Publishing Fund (2022 and 2025) with the Center for Faculty Excellence and Development at Emory University; and the Emerging Scholars with the Political Theology Network. The Michael and Stacey Kohen Endowed Fellowship in Critical Theory and the University of California Humanities Research Institute Award enabled important archival work with the National Association for the Advancement of Colored People (NAACP) anti-lynching papers with the Newspapers and Microforms Library at Doe Library at the University of California, Berkeley. During my time conducting archival research at UC Berkeley, I am grateful for conversations with and assistance by: Dean Rowan, Rebecca Darby-Williams, Marianne Constable, and Christopher Tomlins.

At the University of California, Irvine, my enduring gratitude goes to: Jared Sexton, Frank Wilderson, Rei Terada, and Keramet Reiter. There is an expression in Korean: 스승의 그림자도 밟지 않는다 (One does not even step on a teacher's shadow). It was a unique privilege to have Jared Sexton as a radically different kind of advisor and mentor. Far from establishing a relationship where knowledge had to be simply mastered, Jared cultivated a critical space defined by shared intellectual risk, relentless theoretical questioning, and the necessary edge that comes with excavating underlying antagonisms. In this sense, he was a true first teacher, insisting that the real work of critical thought begins precisely where mastery ends, resolutely opposing the moral critique of stepping on a teacher's shadow. More centrally, he pushed me to inquire into the very constitutions of the shadow, examining its ever-shifting boundaries, their impermanence as an extension of the conceptual limits of thought. This extension on foundational inquiry was, itself, a gift of intellectual generosity that remains unmatched. Frank Wilderson met this theoretical incision at every turn. His guidance demonstrated a relentless type of analysis, achieving full parity with the strenuous effort demanded by the material itself. He left me with two indelible insights. First, the primacy of creative and political commitment. To neglect art and poetry in one's life, he revealed, is to lose sight of these commitments, and, indeed, oneself—a severance where theory becomes a hollow, formal abstraction divorced from its imaginative source, which is the ultimate abolition of the self. Second, he taught the crucial distinction between the academic and the intellectual: that is, there are thousands of academics, but few intellectuals, and thus, ethical clarity is the true measure of scholarly contribution. Rei Terada instilled in me the understanding that critical force often arises from apparent retreat. She demonstrated that this is, in fact, not a withdrawal, but a necessity that allows one to bring the crystallization of aesthetics into vivid focus. Her constant invitation to consider the fundamental structures and conceptual limits of theory affirmed that difficulty itself is often the clearest signal of necessary insight. I offer my sincerest thanks to Keramet Reiter for her continuous support and guidance through the Law and Society Emphasis and for providing a crucial lens to navigate the interdisciplinary landscape of philosophy of law.

The Thurgood Marshall Fellowship in the Department of African and African American Studies at Dartmouth College was pivotal in shaping the early direction of this book. My gratitude extends to the faculty, fellows, and staff present during my time there: Charlotte Bacon, Timothy Baker, Sonu Bedi, Vaughn A. Booker, Veronika Fuechtner, Rashauna Johnson, Azeen Khan, Trica Keaton, Lisa Meehan, Donald Pease, Israel Reyes, and Jesse Shipley. I am particularly indebted to Ayo Coly, whose support and generosity extended well beyond the fellowship. My warmest thanks go to Evelyn Soto, who diligently met with me nearly every day, ensuring no time was squandered in the critical act of writing, and to Derek Woods, who encouraged me to pursue aspects of this project in other forms, including a special issue with *Diacritics*.

At Emory University, faculty, staff, and students have impacted and provided an opportunity for the development of this project. My sincerest thanks and appreciation are offered to Axelle Karera and Calvin Warren for their initial discussions and comments on early drafts of Chapter 2. A special thanks to Calvin, whose virtual presence provided a constant source of both intellectual and professional guidance in navigating the university landscape. I greatly respect his time mentoring students in the Mellon Mays Undergraduate Fellowship Program; I was personally enriched by working with the program's fellows, specifically my advisees, Amal Ali and Mckayla Morrison. Likewise, a heartfelt acknowledgment goes to Jada Brown, Jordan Watson, and Treasure Welle who sparked and sustained enthusiastic engagement in and outside of the classroom. All provided the opportunity to think and read with a fresh mind—a gift that I do not take for granted. I thank the Department of Women's, Gender, and Sexuality Studies, specifically Falguni Sheth, for the invitation to present Chapter 4 at a research seminar. There, the chapter benefited from the questions and discussions posed by faculty and students. I am grateful to Saffy Carson for her research assistance that brought to light important archival details for the court cases presented in Chapter 3. At Emory Libraries, I thank John Morgenstein for his assistance in the very last stages of finalizing this manuscript. I am indebted to Erica Bruchko, who provided immeasurable guidance and support for the archival research necessary for this book. Her fastidious archival expertise has been invaluable. Carol Anderson, Geoff Bennington, Benjamin Brewer, Matthew Chin, Shanya Cordis, Michelle Gordon, Timothy Holland, Lynne Huffer, John Lysaker, Elissa Marder, Ronald Mendoza-de Jesús, Dianne Stewart, and Elizabeth Wilson have been beyond gracious in offering intellectual and professional guidance. With Elissa, I remain thankful for her sustained generosity, unsparing intellectual precision, and support beyond the institution. I am also grateful for Geoff's unique intellectual spirit and for his invitation to edit a special issue on blackness, philosophy, and crisis with the *Oxford Literary Review*—an engagement that, in turn, imbued parts of this manuscript with a deepened valence. My appreciation goes to the leadership team of the Psychoanalytic Studies Program (Elissa Marder, Elizabeth Wilson, and Timothy Holland) for their camaraderie and maintaining such a vibrant and essential intellectual space. Significant thanks goes to Elizabeth Wilson for her professional mentorship and our intellectual conversations amid the shifting titles of academic life.

I thank the Fox Center for Humanistic Inquiry, and Carla Freeman and Mae Velloso-Lysons there, for the Major Works in Review Grant. This grant provided the occasion for a trenchant review from Lee Edelman, to whom I express my most profound gratitude. The manuscript benefited incalculably from both his unsparing comments and detailed inquiries, which demanded an altogether new level of theoretical precision and pushed the work toward its necessary limits—that point of the *real* where the symbolic falters and a valence of desire for the project comes to the surface.

I thank the Tall Trees Society, a work-in-progress seminar organized by David Marriott. Chapter 4 gained significantly from—and was fundamentally reshaped by—the collective insights of those present: Amal Ali, Rizvana Bradley, Scholastique Iradukunda, Jaeden Johnson, Gabriela Puche, and Sara-Maria Sorentino.

From conferences and collaborations to moments of providential support, I thank the following colleagues and scholars for their critical engagement, insights, and generosity (I apologize for any inadvertent omission): Franco Barichesi, Robert Bernasconi, Nicholas Brady, Daniel Butler, Steven Canals, Jamie Chan, Arne De Boever, Patrice Douglass, Omnia El Shakry, Anthony Paul Farley, Jay Garcia, Sheldon George, Nathan Gorelick, Erin Grey, Derek Hook, Alírio Karina, April Kim, Dylan Lackey, Vicky Lebeau, James Martel, Jordan Taliha McDonald, Robert Mesiter, William Mosley, Joi Orr, Tyrone Palmer, Anandi Rao, Rahul Ranjan, Dianne Rubenstein, AbdouMaliq Simone, Dorothy Stringer, Mario Telò, Delio Vasquez, Sigrid Weigel, Michael West, and Amy Wood. A special note of appreciation and respect goes to Douglas Kearney, who was one of the project's very first readers over fifteen years ago, and whose poetic eye provided a critical backbone that has remained since.

The manuscript benefited from an irreplicable group of critical readers: Sara-Maria Sorentino has engaged with at least one version of nearly every chapter that follows. Her humor and depth of erudition (and her formidable command of Marxist critique) provided the best kind of dialectical friction, opening up the possibility of knowledge where I saw none.

Erin Trapp worked with the very earliest versions of several chapters of this manuscript. Providing foundational insight, her reading left no stone unturned, possessing that rare analytical patience that allows the subtle unknotting of a text to take place.

In Prathna Lor, I found a reader and friend who did not simply observe the work, but dwelled within its questions until they yielded unforeseen directions. By holding the tension between poetic intuition and analytic rigor, Prathna transformed the solitary labor of composition into the dialogic experience of the text. Indeed, Prathna both read and listened to several iterations of chapters, offering extensive inquiries and traces to be developed, and thus gifting the book a crucial insight into the very question of reading—a gesture only a poet and analytic thinker together could provide.

My deepest gratitude goes to Jaeden Johnson for undertaking a meticulous reading of the entire manuscript at its near final stage. As one of the manuscript's sharpest readers, his searching comments compelled me to refine and clarify the argument's foundational premises and deconstructive logic. Most importantly, his interlocution pushed the book to elevate the imperative of "un-setting critique," illuminating the text's most crucial theoretical demands and revealing its highest (im)possibilities.

A profound appreciation is reserved for Rizvana Bradley, an incisive and capacious interlocutor whose generosity framed our unexpected exchanges. These encounters served as timely and essential flashpoints, illuminating the conceptual abyss and exposing the limits and fractures where aesthetics meet their racialized underpinnings. Such rigorous engagement gave breath to the book's theoretical ambition and sharpened its intellectual clarity; in the process, these dialogues set a definitive benchmark for the stakes of black critical theory.

Hannah Miller has served as the book's most scrupulous, longest, and generous reader, for which a singular gratitude is owed. Above all, her editorial engagement exceeded any expectations for what is possible through such critical exchanges. Her skills not only allowed the prose to take on its own life—by pushing my thinking and writing to their most rigorous articulation—but also provided the critical distance necessary for the book's core arguments to fully emerge. Her insights functioned as the perfect parallax, allowing me to see the conceptual terrain with a clarity my own proximity had obscured. It was, in fact, nothing short of an analytic event that revealed what the manuscript could become and was driven to articulate.

To Mali Collins and Hans Kuzmich, for their activism and friendship; our necessary intellectual detours and shared critical perspective remain a sustained source of clarity and the brickwork for ethical endurance. And to Ella Lebeau, whose friendship has served as a cornerstone and a source of constant joy and brilliance—grounding the intellectual work in the vital space of everyday life.

To the three individuals who have shaped my mind and its possibilities the most: my sister, for introducing me to the art of plunging into a text and for the abiding lesson that writing is never finished, and yet can always be more exact; my brother, who models a lightness that comes from unparalleled discipline; and my mother, who has been a constant presence, granting the wisdom—the anti-philosophy—to understand life's flux and contradictions, and the profound grace of impermanence.

The deepest integrity of this book's final expression belongs to my partner. Its completion was made possible by the sustained intellectual space of our shared time—a true constellation in which those "stars, densely made and compacted and burning with dark potentialities, often get misrecognized." Thank you for this tether, for the gravitas of shared imperceptible matter, and for constantly cutting through the illusory visions that mask themselves as radical promise.

[illegible]

Introduction

Arrests of "Self-Lynching"

On August 29, 2015, Jasmine Richards Abdullah, one of the main organizers with Black Lives Matter in Pasadena, California, was sentenced to ninety days in jail and three years of probation based on the accusation that she had attempted to "de-arrest" someone during a peaceful protest.[1] Richards Abdullah was arrested on the charge of "felony lynching." In the same year, Maile Hampton was also arrested on charges of "lynching" after endeavoring to pull a fellow protester from the hands of the police during a peaceful demonstration. Hampton, who believes that she was targeted by the police due to her active involvement with Black Lives Matter and the Act Now to Stop War and End Racism coalition, concurred that she had interacted with individual police officers, but urged the public to ask questions as to how the court would proceed in interpreting the charges of the arrest.[2] These contemporary arrests for "felony lynching" are permitted under California Penal Code §405a and 405b, which define "lynching" as the "taking of a person from the lawful custody of a peace officer." The accusation that Richards Abdullah and Hampton attempted to "de-arrest" someone who was held in police custody during a peaceful demonstration signals something more than contortions in the interpretation of the law, and racial antiblack abuses of police power. The startling arrests, which attempted to claim the unlikely incident of a nonviolent protester lynching themselves as a way to circumvent the limited reach of law enforcement, also point to a repetition of displacements that systematically enable the reinterpretation of the penal code, whose original intent was to establish anti-lynching legislation. What is more, this transformation from anti-lynching to "self-lynching," which allowed the courts and law enforcement to place the stress on the act of attempting to de-arrest oneself in the latter half of the twentieth century, suggests that blackness functions as an irredeemable aporia demanding this translation, existing as the constitutive void that enables the very traces in which (anti)blackness is perceptible.[3] Rather than suggesting a transcendental essence or telos of blackness, such a recursive translation reveals a structural psychical dynamic operating within the aporia of the non-being of blackness.

Only after Hampton and Richards Abdullah's arrests in 2015 on charges of "lynching," explicit attention was directed at the egregious (ab)use of the word "lynching" in the context of the historical memory of antiblack lynching.[4] Almost immediately after the arrests, Governor Jerry Brown approved the removal of the word "lynching" from state law.[5] Brown's removal of the term, from a cursory view, might suggest a symbolic reparative gesture that acknowledges the racial terror accompanying the term, practice, and experience of lynching. Despite this delayed correction of the racially charged term, the silence that allowed the word "lynching" to remain inscribed for so long is telling. The removal of the term from written law also stops short of acknowledging racial guilt and fails to signal a correction of conceptual error. Indeed, such a failure of nomenclature exposes the limits of a legal representation that would claim to offer a just interpretation. Instead, the expungement of the term functions to uphold the law's racist reasoning under a renewed liberal veneer. In its evasiveness, the removal of the term "lynching" from the legal text mirrors the conceptual charge of "self-lynching." That is, the dissimulation reinforces the attempt to eliminate any reference to blackness and the racial horrors of lynching, in order to fortify the presence of law, sovereignty, and lynch law. What becomes clear is that "lynching" is never a neutral concept; rather, it remains an expression of white sovereignty or truth. Yet, the removal itself also demonstrates that the term was already conceptually self-referential, requiring blackness neither to possess meaning nor to serve as a referent, but rather as the structural necessary non-referent—the constitutive void—whose foreclosure anchors the symbolic presence of law and white truth. Blackness, then, functions as the anti-referent.

The dichotomy between silence and utterability, erasure and the written law resonates with Drucilla Cornell's critique of the dangers and philosophical difficulties posed by an essentialism of differences within normative jurisprudence. Following the work of Jean-François Lyotard through a feminist lens, she observes, "As Lyotard reminds us, 'injustice is the crime combined with the perpetuation of silence that erases it.' Injustice is itself material, in that harm happens. But it becomes known as injustice in the naming."[6] Jared Sexton captures this dynamic when he describes the white mythology that disavows its origin in theft, thus creating "the crime and its alibi at once"—a structure of illegibility.[7] Jerry Brown's removal of the word "lynching" from the legal framework, examined through the lens of Cornell's work on legal silences, reveals a calculated political chronology. Such a timeline explicitly binds the rewriting of the law—occurring only after the arrest of nonviolent black women protesters—to the persistent harm that legal language perpetuates. Cornell, however, envisions representation as possible within law: "An abuse cannot be fought until it is understood as an abuse . . . The name gave the crime a legal 'reality.'"[8] In contrast, the negation of the term "lynching" does not give rise to a new legal reality; it does not present or produce a new legal representation that would procure an understanding of the past legal and present quotidian abuses attached to the word. This failure to produce such a reality stems not from an inversion of Cornell's argument about the possibility of legal reinterpretation; on the contrary, Brown's removal of the word "lynching" only affirms the enduring impossibility of containing its violence, including its material implications, psychical intrusions, and lethal practices. The mere deletion of the term fails to reckon with the pre-judgment inherent in the word's original use and the organizing principles that enabled the arrests under the charge of "felony lynching" in the first instance. The expungement of "lynching" from legal texts reveals the mechanisms of a dream-work which keeps intact the power relations of these institutional arrangements. Even against the façade of a rhetorical reconfiguration, power relations remain undisturbed and sustain the violence of "self-lynching" as a latent dynamic. Such persistence suggests, I argue, that the legal form is fundamentally incapable of existing without antiblackness; that is, without (anti)blackness as the navel of the dream.

We can understand how "conventional definitions of lynching, virtually without exception, either presuppose or expressly draw a sharp line of demarcation between violence inflicted in the name of the law and that which stands outside or of the law (the extralegal and the illegal respectively)."[9] Consequently, the state's definition or removal of the term "lynching" only perpetuates the illusion of reconciliation and reform while displacing the actual horrors of lynching from the law's historicity. Any expression of the state's racial guilt is, therefore, not an attempt to undo a mere linguistic error. It serves, instead, as an acknowledgment of the state's own formative role in shaping racial terror. Timothy Kaufman-Osborn has explained how the limitations of state reform coeval with the dichotomization of lawful and unlawful definitions of lynching. He writes:

> As one would expect in a criminal code, much the same bifurcation was implicit in the antilynching statutes passed by various states during the late nineteenth and early twentieth centuries . . . Lynching, according to each of these definitions, is construed as a paradigmatic instance of the extralegal or illegal, which, in turn, is typically taken to imply that the aim of reform is to secure state control over the exercise of such unauthorized violence and so bring this criminal practice to a halt.
>
> Such definitions are of considerable utility to those who wish to tell a self-congratulatory tale about the ultimate victory of civilization over barbarism, of the duly constituted forces of law and order over lawless mobs acting absent all authority. However, they are a poor guide to a significant number of lynchings, and they are so precisely because they tacitly rely for their coherence on presuppositions drawn from the logic of the liberal social contract (which, in turn, renders them ill suited to an appreciation of the role of lynching in reproducing the racial contract).[10]

Importantly, Kaufman-Osborn's observations distinguish between legal definitions becoming paradigmatic and lynching as the paradigm. Kaufman-Osborn locates this enforcement in the way lynching sustains a racial contract. While the racial contract is conventionally understood, following Charles Mills, as "a system for which racially determined structural advantage and handicap are foundational,"[11] this definition often hinges on a "conceptual partitioning and corresponding transformation of human populations into 'white' and 'nonwhite' men."[12] I must, however, depart from such a focus. For to focus on the division is to arrive too late. To examine the constitutive violence that enables the contract's very terms, one cannot explain the threshold by simply describing the two rooms it separates. The task, then, is to locate a preceding mechanism that establishes blackness as an ontological condition of non-being. Following Kaufman-Osborn, I thus interrogate lynching as the structural paradigm that both undergirds and precedes this conceptual partition. As *Beyond Abolition* proposes, "self-lynching," too, is part of this founding gesture. In this light, I depart from the idea that lynching simply reproduces the racial contract, which Mills argues maintains a racial order. Instead, I ask that we consider the psychical lynching—a judgment and condemnation *ante legem*—that precedes both the act of lynching and the contract's reproduction. Rather than a product of the law, this originary psychic judgment—the constitutive removal of blackness—constitutes the condition of possibility for both the signifier "lynching" and the legal space of its operation.

At this juncture, we can understand how the logic of racial liberalism necessarily narrows the conception of lynching in order to reinforce the state through reform—a repressive mechanism in the "duly constituted forces of law and order" that abstracts the ways in which the lynching of blackness takes place in the imaginary and through the violence of the *real*. For instance, if the particular aim of reform is the removal of the word "lynching," we must also inquire, as Sexton has, about "the *uses* to which such historical revision is put in the present; the *position* of enunciation from which it is produced and, in turn, helps to fashion; the possible *audiences* of its lines of address; and the political *initiatives* that it enables or disables."[13] Our inquiry must, therefore, extend beyond the kind of enunciation facilitated by such a revision to consider what must remain fundamentally unheard, unsaid, and unthought to maintain the psychical antagonisms that serve as both indelible conflicts and essential bonds in the unconscious structure of antiblackness.

Antiblackness challenges the false opposition between presence and absence, and reveals the limitations of separating the materiality and immateriality of language. Far from a transparent sign, both the word and psychical mechanism of "lynching" function as a force that anchors the law to blackness—a weight producing the very arrests it purports to describe, only to be haunted, possessed, by the materiality of those effects. The "presence" of the black female subject in the arrests of Richards Abdullah and Hampton prompted the necessity of removing the term "lynching." But the term's deletion from legal texts also renders blackness and sexuality—together—absent (or presumes their absence). Such a double movement—wherein presence necessitates removal and removal secures absence—exceeds the scope of a critique of law and a need for juridical intervention. The issue of "self-lynching" in a psychical sense moves beyond legal representation toward an ethical concern regarding the irrepresentability of (anti)blackness. By way of this shift, a deeper question emerges: How do the laws of representation and the representation of law conceal a desire for the destruction and annulment of blackness?

While the state's targeting of nonviolent protesters is not new (protesters from the Occupy Wall Street Movement and BLM have been arrested under the same penal code), the specific arrests of black women for allegedly lynching themselves is profoundly unsettling. These specific incidents present the enduring fact of antiblackness—with its racial, sexualized, and gendered features—not merely as part of the legal structure and the violence of law more generally, but as integral to the laws of violence in terms of time, language, and aesthetics. The following chapters illustrate that the penal code has long functioned to bolster the U.S. nation-state, demonstrating that "self-lynching" is not confined to the mentioned arrests; it also entails the enactment of anti-lynching legislation and succeeding measures. This scope reveals the pernicious, circular manner in which blackness is instrumentalized: first to lynch blackness from being, to posit an imagined self, only then to subject it to criminalization. The instances of "self-lynching" discussed in this book foreground the question of how the self is used and lynched not just in the dimensions of the imaginary, symbolic, but also *by* the *real*.[14] By establishing blackness as both *ante legem*[15] (prior to law) and *contra legem* (against law), this psychic operation marks a fundamental non-relation to the juridical order. It is within this rupture that I trace psychical formations that are themselves a type of custody. The analysis explores the perverse and violent valences (rhetorical, juridical, aesthetic, psychical) of these formations, linking them not only to the contemporary arrests, but also to the *afterlife* of slavery and lynching.

Beyond Abolition explores "self-lynching" as a conceptual structure, rather than as a legal term or rhetorical device. While this structure is illuminated by the first juridical interpretation of the statute—which defines "lynching oneself" as the act of removing oneself from lawful custody—I argue that "self-lynching" precedes this legal interpretation; it is the condition that enables its very formulation.[16] Beyond the appearance of tautology and circular reasoning lies the asymmetrical structural operation through which a prior, extralegal violence performs the foundational work that produces the exact conditions required for the legal text to secure its own authority.

As a conceptual structure, "self-lynching" names the process wherein law projects an imaginary "self" only to pathologize such a figure's imagined criminalization. I extend this legal definition to describe a psychical dynamic in which a "self" is inaugurated and designated within the system of law, only to be made to operate within broader psychical economies of antiblack violence. Such a dynamic reflects the inherent limitations of legal interpretation; the possibility of this "self," I argue, is perpetually withheld from the (non-)being of blackness, even as the concept of the self is usurped to reinforce the capture and captivity of blackness across aesthetics and language. This recursion—at once a projection and a suspension of the self—effectively obscures its primary function of lynching blackness. Because this operation exceeds simple negation, it falls into the stratum of what David Marriott has described as "a black *n'est pas* that in some ways the mind would rather pair off with an *impossibility of signification*" and "that does not represent or aim at *an object*."[17] Foundational to the law and sustaining the onto-political order of antiblackness, "self-lynching" marks the absolute limit of juridical and aesthetic thinking—operating in the register of the constitutive *real*, beyond the representational capacity of both the law's language and the aesthetic form. It is at this limit that *Beyond Abolition* calls for an abolition of the *real*: a radical departure from the foundational logic that requires the destruction of blackness to secure the coherence of the world—a coherence predicated upon the capture and captivity of blackness that the register of the *real* both demands and conceals.

To understand this asymmetrical structural operation, we require a rigorous reexamination of its key conceptual components. "Lynching" and "self" are two terms with very different histories, but they respectively inflict violence and come into meaning through formations of violence. Through the production of their meaning and as signs, they evoke the power to authorize an interpellation that collapses the Other as a (non)self. Placed together, the terms "lynching" and "self" raise concerns about the preservation of the laws of violence and the subterranean movements of desire. The legal term "felony lynching" indicates a juridical obscurity from the outset: it remains unclear where and when "lynching" and "self" intersect in the moment of custody. If the more familiar history of lynching implies capital punishment by a mob or civilians taking the law into their own hand, the constitution of the self within the law is indicative of a different trauma—on the one hand, the violence of transformation, of becoming a subject; on the other, the violence in which the (non-)being of blackness is incapacitated, forced to never appear as self, subject, or life. Indeed, the very violence with which these terms are charged reveals a different register of legislation at work within the language itself: a law that precedes the statute.

In a sense, the law's fixation on a self posited via the scene of "self-lynching" also points toward the centrality of desire. In interrogating how the possibility of "self-lynching" enters conceptual reality through arrest and custody, *Beyond Abolition* reveals that violence is enacted through language itself. In doing so, it highlights the violence at work at the level of reading, translation, and interpretation. Such a reinterpretation—from anti-lynching to the lynching of a self—is not simply a displacement of historical memory, but the repetition of the originary structural violence: the constitutive foreclosure that blackness always faces. Instead of tracing the original intent of the earlier anti-lynching penal code, I examine modern and contemporary contexts to interrogate the historical collusion between lynching and policing as the repetition of this originary displacement—a collusion that fortifies statecraft through the expulsion of blackness. Fundamental to "self-lynching," this recursion animates the possibilities of representational forms and historical memory across time and space, image and rhetoric, *de jure* and *de facto* law. Inescapably, the repetition of such displacements within the successive formations of "self-lynching" presents a desire not only for the arrest of blackness, but also for the arrest of black desire.

On this score, a central concern of this book is why blackness must be the exception across the domains of desire, law, language, and image. Anti-blackness is more than the exclusion of blackness from rights, citizenship, and subjecthood; it performs a fundamental, structural role in shaping law itself. This structural necessity refers to the symbolic structure—the prohibition and ordering principle Jacques Lacan terms the Name-of-the-Father—that establishes the possibility of legal language and social reality. Decisively, as this book demonstrates, the reach of the Name-of-the Father extends to the "laws of law"—the concealed, foundational principles—in aesthetics, language, and the psyche. While I critique liberal notions of state security, law, order, and protection by analyzing recent arrests on charges of "felony lynching," I also probe the psychical, aesthetic, and philosophical tensions between the perception and the event of "lynching the self." These tensions stem from the ontological uncertainty of blackness—a fundamental insecurity of being that furnishes the necessary ground for the violence inherent in the law's current formulations. Consequently, our analysis begins by examining the ways in which the structure of antiblackness denies the possibility of black being as a coherent subject. Ultimately, *Beyond Abolition* moves from a critique of legal language to a critique of Western humanist ontology—a framework that often lends itself to the possibility of reformist *as well as* abolitionist measures at the level of the material symbolic—arguing that this structural interdiction is the necessary condition of the violent maintenance of a racial imaginary and its suppression of (the blackness of) the *real*.

Tracing a pre-history of the arrests—and the legislation that authorizes them—enables us to excavate the distorted images of blackness concealed under representations of the history and historical memory of lynching in North America, specifically California. As we shall see, the point of excavating a "distorted" image is not to recuperate nor reconcile it. To echo Sexton, who elaborates a point made by Hortense Spillers, "it is not enough simply 'to see with greater clarity what the problem is.'"[18] Rather, *Beyond Abolition* explores how the impossibility of blackness becomes constitutive of and for the image. For instance (as the first and second chapters will elaborate), a persistent misconception maintains California's liberal façade as a multiracial and diverse state, supposedly free from the reign of racial terror because it lacked a large black population. This book undoes such mythologies by illustrating not only that black people underwent erasure, but that such erasure is symptomatic of a deeper elimination of blackness as *presence*. In this way, "lynching of the self" does not solely rest on the fantasmatic event whereby a black person is imagined to willfully lynch themselves—twisting actions of self-defense into a riot-turned-lynching—but also dissolves the neat oppositions between presence and absence, self and other.

Thus, this intervention not only delimits a conceptualization of antiblackness in respect to the brick-and-mortar institution of the prison or the carceral structures of the state. *Beyond Abolition* begins with a more unsettling question: Against the staggering images of antiblackness, why must blackness and antiblackness be thought solely at the level of representation—bound to the most immediate references to the prison, the police, rights, and policy? Certainly, these images are carceral in themselves; the function of the image, after all, is to capture and captivate. But what constitutes these images, I argue, is a psychical lynching of blackness that renders it ontologically captive to the image of a self. The question at hand is: Why must one think through the images, translations, objects, laws that hold blackness captive without questioning antiblackness as an axiomatic principle? Why, moreover, must blackness be reduced to such denigration, punishment, and imprisonment—even at the level of the imaginary—in order to *think* and *see* (anti)blackness at all? Does such thought not effectively affirm the logic and wish for policing and lynching to have already taken place as a necessary psychical economy: a pictorial entrenchment (*Vorstellung*) that secures the "knowing" of blackness through its captivity? And why must such "knowing" of (anti)blackness pass exclusively through such paths of reading?

These questions are at the core of *Beyond Abolition*, and they define its stakes. What would it mean to conceive abolition not merely at the material level of general economies, imprisonment, and policing, but also in regard to the psychical *images* that drive a desire for the capture and captivity of blackness? What would it mean to abolish *abolition* as the conceptual nexus that connects notions and images of blackness to freedom and incarceration alike—as the reciprocal logic often instrumentalized to *think* blackness? Rather than considering what recuperative gestures might allow for a reform of representational politics, this book zeroes in on what lies at the edge of abolition: that indeterminable zone between the psychical registers of the symbolic and the imaginary, the unfathomable zone of the *real*. In this regard, I propose that the abolition of antiblackness remains fundamentally unthought as a psychical necessity to maintain the carceral images of blackness that precede and exceed the images and statistics of lynching, policing, and incarceration. In remaining unthought, the maintenance of antiblackness secures the social bonds that cohere a sense of self, history, aesthetics, the political—indeed, the world itself. *Beyond Abolition*, therefore, seeks to excavate what underpins the symbolic appearances of lynching and policing—what mobilizes the lynching of blackness as a *self* in order for a self to be imagined. The question of what qualifies *this* self and its lynching (or rather, what drives their apparent opposition) links together the scenes, images, signs, and letters analyzed in the following chapters of this book and animates these ruminations on the psychical and libidinal economy of antiblackness.

The relations between law and representation, sign and meaning—whose libidinal investments pivot on blackness—point toward the function of the gap, or the caesura, between signifier and signified that requires delimiting a legal and a broader definition of custody, the social control and holding of a person. By expanding the notion of custody beyond the sign of the penal code, its interpretative depth is only fully revealed when the subject-objects of the arrest, and the broader social custody they endure, are caught in a moment of transition. In other words, the signs of "self-lynching" "are not fixed in writing but produced in a subsequent act; they are signifiers without a signified."[19] I argue that custody itself functions as something other than its (pre-)determined legal character, and thus must be understood as a transitional mode along with the subjects of arrest. Custody, then, functions not only as an instrument of the law—one that converts nonviolent protest into "self-lynching"; it also performs a dual operation: custody effaces blackness while sustaining the images and letters through which law, sovereignty, and destiny cohere. Such a superimposition of legal re-inscription and psychic violence is bound together through an interiorized "self-lynching." This logic of self-erasure transforms the "self" into what Barbara Johnson has described as a *selfobject*. In a literary and psychoanalytic context, Johnson explains the notion of selfobjects as an entrapment "in the fictions of the autonomous self as generated by the mirror stage."[20] She writes: "In the early stages of the formation of the self, therefore, other people are not perceived as separate, true objects, but as parts of the self, as selfobjects. The role of selfobjects can be played by other people throughout an individual's life."[21] What is relevant here is how the formation of a self emerges through the extension of a perceived environment—whether physical, fictional, and social—and how this extension becomes internalized in turn. Thus, the mirror image of the self is not simply a reflection *of* a self; it is also a mirage composed of collective desire. Johnson explains further:

> If the child is not appropriately mirrored, is not given the message "what you are is valuable" at this stage, then the grandiose self and the desire to merge with the idealized selfobject do not fade away but become split off and retain their archaic demands. Rather than being progressively reality-tested and integrated, they keep the unfilled hunger for validation intact as an open wound.[22]

Johnson's analysis elucidates how selfobjects sustain a mirage of desire as a fixed *open wound* in the service of an insatiable hunger, while the selfobjects themselves remain split off from a type of reality and symbolic incorporation. Selfobjects are, in other words, necessary to maintain not only fictions of the self, but also the infrastructure of fiction itself. Within the carceral staging of this infrastructure, the subject is compelled to enact its own erasure as the condition of social legibility. Yet, for blackness, such a performance is ineffectual; the "privilege" of self-erasure is foreclosed by a disappearance that awaits, a structural absence that precedes the subject's arrival. In this vein, the self in "self-lynching" must necessarily—and always already—occupy this fractured state, split between subject and object: a position that Johnson, following Spillers, describes as a neither/nor.[23] Crucially, while the selfobject oscillates between subject and object to maintain the fiction of desire, its function indicates a structural castration. This violence takes place at the expense of a virtual self in order to establish the illusion of fiction as an attainable (yet untested) reality. In this way, the "omnipotent selfobject" mirrors the omnipotence of law and the laws of reading the emergent self. Reflections of a split self—and the shards of the fictional whole offered by the reflection—conceal something more occult: the evanescence of a dream-work which stitches together language and writing, writing and letter. That is, the mirroring environment that consolidates fantasies and fictions as a coherent whole masks what has been foreclosed—that which has not yet been written.

Custody, as part of the transitional logic of "self-lynching," also requires further interrogation. On one hand, the concept of "felony lynching," as introduced by California law, rests on a multifarious notion of custody that serves as the operative hinge of the penal code. From the legal vantage, custody is central to the penal code's definition of lynching, not only delineating the transgression that warrants the arrest ("the taking from the lawful custody of a peace office") but also outlining the subject who judges and those who are the objects of that judgment. In effect, custody becomes a means to articulate and maintain sovereign violence by the police, and to mark the racialized grounds on which such violence can be performed and secured. Yet, what becomes "custodial" in the context of the "felony lynching" arrests remains obscured. If lawful custody is historically positioned as a bulwark against the lynch mob or riot, it should theoretically indicate a legal responsibility to shield the captive from *unsanctioned* harm. However, the arrests of Richards Abdullah and Hampton illustrate a perverse reversal of this custodial logic—the captives are *themselves* cast as the source of unlawful injury to their own persons while held by the state. The process begins with an implicit seizure: upon arrest, the state claims the captive's body as its own legal property, effectively "taking" the subject from themselves. Invariably, any subsequent act of self-harm or resistance is read not as a crisis of the self, but as an unlawful "removal" of the state's property from its own keeping. By being perceived as lynching themselves, Richards Abdullah and Hampton are rendered both perpetrator and victim. Such a dynamic does not so much collapse the distinction between these categories as it reveals the originary contamination of law by non-law—a moment where the "custody" of the state reveals itself as the very violence it purports to restrain. This instance marks a moment where what is "outside" (extralegal violence) is structurally constitutive of what is "inside" (lawful custody). Under these conditions, the designation of what (or who) is "custodial" mirrors a narrow discrepancy, not simply between lawful and unlawful action, but more pointedly between extralegal violence, which the law requires, and unlawful violence, which the law forbids. As such, custody serves as a way to facilitate its own misalignment with notions of protection; it serves as a ruse to obfuscate the indistinction between the lawful and unlawful as the exact condition of the arrest.

On the other hand, custody can be understood as fundamentally transitional—a property revealed by the "selfobject's" ambivalent marking of the boundary between lawful and unlawful action. In this sense, custody rests on a psychical process in which others are transformed "into a means for obtaining an end for oneself."[24] Lawful custody, in its use of these subject-objects, opens a space to transform them and hold them as the *thing* of law. As Johnson puts forward, following the work of Donald W. Winnicott, the transitional object is a "paradox of unlocatability."[25] For Johnson, this paradox is as much about object-ness as it is about what a transition exposes: an "expanded middle," an ontological reach through which language renders the difference between and among subjects and objects.[26] It predisposes the theory of transition in transition, so to speak. The paradox of the transitional object opens a space for experience not through phenomenological exposure, but by an implicit agreement—"a contract of nonformulation"[27] in which a subject refers to an object as a thing in an "almost legal dimension"[28] to maintain omnipotence and relationality over the conjured thing. Yet, what provides the subject with a sense of omnipotence is not an image of itself derived from the object-as-other—a standard mirroring—but rather the foundational substitution of blackness-as-property. Under this racial regime, the object (blackness-as-property) does not reflect the subject's (the sovereign's) desire; it secures sovereignty by existing as a quantifiable "thing" of the state. If custody is a transitional site in which those arrested on charges of "felony lynching" have already been rendered as things, then the grounds establishing the apparent boundaries of lawful custody also issue the disavowal of its lawless function.

The definition of custody thus conceals the structural violence of antiblackness inherent in the concept of lawful confinement. Blackness, perceived as an impingement on the symbolic order and the grounds of relationality, allows for an expanded middle—the fortified space established for the human, law, and sovereignty. As this fortified space of sovereignty becomes a paradoxical ground of unlocatability, it obscures its own custodial function. "Self-lynching" is then not only about the foreclosure of blackness as a non-subject, but also very much about the structural necessity of antiblackness that produces the ground and space required for the operations of law, sovereignty, and their relationality. *Beyond Abolition* critically investigates, therefore, the conditions and the racial politics of aesthetics that inform the imaginary scenes and psychical dynamics of "self-lynching."

The book explores the events and images that the legislation ties together to permit arrests of protesters on the charge of a "lynching" of oneself. I use the term "event" loosely here, to convey how the moment of custody and the act of "self-lynching" are perceived and read as a non-event. The concept of the non-event can be understood, on the one hand, with Tze-Yin Teo as "a complex negative of the event"—a formulation which describes it as "that which does not and will not happen; does not wound or leave a mark psychic, epistemic, or material."[29] In short, "the non-event might be the radical other of the event."[30] While Teo's formulation captures the concept's theoretical boundaries, it assumes a subject for whom the absence of a mark is a secondary condition. For the captive, the "non-event" is not a lack of marking, but the axiomatic ground of their (non-)being-in-custody. Consequently, Teo's framework remains limited in understanding the constitutive role of antiblackness. On the other hand, I attempt to unravel how these moments are, in fact, encounters that hold profound psychical functions and produce significant psychical effects as they revolve around the void of blackness. In this vein, these moments are construed as non-events not because of the absence of a wound or mark; rather, as Rizvana Bradley has noted, "black aesthesis constitutes a nonevent, which bears the absolutely unassimilable."[31] This reading affirms that the non-event, within the black critical tradition, is not the absence of a mark, but the mark of an ontological and political exclusion that cannot be assimilated by, or sublated within, the systems of knowledge or aesthetics.

In placing these scenes (or moments) together in the following chapters, I show how the psychical state of lynching, with its accompanying desires, wishes, fantasies, dreams, must take custody of an imagined and projected self. The book pursues this analysis as a question of political meaning, extending beyond a mere question of legal definition. There is also a philosophical dimension at stake, as the work reflects on how the (non-)meaning of blackness is continuously and necessarily with(held). This philosophical concern is instantiated within the custodial apparatus, which, I argue, executes both institutional restraint and the psychic custody that holds blackness captive. At the heart of each chapter is the question of what constitutes and conditions the custodial—what decides the lawfulness of an arrest—and how these mechanisms are buried by the racial sovereign grounds that authorize the arrest of a (blackened) self. At once, the extirpation and projection of blackness constitute a "self-lynching." By extension, the necessity of this process confirms that "self-lynching" is not an aberration of the law, but the structural mechanism that underwrites the onto-political order of antiblackness, the very pulse of the legal system's authority. Throughout these chapters, I expand on this term to illustrate how the psychic consequence of its drives materializes not only a latent mode of lynching, but also facilitates the systematic misreading and denial of lynching's proper representation—a representation that is structurally precluded by the state's custodial vision.

"*Show* Me Black Death . . .": A Note on and Against Method

The violence of representation is often misunderstood as something that can be grasped through the representation of violence. The lynching of blackness and antiblackness does not escape this woefully narrow view. During my research for this monograph, several of my academic conference presentations on the lynching of blackness and the recent arrests were met with the question: "Is it possible to delink (the ontology of) black death from the police arrests of 'felony lynching'? Must we think about policing and black death together?" Sometimes, the questioning went even further: "How many black people have *actually* been lynched in California?" or "Show me black death—*in numbers*. Only then can we understand the scope of its violence." The frequency of these remarks and the ease with which they are made suggest a host of problems. Under the veneer of empiricism, data, or ethnographic knowledge, there lies a deep well of racial anxiety, hostility, and antagonism toward the question and significance of black life, of black presence and absence. But these misgivings are also telling in another way: in the perverse demand *to be shown* black death, antiblackness, or blackness, the claim is that one *can see and know* (anti)blackness, understand it, grasp it—fully exhaust it. At the core of our investigations into lynching and arrest is the interrogation of this desire to simultaneously keep blackness within reach but also under exclusion, eradication, and suspension, as a way to maintain a sense of knowledge and truth through representation—even against, or in spite of, one's racial doubt. Indeed, as Frank B. Wilderson has submitted: "In life, identification is limited only by the play of endless analogies, but death is like nothing at all."[32]

The assumption that (anti)blackness can be understood—whether through analogy or by placing it in proximity to or as something more material, quantifiable, intelligible—presumes too much (or too little) about blackness as both presence and absence, as either/or. Nonetheless, at this juncture, we can submit more directly that antiblackness is not something which can be simply overcome or redressed by the political language and discourses of abolition. As Daniel Butler has explained, "We often synonymize the term 'antiblackness' with racism directed at black people, but this too easily conjures the fanciful idea of lamentable othering for which we atone by 'doing better' next time."[33] At issue then is not only the recognition that language and discourse themselves require us to plumb more critically the void of blackness. Also at stake is the need to rethink the notion that antiblackness is simply a moral dilemma of racism or the "othering" of black social identity. Instead, we must track the more fundamental role and function (anti) blackness performs within the structure of the unconscious. Hence, "self-lynching" becomes pernicious precisely because it operates in the registers of language and the unconscious, necessitating a mode of thought that invariably begins at the level of meta-psychology.[34] Because the repetition of this charge reflects the ways in which (anti)blackness structures the psyche, it reveals that the collective unconscious and imaginary are themselves predicated upon a blackness that is quintessential to the conditions of their thinkability—yet remains unthought within the axioms, frameworks, and articulations of the theories themselves. The following chapters, therefore, labor within this very unthinkability, navigating this impasse to unmask the "self-lynching" charge not as a legal anomaly, but as symptomatic of a sovereign order that survives by what it refuses to think.

In these preliminary remarks, I aimed to show that the complex connecting lynching, the carceral, and antiblackness is irreducible to solely the juridical and representational. Many of the terms and conceptual frameworks commonly utilized to analyze lynching, the carceral, and antiblackness as political concerns must be interrogated, delimited, and unsettled. Only then can we situate them as rhetorical, aesthetic, philosophical, and psychical figures and objects forwarded by the uncertainty of blackness and indexed by the gratuity of antiblackness.

If *Beyond Abolition* places pressure on the notion of a political horizon itself—since the precarious edge of black (un)freedom troubles any semblance of futurity or telos—then we are also tasked to inquire, as Hayden White has, about the conditions that steer "history as fulfillment."[35] To be sure, this book is not a historical study. However, I find a productive resonance in White's critical probing of historical reconstructions and their forms. While White's project centers on the narrative structures of Western historiography, I transpose his insights to cast light on the indeterminacy of blackness—a site where the "reality" of violence and its "manifestation" in law are most forcefully decoupled. "The difference between a reality and its forms of manifestations can be discerned."[36] For White, this difference is not just a matter of the "thing represented and its representation. It is this difference that makes possible the critical comparison between one representation of 'the past,' or any aspect of it, and another."[37] He explains further:

> The belief in the commensurability of different representations of any aspect of the past hinges on the prior belief in a past to which all representations of it can be referred and differentially assessed as to their validity and their status as contributions to our knowledge of it. But the real past is not, of course, accessible, except by ways of its representations—indexical, iconic, or symbolic, as the case may be.[38]

White's identification of the past as a "real" accessible only through its manifestations finds its extreme limits in blackness—through which representation does not merely fail to reach the past, but actively produces one that necessitates black death. Methodologically speaking, *Beyond Abolition* begins and contends with this paradox: the aporia of blackness underpins representations of history in the face of the impossibility of reconciling the past with the present—and vice versa—in all of blackness's (in)commensurate forms. Significantly, what this suggests is that blackness is not simply a lack or absence that must or can be overcome or "re-represented" into intelligibility. Rather, blackness, and the nefarious ways in which it becomes lynched as a self and subject, functions as an essential part of structuring modern conceptions of the images, objects, signs, and subjects of law, history, value, and even the unconscious. Throughout this book then, we will contend with questions of the material symbolic not as a way to seek out or retrieve the immaterial "truth." Quite the contrary, we will challenge the false oppositions and the presupposed diremptions between the material and immaterial, presence and absence.

In light of these goals, presenting the chapters in chronological order—commencing with a pre-history of the recent "lynching" arrests—seems contraindicated. Yet much of our focus will be directed at the traces, fragments, and non-appearances of (anti)blackness: those elements that are woven into, yet often occluded by, the tapestry of the penal code that still authorizes present-day arrests. We attend to the philosophical, aesthetic, and psychic questions that follow from these occlusions. Saidiya Hartman might describe such an approach as the effort to:

> "brush history against the grain" [which] requires excavations at the margins of monumental history in order that the ruins of the dismembered past be retrieved turning to forms of knowledge and practice not generally considered legitimate objects of historical inquiry or appropriate or adequate sources for history making and attending to the cultivated silence, exclusions, relations of violence and domination that engender the official account.[39]

Extending Hartman's critical insight, I argue that the convergence of blackness and ruination is foundational. We must therefore ask: Why is this coupling a prerequisite—a lethal ground—for the production of thought itself, including the very objects and concepts that constitute it? Furthermore, in the context of the deadly judgment of the self, why does the convergence of blackness and ruination provide the psychic backdrop for the images and narratives of history? Thus, while I am doubtlessly indebted to the archive and historical research that precedes and shapes this project, the hermeneutical labors presented here aim to explore the relationship between the (non-)meaning of blackness and the (antiblack) desires that escalate into the lynching of blackness—a repetition across time, space, and psychical registers in the *afterlife* of slavery and lynching. The two are not mutually exclusive: at issue is what blackness elicits *in form*, but also how blackness *informs* desire.

To grasp this constitutive relationship between blackness and desire, the book requires a methodological shift. This means, again, that I am less concerned with establishing a historicity or "a more accurate depiction" of history than with what is happening at the level of the drives, which forcefully compel (anti)blackness into a set of appearances and representations as the objects, images, and texts that are themselves structures of disavowal. As we will demonstrate, the psychic and symbolic work of blackness's dissimulation—the ability of meaning, self-image, and sovereignty to appear stable—is predicated on the violent exclusion of blackness back to the *real*. The perpetual lynching of blackness ensures the functional division between the imaginary and the symbolic. In this regard, the conceptual figure of "the slave" only achieves coherence as a symbolic signifier through the prior, foundational repudiation of blackness as the disruptive excess it cannot fully assimilate.

In this way, *Beyond Abolition* argues that race puts blackness back to the *real*; in effect, the *jouissance* of "race" at the intersections of the imaginary and the symbolic gestures to that placement, the blackness of the *real*. Blackness is inextricable from the symbolic representation of "race" or "the slave." That is, a slave is not the same as blackness, but blackness is absolutely fundamental to the *meaning* of the slave. As *Beyond Abolition* will contend, the lynching of blackness dissimulates the work between the imaginary and the symbolic to procure the possibility of meaning and appearances—not only for the figure of the slave, but also for the very formations and images of self, being, and sovereignty.

To reflect on what the archive, images, and objects of history and the law can or cannot say is to destabilize the boundaries through which desire, judgment, violence, and blackness are thought to be mutually exclusive and equal. Still, if we are to take seriously into account the psychic life of (anti)blackness, we can neither isolate nor reduce it solely to the level of fantasies. Too often, scholarship on power, subjection, and violence describes the operations of colonialism and settler colonialism, slavery, and lynching as symptomatic expressions of fantasy—fantasies of conquest, antiblackness, dominating the Other—without apprehending fantasy as the privileged site of accessing what has been silenced, erased, displaced. There is a great deal of irony in the sense that this brings fantasy, its image and meaning, to a subjective, as opposed to a dialectical, standstill. At best, this limited view capitulates to a reading or rendering of the ego formation of power, even though it takes for granted the unconscious as a structure; at worst, "psychic life" takes on an imagined character and life of its own, where the role of fantasy is assumed to have explanatory power *over* power. The parapraxis—this slip—reveals a disavowal between the scholar and scenes of violence: the fantasy of fantasy becomes so effective that matters of identification, *ressentiment*, fragmentation, et alia seemingly dissipate. The image of fantasy hijacks the scene of reading, leaving the "psychic life" of (anti)blackness, power, and violence examined exclusively at the level of representation.

To that end, the book takes its cue from Frantz Fanon's incisive observation: "When we assert that European culture has an *imago* of the black man that makes him responsible for every possible conflictual situation, we have kept within reality."[40] In the following chapters, Fanon's conceptualization of the *real*, one that differs from the *real* in Lacanian terms, will be crucial. It allows us to discuss how fantasies render the *real* and reality indistinguishable, while simultaneously addressing Fanon's grave concerns regarding the impossibility of moving beyond the exposure of blackness to the *real*. For now, Fanon makes us aware that, indeed, an *imago* of blackness has its place in culture, and is neither unreasonable for nor free from the duress of a collective unconscious.

In this regard, it is worth noting the interdisciplinary and transdisciplinary nature of this project, which is equally informed by, challenges, and departs from tenets of critical theory, psychoanalysis, and poststructuralism. The critical methods of black studies, in particular black critical theories and Afro-Pessimism, have a large influence on the philosophical framework guiding my investigation of "self-lynching" as a psychical dynamic. Specifically, the works of Frantz Fanon, Rizvana Bradley, Patrice D. Douglass, David Marriott, Jared Sexton, Sara-Maria Sorentino, Calvin Warren, and Frank Wilderson, among others, are formative for my own interrogations of the impossible disimbrications between the anteriority of blackness and symbolic placements (whether that placement is the law, aesthetics, politics, or ontology). Their work resonates in varied but critical ways with the intellectual goal of the book series "Inventions: Black Philosophy, Politics, Aesthetics" this monograph is part of: "The critical task of any aspirational black philosophy is its ability to tell apart blackness from its mirages and impossibilities."[41]

But already, the umbrella of black studies or Afro-Pessimism might be too broad to define the analysis and critique launched in this book. In fact, this book finds its most crucial questions in the moments of abstraction, tension, and pressure arising from black studies' internal debates and external engagements—at the disciplinary boundaries and structural core of black studies. In this way, the congruencies and differences between Afro-Pessimism and psychoanalysis prove to be particularly useful. As Sexton clarifies, Afro-Pessimism "is a reading of what is gained and lost in the attempt—the impulse—to delineate the spatial and temporal borders of anti-blackness, to delimit the 'bad news' of black life, to fix its precise scope and scale, to find an edge beyond or before which true living unfolds."[42] Sexton offers a critical reorientation through a reading that shifts the analysis of blackness and antiblackness "from the empirical to the structural or, more precisely, from the experiential to the political ontological,"[43] thus reminding us that a reorientation of reading can expose the simultaneous pleasures and horrors underscoring the paths of reading, writing, and thinking themselves.

Sexton's discussion of reading as a way to expose and place together the intricacies of language, desire, and blackness echoes Vicky Lebeau's critical reflections on the necessary self-reflexivity of psychoanalysis as method and approach. She explains: "Psychoanalysis can lay claim to a language and a domain of its own . . . Yet neither language nor domain stand alone. Psychoanalysis is intertextual, forged through a range of disciplines and systems of thought which keep it open to the cultural objects it attempts to understand."[44] Complicating the idea of method, she explicates, "In fact, the very idea of application—from the Latin applicare: to join, to fold together—is troubled by the concept of intertextuality."[45] Together, psychoanalysis and Afro-Pessimism offer a distinctive intertextuality that shifts how we approach time, language, and representation. This necessitates an interrogation of the very conditions that allow these domains to speak, become legible, or even become possible. Thus, our investigation into the pre-history, memory, and reported practices of lynching aims to unsettle the terms and conditions that govern the seeming appearances, disappearances, and non-appearances of blackness—phenomena organized by the psychical states and drives that preserve the libidinal investment in antiblackness. I analyze how, as a larger complex, "self-lynching" forms the infinite modes of policing, capture, and captivity that maintain the uncertainty of blackness as non-being. In this structural foreclosure, blackness is precluded from the category of what constitutes life, a distinction necessary to analyze the political and ontological meaning (and meaning-making) of *afterlife* discussed throughout this book.

In the last decade, there have been representative publications that engage with the intersection between law and antiblackness. Contemporary examples include, but are not limited to, Sora Han's *Letters of the Law* and Anthony Farley's corpus of essays that ruminate on the structural dynamic of "white-over-black." The central thesis in Han's *Letters of the Law* is that the fantasy of colorblindness is a foundational gesture of American law.[46] However, the notion that the law writes itself according to this fantasy suggests two critical points: first, it assumes the law is merely blind to its own antiblackness, raising the question of whether the law can ever "see" its own violence; and second, it forces a speculative inquiry into what it would mean if the law could truly "see" race—and, in turn, how such a truth would be instantiated. This speculative "if" places questions of black (un)freedom and justice under the telos of juridical law. In this regard, Han's work enacts a "suture" where there is actually an unbridgeable rift: by collapsing the interval between Afro-Pessimism and Black Optimism, she disavows the constitutive gap that makes the legal fantasy possible in the first place. By positing the law's own "blindness" as a threshold to be crossed through a new kind of "vision," Han's work effects a false closure—recasting the structural antagonism of antiblackness as a representational crisis that implies the law can be "fixed" through better letters.

Beyond Abolition departs from such a standpoint, making this divergence one of its central concerns. The book argues that the anteriority of blackness extends beyond juridical law to the very symbolic law that secures and makes possible all legal revisions, reforms, and interpretations. Moreover, as essential psychoanalytic insights tell us, vision is never innocent—not due to fantasy or willful blindness, but because of how "the unconscious (formed by the dominant order) structures ways of seeing and pleasure in looking."[47] Vision—from seeing, looking, gazing to the faculty of thinking and the imagination—is always tied to desire. That blackness is the constant exception to desire indicates the impossibility of abolition, if desire is inextricable from the social link, or what Lacan has described as the "desire of the Other" (Chapters 5 and 6). *Beyond Abolition*, thus, rejects the notion that the desire for colorblindness is law's founding gesture; it does not assume that a more critical representation of the law can lend itself to "see better," or (to evoke Sexton vis-à-vis Spillers once more) "to see with greater clarity." For, to demand that the law "see with greater clarity" is to mistake a more precise aim for a more just vision.

In a related but distinct engagement with the structural forces of antiblackness, Farley's corpus offers a critical framework focused on the repetition of the foundational racial dynamic itself. Throughout his work, Farley theorizes the repetition of "white-over-black" as a structural dynamic indicative of the desire to "perfect slavery" within the post-emancipation shaping of modernity. He productively links this repetition and what he sees at the level of the imaginary—dreams, screen-memories, and wishes—arguing that the institutional materialization of segregative practices, "white-over-black," is intertwined with the desire for "slavery's perfection."[48] While, to some extent, *Beyond Abolition* resonates with Farley's investigations into the collusion between the material symbolic and imaginary, it departs from an analytic that reads the political, aesthetic, *and* psychic solely *through* the production of discursive formations of race, including the dynamic of "white-over-black." The risk of viewing the "perfection" of slavery through this lens is that "white-over-black" might be misconceived in positive identitarian terms. This critical hesitation ensures that we do not mistakenly substitute the slave (as a legally constituted status of negation and political object) for blackness (as the anterior, inescapable designation that secures the meaning of the slave). The lynching of blackness, as maintained throughout this book, is precisely this necessary anterior condition that precedes and secures the symbolic's coherence, dissimulating the instability between the imaginary and the symbolic to procure the possibility of meaning and appearances in the realm of being and sovereignty—including the segregative dynamics that make "white-over-black" apparent.

Grounding the analysis in these anterior ontological distinctions rather than juridical definitions serves to clarify the book's methodological trajectory. That is, by prioritizing the psychical and the structural over the procedural, this project situates itself outside the conventional boundaries of the discipline. Stated more pointedly, *Beyond Abolition* is not a legal theory book. Although a significant portion of the book examines the word, application, and operation of law, the aim of this book is neither to theorize developments in legal interpretation and analysis, nor to speculate on the potential of the application of law. In this way, Walter Benjamin's dialectical approach in "Critique of Violence" ("Zur Kritik der Gewalt") is crucial. His ruminations on the founding instance of violence as suspended over an abyss allow for an interrogation of what underlies not just the violence of the law, but also the constitutive violence that authorizes antiblackness across the register of aesthetics, language, and politics. Benjamin is, indeed, cautious of another dialectic: a dialectical law that he sees trapped in the interaction between law-making and law-preserving violence—what he describes as "that law of its oscillation."[49] He elucidates that any critique of violence rests on the evaluative criteria which establish and uphold the law. As Sigrid Weigel observes,

"It is this violence, as always inscribed in lawmaking which turns a legal-theoretical discussion of violence's character as a means into a discussion of the 'gravely problematic nature of all legal violence.'"[50] The laws of violence, thus, require a more critical hermeneutic approach that moves beyond the analytic frame of positive law and its legal application. Likewise, a similar pressure must be placed on the illusory horizons that project the enclosure of the laws of violence—which is to ask what it might mean to move *beyond* abolition. Moving beyond abolition proposes, as Benjamin does, a dialectical reflection on the philosophical possibility of pure violence that would mark the absolute ending of the cycle of law-positing and law-preserving violence. It is by discerning this critical presupposition—this idea of pure violence—that the critique of violence, and the movement beyond abolition, becomes possible. The history of violence thus carries within it the resources for its own rupture. To be sure, this rupture is not to be misconstrued for a higher Marxian or Fichtean synthesis; it produces no reconciliation, but rather indexes the point where the dialectic itself fails. The move beyond abolition is thus found in this very impasse—a dialectical turn that does not resolve the tension but instead subverts "pure violence" as an ideal. In this turn, Benjamin notes a messianic act that exceeds the connotations of religious and mythic intervention: "But if, with respect to violence, its standing resource [*Bestand*] as pure immediate violence is also secured beyond law, this proves that, and how, there is a possibility of revolutionary violence."[51] Beyond the abolition of state power and the mythic violence that might characterize abolition in the popular imagination or as common political sense, Benjamin calls for a divine violence, a violence that "is law-annihilating."[52] Such "un alloyed" violence would destitute the power of laws in their law-making and law-preserving capacity. The de-posing of law would include the annihilation of the extant abolition already at work in the alterations that permutate from the logic and imposition of legal institutions.[53]

This lateral move, from the violence of the law to the monopoly of state power, parallels the shift that Fanon describes: from the ontological violence that threatens blackness to its manifestation as everyday antiblackness. As he notes, "In a sense [blackness] has to embody hatred. This is why the Americans have replaced lynching by discrimination."[54] By Fanon's account, blackness as the embodiment of hatred precedes itself. And yet, the conversion from the non-being of blackness to blackness serving as the pinnacle of hatred also reveals a dialectical law concealed within and underneath the disparate manifestations and economies of antiblackness. Fanon demonstrates that antiblackness paradoxically unifies diverse appearances, acting as the shared guiding principle that structures reality and its subsequent iterations. *Beyond Abolition* builds on these insights to reconceptualize antiblackness through the "self-lynching" of blackness—grasping it not merely as a consequence of the law, but as foundational to the self-sustaining logic in which blackness is suspended as a self while simultaneously structuring the concepts of the modern state, sovereignty, and abolition. The ultimate aim of *Beyond Abolition* is to identify the singular, law-like violence that underlies all varieties of antiblack practices and forms—from the racial state system to the immediacy of blackness to the *real*. This immediacy, distinguished from "the blackness of the *real*," names the unmediated structural condition of blackness: its status as a site perpetually deprived of the symbolic and legal buffer afforded to the Human. Such a condition of being without mediation simultaneously constitutes the exposure of blackness to the real and confirms that the *real* itself is structured by antiblackness (the blackness of the *real*). Understanding this structural immediacy—the irreducible law of black social death—thus becomes the necessary philosophical step for any critique that seeks to move beyond the limitations of historical abolition and toward addressing the ontological foundations of racial governance. Imperatively, this work demands a dialectical and deconstructive rigor to be applied to the critique of antiblack violence itself—a critical rethinking that foregrounds the failures of analyses treating this violence as an event or contingency rather than as a structural precondition of the modern world. The stakes lie in demonstrating how the act of its critique must be conceptually *de-posed* from the law-like compulsion of merely reformulating the terms of black suffering—a compulsion which only reinforces the internalized violence and fatal enclosure of "self-lynching." Otherwise, the critique of antiblack violence risks its own betrayal, lynching itself through the very logic it intends to abolish. *Beyond Abolition*, therefore, does not offer a recognizable political program; instead, it commits to the ceaseless methodological unsetting (*Entsetzung*), insisting that antiblackness be treated not as a symptom of a dialectical law, but as its foundational, irreducible condition.

Contested Ground: Defining and Clarifying Use of Terms

Already, I have mentioned a few technical terms such as the symbolic, imaginary, the *real*. In the following section, I offer a non-exhaustive glossary of key concepts (or interventions) that ground the book. While these terms carry a specialized and often technical lineages, a central objective of *Beyond Abolition* is to demonstrate how (anti)blackness, as an analytic lens and hermeneutic approach, challenges their accepted frameworks and forces us to fundamentally rethink their common definitions and conceptual reach.

Real Abstraction

In the concluding chapter, I focus specifically on the notion of "real abstraction" as it has been developed within various Marxist discourses. However, as the term "abstraction" is threaded throughout the book, its definition cannot be treated as a transparent or self-evident category. Although Karl Marx himself did not technically coin the term "real abstraction," the notion of abstraction was central to his conceptual analysis of social relations and materialism. For Marx, social relations necessitate the abstraction from the particularities of the concrete to a point where abstractions take place not just at the base of society. The social relations and material forces of production—the base of society—determine and are reflected in the superstructure of ideology and culture. Significantly, Marx highlights that real abstractions themselves are not things. As Sara-Maria Sorentino has explained, "Instead [real abstractions] point to the 'supra-sensible' (*Capital* 165) conditions that Marx traces between time, money, labor, and wealth, and which through a 'social synthesis' (Sohn-Rethel) proceed 'behind the backs of the producers' (*Capital* 135)."[55] Take for example Marx's reflections about the dual characteristics of a revolutionary movement that "finds both [their] empirical and [their] theoretical basis in the movement of *private property*."[56] I quote at length to show his rhetorical deployment of "abstraction" and how he situates it in relation to what he sees as "real." Placing these concerns together anticipates how the concept of real abstraction will be used by later theorists. Marx writes:

> This *material,* immediately *sensuous* private property is the material sensuous expression of *estranged human* life. Its movement—production and consumption—is the *sensual* revelation of the movement of all production hitherto—i.e., the realization or the reality of man. Religion, family, state, law, morality, science, art etc., are only *particular* modes of production, and fall under its general law. The positive transcendence of *private property* as the appropriation of *human* life is, therefore, the positive transcendence of all estrangement—that is to say, the return of man from religion, family, state, etc., to his *human,* i.e. *social* mode of existence. Religious estrangement as such occurs only in the realm of *consciousness,* of man's inner life, but economic estrangement is that of *real life*; its transcendence therefore embraces both aspects. It is evident that the *initial* stage of the movement amongst the various peoples depends on whether the true and for them *authentic* life of the people manifests itself more in consciousness or in the external world—is more ideal or real. Communism begins from the outset (*Owen*) with atheism; but atheism is at first far from being *communism*; indeed, it is still mostly an abstraction.[57]

While Marx explores more closely how the conversion from the concrete to the abstract takes place through social relations in his later essay "Grundrisse," I quote here from his earlier work because it illustrates the interdependence between abstraction and the external world, estrangement and movement. These reflections on "the positive transcendence of *private property*" also anticipate the discussions in Chapters 1, 3, and 6, where I elaborate on the implications of a notion of transcendence which remains, in my view, unduly metaphysical. For now, Marx shows us that the particularities drawn from a concrete totality require no conscious intellectual labor to conceive their abstraction; the movement of social relations performs this abstraction instantaneously. Until one decidedly does something with their interpretation of the external world, the movement of communism—that is, the actualization of putting communism into movement—remains an abstraction, an atheism, an idealism—"more ideal or real." In this sense, Marx's use of the word "real" is situated within the material realities of social relations. The concrete acts as an index to caution against idealism—not just by way of discussing and responding to material conditions, but also in respect to abstractions themselves. Thus, to assume that Marx conceives abstractions simply as products of the mind or an ideology would be an idealism that he himself rejects. For Marx, abstractions emerge through social and material relations and are irreducible to the ideas that capitalism might bestow upon real, concrete particularities. As such, Marx maintains that "it seems to be correct to begin with the real and the concrete, with the real production."[58] As he avers in "Grundrisse":

> The concrete is concrete because it is the concentration of many determinations, hence unity of the diverse. It appears in the process of thinking, therefore, as a process of concentration, as a result, not as a point of departure, even though it is the point of departure in reality and hence also the point of departure for observation [*Anschauung*] and conception. Along the first path the full conception was evaporated to yield an abstract determination; along the second, the abstract determinations lead towards a reproduction of the concrete by way of thought.[59]

Categories of abstraction, thus, appear *through* (not *as*) the real act of production and material relations. However, as Marx clarifies above, the social and material conditions (the concrete) are inseparable not just from the production of thought; material conditions also influence the way in which some forms of thought, such as abstract concepts, take on an ideal form.[60] Alfred Sohn-Rethel expands on this, noting that the "social existence under conditions of commodity production" and intellectual labor together construct varying degrees of abstractions. He explains that real abstraction and its ideal reflection are two aspects of a single process: "The abstraction comprising both aspects is one and can only be one. Its two aspects or parts can be related in no other way than in a context of conversion, the real abstraction being converted to its ideal reflection into intellectual form."[61] Sohn-Rethel specifies further that in the "real life" of capital, "the ideal abstraction blots out the real abstraction so as to make it unrecognisable."[62] Importantly, Marx indicates that the real abstraction of the base does not materialize as abstraction *itself*; such an idealistic claim would be to ignore the concrete, material nature of capital relations. The abstraction inherent in the material forces of production is distorted when it is filtered through ideal forms of thought, yet these forms are distinct from the *real* abstraction of the base. To treat real abstraction as if it is materialized directly and visibly as an abstract entity would offer an inappropriately idealistic account of how capital relations operate. Rather, real abstraction can be understood in the Marxian sense "not as a mere mask, fantasy or diversion, but as a force operative in the world."[63] This operative force stems from the seeming contradictions between labors of the mind and the social and material relations of the external world. In this way, real abstractions are, as it were, "born from difference."[64]

As another example of "the debate on Marxian uses of abstraction,"[65] Slavoj Žižek, following Sohn-Rethel, explains that "before thought could arrive at pure abstraction, the abstraction was already at work in the social effectivity of the market, already at work in the act of commodity exchange."[66] He clarifies further:

> If, then, the "real abstraction" has nothing to do with the level of "reality," of the effective properties, of an object, it would be wrong for that reason to conceive of it as a "thought-abstraction," as a process taking place in the "interior" of the thinking subject . . . or, to quote Sohn-Rethel's concise formulation: "The exchange abstraction is not thought, but it has the *form* of thought."[67]

At the same time, he notes that "'real abstraction' is unthinkable in the frame of the fundamental Althusserian epistemological distinction between the 'real object' and the 'object of knowledge' insofar as it introduces a third element which subverts the very field of this distinction . . . in short: the symbolic order."[68] Žižek thus demystifies "real abstraction" as pertaining to the materialism of reality and objects—a relevant point for our analysis in Chapter 6—and shows that the exchange of abstraction is perceived to have the *form* of thought. This suggests that "real abstraction," in the Marxian sense, should not be confused with a simple materiality; rather, it is precisely that which undoes the false oppositions between materiality and immateriality, concrete reality and ideology.

By no means an exhaustive account of abstraction and real abstraction according to Marxist thought, these preliminary notes will help us consider how conceptions of abstraction can become an idealized form in response to the perceived contradictions of knowledge and materialism, thought and social relations. However, this tradition, even in its most sophisticated formulations, risks presupposing a universal social totality which antiblackness fundamentally undoes, thus requiring a methodological commitment beyond the limits of capital's "real abstraction."

The Imaginary and the Symbolic

While various psychoanalytic traditions are alluded to throughout the book, I draw significantly from Sigmund Freud, Jacques Lacan, and Frantz Fanon, even as I occasionally depart from or challenge some of their concepts. Their influence on my use of psychoanalysis stems primarily from their emphasis on the unconscious and the objective of delineating a metapsychology—a theoretical framework that moves beyond empirical clinical observation to map the structural, dynamic, and economic conditions of the psychical apparatus. Central to this project are the imaginary and symbolic—two of the three fundamental orders Lacan identifies as structurally interdependent. Following Lacan, the imaginary in *Beyond Abolition* can be understood as the register of psychical images and perceptions (e.g., fantasies, phobias, anxieties) and the dynamics that enable and facilitate them. What occurs at the level of the imaginary shapes one's sense of material reality, a sense which is itself constituted and structured by the symbolic order: the register of representation, law, and language. These orders are necessarily bound to one another; the process through which one arrives at meaning in the imaginary is shaped by the symbolic, and vice versa. If the imaginary and the symbolic illuminate the intersection between meaning and material reality, then the *real* and the symbolic together elucidate the limits of language due to the impossible reach of the *real* which resists symbolization. The irrepresentability of the *real* is thus essential to the central argument of *Beyond Abolition*. It is precisely the exclusion and disavowal of this unsymbolizable *real*—the blackness of the *real*—that ensures the functional division and coherence of the imaginary and symbolic orders.

The Real and Real-Fantasy

Throughout *Beyond Abolition*, we explore how the symptomatic screening and misrecognition of antiblack violence is indistinguishable from the violence of (blackness of) the *real* and the real-fantasies of antiblackness. We can understand the *real* in two ways. First, Lacan views the *real* as the order that supports the imaginary and the symbolic, yet "may well not be determined."[69] For Lacan, the *real* is not the hole in reality and in the representation of reality; instead, the *real* is what exposes that hole by "something that oscillates in the interval."[70] In this way, Lacan explains that "the real has to be sought beyond the dream—in what the dream has enveloped, hidden from us, behind the lack of representation of which there is only one representative. This is the real that governs our activities more than any other."[71] For Fanon, however, the *real* is not simply a limit-point that exposes the gaps in representation. The exposure of blackness to the *real* points to a hole in both being and representation that is not merely a general function of revealing the limit of the symbolic; it is a specific structural condition whereby blackness is perpetually deprived *of* and *by* the symbolic, not just through a lack in the formation of the subject, but also through the structural lack of mediation afforded to the Human. This condition uniquely renders blackness structurally vulnerable to the violence emanating from the unmediated violent *real* and the laws of antiblackness. Thus, the buffering mechanisms of the symbolic—social contracts, legal protection, and the "security" of the state—are fundamentally unavailable for blackness. The interplay between the imaginary and the symbolic sits at the cleavage between the *real* and the irrepresentability of blackness. This is why for Fanon "analyzing the real is always a delicate task."[72] For blackness is not simply a problematic at the register of the *real*; the exposure of blackness to the *real* indicates a violence that, for Fanon, further obscures the distinction between the *real* and reality, and dissimulates the work between the imaginary and the symbolic. In this vein, Fanon raises concerns about the image, the *imago*, and aesthetics in relation to the *real*—placing the *real* in tension with the (il)logic of fantasy.[73] Unlike Lacan, who declares "that it is in relation to the real that the level of phantasy functions: the real supports the phantasy, the phantasy protects the real,"[74] Fanon identifies the impossibility of reality-testing where the real fantasy of blackness and reality become indistinguishable. In this light, the *imago* of blackness, birthed from the antiblack fantasies of culture, makes blackness the locus of generalized societal anxiety. This structural positioning compels the realization that blackness is made "responsible for every possible conflictual situation, we have kept within reality."[75] Fanon thus sees the cultural and collective fantasies of (anti)blackness—where blackness is posited as the source of every possible conflict—as the exact scaffolding that maintains a sense of "reality" for the human. His interrogation of the real-fantasies, and how those fantasies distort the reality of (anti) blackness, raise concerns central throughout the book regarding the forms that abstraction may take. The question of forms and abstraction together, we will come to see, further elicits the possibility of impossibility regarding transformation—the psychical shifts, mechanisms, and processes through which symbolic and imaginary elements accrue value, a value defined by its positioning against other differences.

This impossibility reflects the "self-lynching" of blackness in at least two ways: first, the pathologizing of blackness at the level of the imaginary (via collective fantasy) maintains a semblance of reality, law, and order; and second, the impossibility of transformation speaks to the recursive nature of displacement, deferral, and erasure that is evident in the "self-lynching" of blackness. These displacements are sinews of a structural order that sustains itself through the unrepresentable violence of the *real*. This particular type of truth reveals the violence (of the blackness) of the *real* to be the unsymbolizable precondition that both founds the possibility of recognition for the Human and simultaneously ensures its perpetual, internal failure to account for the being of blackness.

Dream-Work

Dream-work is a key concept in Chapters 1, 5, and 6. Since Freud's conceptualization of the dream-work, scholars in psychoanalysis, Marxism, aesthetic theory, and black studies have taken up the concept to evoke processes of transformation that subtend or are latent to representation—such as the appearance of images, forms, structures. Central to Freud's framework is his emphasis that what one sees might signify something radically different; the psychical mechanisms that conjure the appearance of forms stem from the unreachable "navel of the dream." Freud is very clear about the conflation between dream-thoughts and dream-work, a slippage that lends itself to further confusion between an interpretation that takes place at the level of representation and the attempt to articulate the relationship between the unconscious and the psychical mechanisms that make such representations possible. He writes:

> The dream-work is not simply more careless, more irrational, more forgetful and more incomplete than waking thought; it is completely different from it qualitatively and for that reason not immediately comparable with it. It does not think, calculate or judge in any way at all; it restricts itself to giving things a new form. It is exhaustively described by an enumeration of the conditions which it has to satisfy in producing its result. That product, the dream, has above all to evade the censorship, and with that end in view the dream-work makes use of *displacement of psychical intensities* to the point of transvaluation of all psychical values. The thoughts have to be reproduced exclusively or predominantly in the material of visual and acoustic-memory traces, and this necessity imposes upon the dream-work *considerations of representability* which it meets by carrying out fresh displacements.[76]

In a note that accompanies this explication of the dream-work, Freud further stresses the distinction between the dream's manifest content, latent content, and the dream-work. But he also implies an attachment to the confusion that allows for reading and interpretation at the level of forms:[77] "At bottom, dreams are nothing other than a particular *form* of thinking, made possible by the conditions of the state of sleep. It is the *dream-work* which creates that form, and it alone is the essence of dreaming—the explanation of its peculiar nature."[78]

Though the book will, at times, highlight how the "self-lynching" of blackness complicates standard readings of transformation, I take seriously Freud's emphasis on "a particular form of thinking" that can overwrite the mechanisms of the dream-work, thereby obscuring that which remains unthought across various modes of representation and appearance. In our case, the unthought of blackness and the lynching of blackness from "a particular *form* of thinking" lead to a critical tension between the misidentifications and misrecognitions required for recognition as such and the (non)knowledge of blackness. This distinction—between the conditions of general recognition and the non-knowledge of blackness—is pivotal to the framework of *Beyond Abolition* because it allows us to discern how such forms signal a very particular type of (non)knowledge of blackness, which, in turn, exposes a truth about the violence (of blackness) of the *real*. This might align with Freud's well-known maxim of dreams as the royal road to the unconscious. But as Jonathan Lear points out, "What [Freud] actually says is: 'The *interpretation* of dreams is the royal road to a *knowledge* of the unconscious *activities* of the mind.'"[79] Lear explains further, "This activity yields a very special kind of knowledge: not theoretical knowledge of a hidden realm, but practical knowledge of how to take split-off aspects of one's own imaginative activity."[80] Lear's insight parallels *Beyond Abolition's* own investigation, which seeks what is latent to the interstices between being and the imaginary, and asks how the "self-lynching" of blackness subtends this imaginative activity. Equally significant is the distinction between seeking and retrieving some hidden content versus the (non)knowledge that animates psychical forms and content. Part of *Beyond Abolition*'s endeavor is to articulate the relationship between the (non)knowledge and (non)meaning of blackness and "self-lynching" as the conditions that (re)produce the possibility of the knowledge and meaning of forms and appearances.

Image and Form

Image and form, no doubt, have their immediate resonances within a visual register and within aesthetics. However, as discussed above, these terms also carry a specific psychic valence. For Georges Didi-Huberman, the exploration of images is inseparable from the formation of knowledge. In reference to the German art historian Erwin Panofsky, he says: "'The relation of the eye to the world' is in truth a relation of the soul to the world of the eye."[81] The seeming unity between the eye and the world leads Didi-Huberman to question the coherence of this relation—the split that constitutes the image—by meditating further on the role of the unconscious.

> To split the notion of the image would be, first, to return to an inflection of the word that speaks neither of imagery, nor of reproduction, nor of iconography, nor even of "figurative" appearance. It would be to return to a questioning of the image that does not *yet* presuppose the "figured figure"—by which I mean the figure fixed as a representational object—but only the *figuring figure*, namely the process, the path, the question in action.
>
> [. . .]

> We must, by opening the box [of representation] open its eye to the dimension of an expectant gaze: wait until the visible "takes," and in this waiting try to put our finger on the *virtual* value of what we are trying to apprehend under the term *visual*.[82]

Aside from the relation between the world and the eye, the relation between the "eye" and the "I" alone indicates a myriad of dynamics operating from within and without. What I infer from Didi-Huberman's emphasis on the *virtual* value that precedes the visual is how together the acts of waiting, processing, and articulation can project an image even if it is only a temporary and fleeting impression. Thus, there is an image that might be represented in the visual register, but there are also images that precede their representability. A trace (whether virtual, immaterial, or psychic) can be construed as an image, even if its vicissitudes are not represented or representable. For instance, while Freud describes the instinctual representative (*Triebrepräsentanz*) as "a psychical representative"[83] (*psychische Repräsentanz*), he also clarifies that what "is represented in mental life by an instinct"[84] does not necessarily correspond with what symptomatically manifests—the appearance—as a result of the drive. *Beyond Abolition* will frequently examine this dynamic between the drive, its vicissitudes, and the manifestation through which it takes form—whether that form is law, an aesthetic choice, or language. The "self-lynching" of blackness animates the various psychical dynamics under examination, enabling the relation between the world and the eye, and the image conjured by the sovereignty of the eye and its relationship to the world.

What constitutes the image (say, the content—whether psychic, virtual, or material), thus relies on a combination of psychic, sociocultural, and political forces and dynamics. In the case of artistic images, it also includes the craft of techniques as a way to "reveal" or frame representations of reality, truth, and knowledge (*technē*). Undoubtedly, images are forms, but not all forms are images. Since Bradley's watershed monograph, *Anteaesthetics: Black Aesthesis and the Critique of Form*, the evocation of forms cannot be, in my opinion, taken for granted. As Bradley astutely outlines, the recursive dissimulation of blackness takes place both in the interrogation of forms (and formalism) and the productions of forms. The endless mirroring of this twin movement gives rise to, on one hand, the unthought of blackness, and on the other hand, the way in which (anti)blackness is constitutive of forms, a logic of valuation, the metaphysical violence of ontology, and, more generally, what Bradley sees as "a racial regime of aesthetics."[85] Like Bradley, I ask how "blackness poses irresolvable problems for form, which no amount of formalist interpretation can fully reconcile."[86] To define form, then, seems somewhat incongruous with this examination of the ways in which blackness is anterior to the conditions of form and its possibility. Still, to presume form as given might miss the point of how "blackness is the condition of (im) possibility for form."[87]

In *Beyond Abolition*, I refer to form often in the aesthetic sense of an appearance, composition, or structure that precedes its content, as well as the way psychical forces and registers determine their forms (e.g., dream-thoughts, wishes, fantasies, phobias, etc.). While appearance is often translated in a Hegelian context as *Erscheinung* (the manifestation of essence in the phenomenal world), my focus is on the critical movement between *Darstellung* (presentation) and *Vorstellung* (representation). G.W.F. Hegel, though only referenced sparsely throughout the book, remains nonetheless formative for his extensive meditations on this inextricable relationship. That is, the movement from something like a thought-form (or picture-thought), a psychical representation (*Vorstellung*) as contingency, to the rational presentation (*Darstellung*) of a system or structure raises a critical imperative to seek what has been rendered as abstractions (and how) as opposed to effects of knowledge.[88] This imperative—to trace the necessary emergence of structural coherence from contingent conditions—is echoed in Lacan's structural account of subjective formation. Hegel invites a dialectical thinking and reading of seemingly contradictory forms just as Lacan recalls the "total form of the body"[89] as an imaginary *Gestalt*, stemming from a misrecognition (*méconnaissance*). These apparent diremptions compel us toward a task similar to Gillian Rose's provocation of "failing towards form."[90] More relevantly, however, they align with the political urgency of George Jackson's "growing spiral of contradictions."[91] I interpret this task as maintaining the struggle inherent in contradictions while simultaneously excavating what animates their seeming oppositions, rather than escaping into the easement of their abstractions. In this sense, a central investigation of *Beyond Abolition* explores how the "self-lynching" of blackness provides the ground-wire for the appearance and contradiction of forms while also questioning the unconscious desire for their abstractions.

Outline of Chapters

Each chapter in this book examines the distortion of "self-lynching" in the symbolic and imaginary that creates the central paradox according to which blackness inhabits a position of both elision (structural non-being) and accrual (material accumulation). This paradoxical status manifests primarily in the form of policing and punishment, but also as a fundamental position of capture and captivity in and for the image of sovereignty and the *self*.

Chapter 1, "'Crimes of the Blackest Hue': Policing, White Justice, and the Antecedent Violence of Popular Sovereignty" reexamines the relations between slavery, lynching, and the criminalization of blackness not simply for their historical ties to policing in the United States, but in the context of what Marriott has poignantly coined the "occult presence of racial slavery."[92] The psycho-social bond of racial slavery haunts California and the American West as a projected ideal toward which the nation-state continued to direct its regime of racial terror under the cover of westward settlement in a post-Emancipation context. The chapter also illustrates how antiblackness undergirds the dream-work of sovereignty, binding together a collective sense of white justice that could be exercised and justified through practices of lynching. By revisiting the debates around slavery, the reinforcement of fugitive slave law, testimony exclusion laws, and lynching as a practice of "frontier justice," the chapter interrogates the language of sovereignty, truth, and justice in the context of California statecraft being projected as a liberal horizon. The chapter conceptualizes antiblackness as an antagonistic position in the eyes of positive law—as both *ante legem* and *contra legem* to the discursive frameworks through which law and society cohere. It is here that the chapter introduces lynching as castration in the racial imaginary: a prohibition in the symbolic order that has yet to encounter a real abolition. This prohibition extends into the economic domain, where the slave's radical incapacity and non-value consolidate into a form of liquidity that substantiates the groundless subject of capitalism. The chapter argues that the financialization of capital relies upon this "extravagant expenditure" of blackness, treating the (dis)appearance of the slave as a libidinal and metaphysical necessity that sustains the dream-work of Manifest Destiny.

If the symbolic order's ultimate limit is the *real*—defined by Lacan as the impossible ("the opposite of the possible is certainly the real, we would be led to define the *real* as the impossible"[93])—then any abolition pursued strictly within the symbolic register must confront this radical uncertainty. The chapter uses this provocation to speculate further on the relationship between the antiblack screens of liberalism and sovereignty, and blackness as fundamental to the formation of the image, thereby leading to the next chapter, which deals with concerns of sovereignty and the image more extensively.

Chapter 2, "At the Edge of Presence: Antiblackness and the Image of 'Self-Lynching,'" explores the role of racialized sexuality and desire in the historical memory of antiblackness and the order of law. It does so in two ways. First, by expanding on the previous chapter's meditations regarding the dissimulation of antiblackness under the political banners of sovereignty and lynching as a right, this chapter extends its analysis to the formations of memory, the historicization of lynching, and the enactment of the antilynching legislation in California. Given how fundamental antiblack sexual politics were to lynching's regimes of terror, the chapter contends that the libidinal violation of blackness, namely that of black desire, was both a product of and inherent to lynching. Antiblack sexualized fantasies were thus central to the ideological apparatus and psychic terms of lynching in California. This is particularly evident in the enactment of the penal code and the fact that the code's own history is *re-membered* through the lynching of two white men, John Holmes and Thomas Thurmond. The penal code has often been referenced as the state's response to the spectacle of the Holmes and Thurmond lynching, which produced a flood of media images and responses. The Holmes and Thurmond lynching usurps the origins of the penal code as part a foundational myth, while the labors of two black political advocates, Delilah Beasley and Frederick Roberts, whose efforts were integral to the passing of this bill, are systematically denied. The legislative intent of the penal code, designed to shield racialized subjects from extralegal discipline, is thus undermined. The state's defense of sovereignty not only folds into the logic of law's racial authority; it is also sustained through the instantiations of whiteness at the site of blackness's disfigurations.

The second part of the chapter interrogates the image and the racial limits of representation by using the photographic work of contemporary artist Ken Gonzales-Day.[94] Gonzales-Day uses digital media to (re)produce and reimagine historical images of lynching sites. Removing the victim's body from the image, the artist asks the viewer to imagine the racial figure of the murdered victim, while simultaneously acknowledging that not all victims were of African descent. However, the disfigurement of blackness remains inherent in the imaging of lynching violence—even in the attempt to recuperate the racial figure—due to the indelible force of antiblackness on the historical memory of lynching. By placing these images together—the historical memory of Thurmond and Holmes and Gonzales-Day's digital art—the chapter unpacks how an imagined presence of a "self" signals the desire for both sovereignty of the image and the image of sovereignty.

Chapter 3, "Untranslatability, Resistance: The *Afterlife* of 'Self-Lynching,'" considers the strange and estranged forty-year gap between the anti-lynching legislation's enactment and the first two court cases making use of this law (1969, 1999). Both cases relied significantly on the misinterpretation and distortion of the statute's original intent. The chapter illustrates how the seeming absence of documented lynching violence in the State of California is not simply an outcome of the juridical restrictions which determine when a case can be prosecuted and judged under this specific statute; the interpretation of the penal code in the two court cases also signals blackness's irrepresentability in the juridical racial imaginary, thus enabling the translation from the statute's original legislative intent of anti-lynching to the notion of "self-lynching." A fundamental question here is how the terms "untranslatability" and "resistance" labor differently in respect to blackness. The chapter considers the untranslatability of blackness in the various registers of "resistance" in law, representation, and the psychic economies of antiblackness. It further reflects on how the transience of such a translation casts an impossible "self" via a mode of lynching in the juridical imaginary—a type of foreclosure that precedes and operates beyond the orders of *de jure* and *de facto* law.

Chapter 4, "High-Tech Lynching": Irony, Sexual Difference, and Toni Morrison's the 'Metaphor of Itself,'" departs briefly from the genealogy of the penal code to continue its conceptual ruminations on blackness, resistance, and language through the image of "self-lynching." The chapter revisits Clarence Thomas's characterization of Anita Hill's testimony during his Supreme Court confirmation hearings as a "high-tech lynching." The chapter explores Thomas's rhetorical usage of the term, showing how it reproduces the logic of lynching while simultaneously reducing it to a representation trope. Following Toni Morrison's readings of Thomas's remarks and the media representation surrounding the event, the chapter engages her observations that Thomas uses "lynching as the metaphor of itself." However, the chapter pivots to examine the structural divergence between irony and metaphor as substitutive images. The discrepancy, I argue, mirrors the gap between what is considered irreal or real in the schema of antiblack social fantasies of knowledge and truth. The chapter further examines this racial representational logic by asking how blackness is put to work in the semblance of signs and signifiers of racial and sexual difference and the hallucinatory effects coterminous with them.

Chapter 5, "Beyond Abolition: Unhomeliness, Perversion, and the Arrest of Jasmine Richards Abdullah," centers on the question of the real-fantasy and its role in the violent exposure of blackness to the *real*. This chapter focuses on the events surrounding Jasmine Abdullah Richards's arrest for "self-lynching." The escalation of events—and the identificatory desires, anxieties, and projections that facilitate them—expose the uncanniness and perversion underlying the arrest. However, this perversion is not strictly an effect of antiblack police violence in the practice of law and order as it is commonly understood. On the contrary, the chapter asks what conditions give rise to the appearance of the arrest of blackness *as* uncanny (or as Freud might say, *unhomely*), and whether blackness can ever find homeliness (with) in language. In this sense, the language of law and rights is once again under scrutiny, though less as a framework of principles and values and more as a telos. Abdullah Richards's arrest not only signals a perversion of antiblack policing, law, and order, but also shows how perversion maintains and justifies antiblackness as the limit to reason and being, meaning and interpretation. The chapter argues that the conversion from an imagined rioting to the perception of Abdullah Richards lynching herself brings into sharp focus the question at what level the abstraction of (anti)blackness is conceived and sustained as a foundational logic.

Chapter 6, "Black Abstraction?: Real Abstraction, the Artworks of Melvin Edwards and Torkwase Dyson, and the Abolition of the Real," argues that our inquiries into "self-lynching" in aesthetics, politics, historical memory, and language elucidate the fundamental function of real-fantasies of antiblackness. This chapter puts the notion of real-fantasies in tension with conceptions of abstraction—specifically within Marxist readings of real abstraction and race. It pursues this final set of questions by turning to the artists Melvin Edwards and Torkwase Dyson, who engage with both the abstraction of lynching and lynching as an abstraction in their works. Arguing that abstraction remains a mechanism that brings what blackness is *not* into appearance, the chapter argues that abstraction is never unmoored from a structure of disavowal. On this score, the book concludes by meditating on a question similar to the one it began with: What might be both concealed and brought into view at the edge of abolition where the recursive movement of "self-lynching" takes place? The book leaves us with a final provocation: the abolition of the *real*—the un-setting of the traumatic core that sustains blackness's interminable descent. If the "self-lynching" of blackness provides the conditions for the structural and psychical coherence of the world, then abolition cannot be found in the symbolic or imaginary registers alone. It is here, in this *beyond abolition*, that the particular form of thinking that constitutes our world is finally rendered impossible.

One

"Crimes of the Blackest Hue"

Policing, White Justice, and the Antecedent Violence of Popular Sovereignty

The contemporary stakes of "self-lynching," as established in the Introduction, are less a series of historical contingencies than they are symptoms of a fundamental structural logic that demands a genealogical investigation. To that end, this chapter performs a genealogy not of origins, but of translation. Unlike the pursuit of a historical moment or a linear causality—which might falsely suggest a redeemable alternative—this genealogy tracks how antiblackness, as a non-subsumable foundation, is structurally rendered legible across the material, economic, juridical, and psychical domains.

Central to this process is what David Marriott identifies as the "beautiful perfection" of black death: a status where blackness is positioned as *ante legem*.[1] In this modality, "being is always already dead and so cannot be killed," yet "as property, it can be punished according to the forensic rules and pronouncements of the forum, a law that can be re-enacted each time white desire needs to defend or affirm itself *as the right law of the living*."[2] By tracing this foundational prohibition of blackness, the chapter explores how the *ante legem* (and *contra legem*) position of blackness is translated into the specific psychical and material apparatuses of U.S. sovereignty. In this translation, the structural force of "self-lynching" constitutes blackness's castration and displacement, rendering the possession of a self for blackness impossible.

Such a translation reveals lynch law as a direct extension of antiblackness—an un-settable foundation. Far from a remediable instability that might eventually be corrected or reformed, lynch law signals the structural impossibility of blackness—a current that necessitates a "rotten" cycle of repetition between law-preserving violence that eventually destroys law-making violence.[3] In this way, the "self-lynching" of blackness prevents the state from ever "setting" itself in a foundation of justice. Precisely because antiblackness establishes an un-settable foundation,[4] the law must compulsively reenact a violence sustained by the antiblack dream-work underlying liberalism and westward expansion. As I argue in this chapter and throughout *Beyond Abolition*, antiblack violence cannot be "set" or "fixed" into a stable past; instead, (anti)blackness functions as the very violence that makes the law possible while ensuring its *afterlife* persists as "a mode of translation."[5] In this register, (anti)blackness can never be fully codified, resolved, or relegated to history. Rather, the translation manifests as a recurring psychic demand—appearing "each time [as] white desire [needing] to defend" itself. By tracking this circular psychical movement, the chapter moves beyond mere historical documentation to demonstrate how this structural operation maintains the un-settable foundation upon which the modern racial state is built.

In 1834, amidst the era of escalating anti-abolition riots—a violent backlash against the radicalism of militant abolitionism within the broader Age of Reform—newspapers such as *The Galenian* justified "lynch law" as the right of *the people* to exercise popular sovereignty when the courts were unable to uphold the rule of law on behalf of the community's good. *The Galenian* described an accused murderer, Patrick O'Conner, who "had committed crimes and misconduct '*of the blackest hue.*' . . . 'His whole character,' the paper implied, made any alternative to lynching impossible."[6] The force of *The Galenian*'s justification resides in its racialized rhetoric. By framing the offense as "crimes and misconduct of the blackest hue," the paper suggests that the crime itself is contaminated by blackness—a judgment the paper assumes to be natural and self-evident. It is not simply that O'Conner committed morally reprehensible crimes, but that the *hue* of those crimes—their "blackened" nature—contaminates his entire character, his very being, to a superlative degree. Such a judgment draws its explanatory power from the naturalization of antiblackness, which functions as the unquestioned backdrop of the social order, allowing the paper to justify extralegal violence without ever having to explicitly name race. What is clear from the headline is that because crime and misconduct are "blackened," the only legible response becomes the most severe and lawless punitive measure: lynch law. "The blackest hue" is thus presented not as a description, but as a condition of unfettered lawlessness that demands the reciprocal violence of lawlessness itself.

A stark tension emerges here between event and perception: lynching as an expression and exercise of lawless violence, and the imagined lawlessness of blackness that ostensibly contaminates one's being to commit the most "blackened" crime. Such mirroring—wherein lynching reproduces the very lawlessness it claims to reprimand—signals a more fundamental, racialized judgment. By telegraphing a judgment of O'Conner's "character" as "natural" or even divine, the paper effectively divides those rendered redeemable by law from those who are not, those who are human from those who are nonhuman. This constitutes the first translation of the genealogy: the rendering of the foundational prohibition into a psychical mechanism tethered to an ontological judgment. Reflected in "the blackest hue," this perception pervades the subject's entire character, implying that blackness provides a sufficient reason to justify lynching without recourse. Even in the absence of any explicit referentiality, blackness provides this reason via the architecture of race. In this register, blackness facilitates an interdependency between "race" and "reason"—a racist reasoning—that does not just support lynching and makes "any alternative to lynching impossible"; it also animates the capacity for these two poles to coalesce even in the face of their own glaring contradictions.

"Crimes of the blackest hue" opens up a problematic that is central to this study: What are the psychical dynamics and relations that structure "self-lynching"? What constitutes a self within the psychical mechanisms of lynching? And in what ways does the "self-lynching" of blackness constitute a founding gesture within and outside the law? Reading "crimes of the blackest hue" as symptomatic of a deeper uncertainty essential to lynching—as a phenomenon oscillating between the legal and extralegal—compels an understanding of more than just the representational value of the symptom as a figure of judgment; it necessitates a tracking of how such a symptom accrues meaning from the imagined life of sovereignty. In this chapter, my aim is to interrogate how "self-lynching" as a psychical dynamic underscores the meaning-making of both positive law and lynch law, alongside those notions of sovereignty coterminous with lynching itself. In the analysis that follows, the accrual of sovereignty is shown to stem from the lynching of blackness as a possible self. Such a foundational foreclosure of blackness renders impossible any function of blackness as a sign of continuity, coherence or stable meaning. Instead, the foreclosure animates the possibility of what the system mistakes and misrecognizes for a sign—appearing explicitly as criminality or figure of investment, or implicitly as the constitutive "outside" against which sovereignty defines itself. These figures reveal themselves as images that provide the illusion "of continuity, coherency, and meaning in place of the fantasies of emptiness, need, and frustrated desire that inhabit our nightmares about the destructive power of time."[7] The perceived stability of these images, however, remains merely the symptom of a constitutive necessity to conceal antiblackness as the foundation of the system. What is projected as the integrity of sovereignty reveals itself, in this light, as the "self-lynching" of blackness—a process that confirms the foundation of sovereignty through the enforced non-being of blackness.

Fantasies of blackness are essential to the imagined life and dream-work of law, sovereignty, and their possibilities, as the newspaper headline demonstrates. "Crimes of the blackest hue" functions as an inscription—an enunciation of lynch law where, as Hayden White might explain it, "the text summons up a 'substance,' operates in the domain of memory rather than in that of dream or fantasy, and unfolds under the sign of 'the real' rather than that of 'the imaginary.'"[8] What this tells us is that blackness as an imagined yet consolidated figure turns the communicative act of law, specifically lynch law, from its unwritten form into an event to secure an imagined truth against a perceived limit. As Cornelia Vismann observes, this mediatic relation of law produces epistemic objects where "they not only fix a result but also shed light on their own development, on that which precedes grand acts of writing . . . they allow access to that which came before the law, the legally binding verdict, the issued deed."[9] Vismann brings to our attention the production of epistemic objects which are essential to the law of "writing up while writing *along*" but nonetheless establish law's validity. "Crimes of the blackest hue," as an inscription before the law, materializes the terroristic extralegal rituals of lynching just as it purports a constructed meaning of blackness. As an inscription before the law, the phrase functions as a timeless figure among many in the *afterlife* of slavery and lynching.

Reading this phrase as part of the meaning-making of lynch law points to how such signs and symbols remain inseparable from the dream-work of white sovereignty—the manifest content which stands in for and obscures the psychic life of antiblackness. In this chapter, I interrogate how notions of Manifest Destiny and its fantasies of sovereignty illustrate the manifest content of an antiblack dream-work even in regard to, or in spite of, the dissimulation of blackness. The tensions and drives that weave together this dream-work of sovereignty are crucial to understanding the *afterlife* of slavery and lynching. The dream-work speaks to the nature of *afterlife* in both its ghostly existence and psychical survival (or what Walter Benjamin describes in his use of the notion of *afterlife*, *Fortleben*, the survival of not just life after death or an end, but the continuation of living enabled by a translation that invokes the "stage of a continued life").[10] Manifest Destiny, as an index of the dream-work of sovereignty, is, thus, interdependent with this notion of *afterlife*, a translation that rests on the untranslatability of blackness (see Chapter 3). Yet as I hope to make clear, the dream-work of sovereignty does not simply reveal a "latent content" of antiblackness. Rather, blackness and antiblackness fail to appear as the content of the dream-work precisely because they are unlocatable across the registers of Sigmund Freud's now well-known triangulation of manifest content, the latent dream-thought, and unconscious wish.[11] Thus, instead of embracing the "standard notion of penetrating deeper and deeper into the core of the dream"[12] to bring a latent meaning to consciousness, our aim here is to ruminate on the impossibility of blackness coming into appearance. We move beyond the separation and binary of presence and absence to excavate the a priori conditions that render blackness as unknown (and unknowable) to the foundation of law.

To this effect, the founding gesture animating the dream-work and underlying the signification of lynching rests on an indeterminate ontology of blackness. An ontology of blackness read as interchangeable with criminality functions as a method for unifying extralegal meaning, ritual, and judicial commitments of what is deemed "people's justice." As a medium, the sign of "the blackest hue" becomes jurisgenerative, authorizing the use of lynch law and the consequent suppression of the courts. Perceived as a threat to the illusion of whiteness, blackness functions as a screen for the ontological projection of criminal fabrications and legal fictions. What is rendered as "the blackest hue" extends the signifying chain of lynch law, wherein "the *imagined* instant of unified meaning is like a seed, a legal DNA, a genetic code by which the imagined integration is the template for a thousand real integrations of corpus, discourse, and commitment."[13] For Robert Cover, the fleeting unification of meaning internal to law is telic: "the too fertile forces of jurisgenesis"[14] imply the objective to evolve in an orderly fashion "like a seed" or "legal DNA." While Cover addresses legal meaning through precept and principle, his logic applies with equal force to lynch law.[15] Lynch law, manifesting its signification from this seed, exacts the extrapolation of appearance from its very concealment that generates meaning. In this regard, the disclosure of appearance within lynch law—a system with antiblackness at its kernel—includes the representations and formations of "popular sovereignty." This initial analysis tracks the translation of antiblack prohibition into a psychical and ontological mechanism. Before examining the economic manifestation of an antiblack dream-work, one must pause to consider the relationship between this dream-work and the instantiation of whiteness as sovereignty. The structural prohibition of blackness, having been rendered psychically legible as an ontological judgment, is necessarily incorporated into the formal (and extralegal) apparatuses of positive law. This next section traces how the *ante legem* position of blackness is translated into the practices of lynch law and Manifest Destiny—mechanisms that simultaneously claim to uphold white justice while generating their own sovereign power.

Manifest Destiny: A Dream-Work of Sovereignty

"I am not a prisoner of History. I must not look for the meaning of my destiny in that direction."
—Frantz Fanon[16]

Perceived as an uninhabited space and free territory, the American West provided an ideal destination in the collective fantasy of Manifest Destiny. The horizon of westward expansion, indeed, was envisioned as the space to perform "popular sovereignty" or "community justice" liberated from the oversight of an established criminal justice system; it simultaneously marked the possibility of economic growth, stability, and independence amidst the ruptures of the Mexican-American War and the Civil War. This tension is clarified by David A. Johnson, who explains that "the practice of vigilantism in newly settled territories revealed profound tensions attending the growth of capitalist institutions on the frontier" while "the subsequent suppression of lynching was closely related to the ongoing development of a frontier region's society and economy, and to the establishment of an American criminal justice system and the particular meaning it gave to the concepts of authority, criminality, and justice."[17] As a site of lawless freedom and economic promise, the Western frontier became a fecund space for the larger racial imaginary of the nation-state—a domain where the abolitionist ethos of the Northeast could be systematically dismissed. The ambiguity of political and geopolitical boundaries also rendered tenable, or at least morally unquestionable, the desire to corroborate pro-slavery sentiment and manipulate the administration of fugitive slave law. Reinforcing the segregation of black life and other informal iterations of slavery, these porous boundaries meant that "hundreds lived in slavery despite California's formal ban on that institution."[18]

In the first half of the nineteenth century, California, and the imagined uninhabited space of the American West more generally, served as an unregulated site in the nation's racial imaginary, thus positing the mirage of a new dawn: a racial liberalism facilitated first by the abolition of racial slavery in the new Mexican Republic and later by the unrealized promises of Reconstruction. The unregulated space staged the opportunity to transplant the nation's insidious desire for and libidinal commitment to the lawful racial subjection, subordination, and segregation of blackness under the guise of collective sovereignty and "popular justice." As Christopher Waldrep explains, "When California joined the Union as a free state in 1850, the South lost a political battle, but in the long run, Southern white racist supporters of vigilantism and lynching gained immeasurably more from California's support of extralegal violence."[19] The legitimization of vigilantism, as Waldrep elaborates, provided a dual purpose: it motivated westward migration *and* simultaneously provided a legalistic defense for localized racial violence (or "lynch law") that undermined the abolition movement's opposition to chattel slavery. Within this logic, an opposition to chattel slavery on moral grounds remained compatible with a championing of popular sovereignty and the right to pass extralegal judgment without due process, based on the belief that citizens could justly circumvent established judicial apparatuses.[20] Consequently, the apparent contradiction of the pro-lynching abolitionist reveals itself as a functional alignment of values. Carol Anderson observes how summary punishment and the right to bear arms among white citizens were inextricable, reinforced by state legislations that encouraged "white citizen patrols 'to seize arms found in the homes of slaves and free blacks,' and those caught trying to bear arms could be 'summarily punished.'"[21] As she explains further, "Statute after statute barring ownership or even the use of weapons, unless approved by whites, made this right, even for free Blacks, race-contingent and conditional."[22] In this vein, the abolitionist stance was defined by its narrowness: just as one could oppose the institution of chattel slavery yet still endorse lynch law, one could also hold anti-slavery values while favoring the coercive labor system of peonage, therefore rejecting legal ownership of individuals without abandoning the impulse of racial control.[23]

Peonage, a system of debt servitude inherited from Spanish-colonial and Mexican rule in the Southwest, maintained Latine and Native American populations in bondage. These localized practices exacerbated the ideological debates of the sectional crisis due to the ongoing legal and practical indistinction between chattel slavery and the weaponization of debt and involuntary servitude to suppress black freedom. These professed contradictions indicate not only the juridical conditions that would actively suppress the possibility of black self-ownership in the face of white popular sovereignty; they also speak to how such "values"—*de jure* or *de facto*—figured claims of blackness simultaneously as they displaced the ways in which blackness would be forced to (dis)appear symbolically.

The foundational prohibition of blackness is not only translated into a psychical and juridical mechanism, but also manifests in the economic domain through the paradox of the slave's body. This translation reveals how blackness's non-value is instrumentalized in the financialization of capital, structuring the very conditions of speculative value and expenditure. Indeed, California emerged as exceptional in its capacity to respond to the nation's racial antagonisms through the perpetuation and fortification of extralegal violence—a vigilante justice which functioned as an extension of the nation's political and psychosocial ties to slavery and segregation. Stephanie LeMenager's work regarding the contested boundaries and visions of the "American West" points to how the imagined site west of the Mississippi impacted the meaning-making of the nation-state, modernity, and white selfhood. Specifically, she observes that "slave value was intimately linked to the territorial annexation that came to be understood as U.S. Manifest Destiny,"[24] a process that gave the nation its territorial shape. At the nexus of migration, the horizons of the Western frontier, and the racial imaginary of the nation during the 1820s and 1830s, LeMenager demonstrates that the mobility of slaves stabilized their value across regional markets, securing a new economic niche for planters in the Upper South.[25] Such a logic, LeMenager points out, evinces a foundational yet unsettling tenet of capital and finance: while slaves posed "a more likely speculative risk than land,"[26] they constituted a superior investment. To this end, slave ownership was more than a sign of capital in terms of property and production; the exchange value derived from the legal and illegal slave trade was "linked to short-term capital gains" relying on "buying [slaves] for future resale rather than for use."[27] LeMenager further observes the unique backdrop of the Mississippi Valley and its role in producing "imaginary nations within nations, fantastic empires, and mutant semi-national confederations" that made the South *western* and the West *southern*.[28] The political economy of the Mississippi slave trade also underwrote a strong sense of white mobility. Unequivocally, the sense of white mobility, capital, and financial gain radiated not just across the South and Southwest, but also permeated the North and Northeast. Slaves—essential to the supply of labor yet even more vital as speculative assets—attained a high in speculative value precisely as other forms of property and commodities declined in worth.[29]

LeMenager raises the critical point that the speculative value of the slave—and its role in the westward expansion—rested upon the hydraulics of fantasy and conjecture. From within this circuit of projection and expansion emerged "a relatively new category of person whose sole purpose was to facilitate the movement and transference of slaves from centers of supply to centers of demand."[30] While LeMenager's analysis provides a necessary economic grounding, its emphasis on the slave's speculative value—the perception and projection of the slave—risks naturalizing the violent, foundational conditions that enable such figuration. Specifically, the focus on exchange value obscures the slave's forced absence and the function of that absence in the generation of value. This oversight masks the underlying violence requisite for constructing both the slave's speculative value and the new categories of personhood tied to the fantasies of Manifest Destiny and westward expansion. Nested within this economic calculus is a more fundamental interrogation: Where is blackness located if the slave's presence is registered exclusively as an asset of exchange value? More critically, what is the ontological function of blackness—what does it effectuate—within this expansive landscape of destiny and capital? The relationship between the speculative value of the slave and the slave's role and function in the projections of white "destiny" against ever-expanding regional slave markets only begins to encounter the "vertiginous absence" of blackness.[31] At stake in the intersections between lynch law, the liquidation of the slave, and the teleology of Manifest Destiny is the expression of white selfhood and white sovereignty contingent upon the incapacitation of blackness.

Take, for instance, LeMenager's reading of John Murrell's slave-trading practice, where he "counts on the high value of slaves in the 1830s and the greed of investors to carry off his transactions, which resemble the transactions of legal slave traders in every detail save beginning and end."[32] Murrell's "sale pitch," used to coerce the enslaved, betokens the double-bind of a debt that places (re)captured black life into the dire straits between (un) freedom and death: "If I steal you, and carry you off, and sell you four or five times, and give you half the money, and then leave you in a free state, will you go?"[33] As LeMenager indicates, the slave might agree, but the trade-off is that "black self-ownership has become equivalent of not having a body."[34]

> There is an economic logic here: as a capitalist or new owner of himself the slave has been removed from the hyper-embodied labor sector. But this logic takes a cruel turn because . . . the social convention of race insures that the black body will always be marked. In attempting to achieve freedom, Murrell's slaves become only too remarkable. When a particular slave Murrell handles begins to be widely recognized, the thief must make good on his sleight of hand and cause that slave to disappear.[35]

Whether contracted formally or informally, signs of black self-ownership in the context of the sectional crisis engendered the slave's "disappearance" at the material level of the body. Yet, a central tension remains: Does "the social convention of race" continue to guarantee the marking of the black body even when the body is disconnected from the "hyper-embodied labor sector" and its corresponding symbolic circuits of labor power and market value? What is elided in LeMenager's analysis is why would the slave consent to the inevitable consequence of his/her own disappearance—a trajectory that regularly culminated in death under the "promise" of freedom. As Sarah Haley has carefully parsed out, the very logic of consent is a category of error in this context: "The dichotomy between willingly leaving and being kidnapped is faulty, as it assumes she had the freedom to make a willing choice."[36]

With this in mind, what is at issue is less a psychological explanation for the slave's particular "choice" than the structural conditions that enable an impossible forced choice, or what Jacques Lacan describes as the *vel*.[37] The impossible forced choice is not just about coercion into a false freedom; it reflects the slave's impossible position that makes such exchanges possible in the first place. As Sara-Maria Sorentino explains, the slave's radical "absence—the incapacity of the slave; the nothingness of blackness—coheres in the liquidity of the slave in order to substantiate natural necessity, which itself can be considered the cover for the groundlessness of the self-determined subject of capitalism."[38] Sorentino is crucial here for theorizing blackness not merely as a consequence of history or as a feature of race, but as a condition that "precedes the history of race, standing in for a system of legibility."[39] Within this theoretical frame, the signifier of the body in respect to race is shrouded in subterfuge before it can be rendered as value—speculative or otherwise. This condition anchors Sorentino's analysis of the triangulation of the slave's liquidity, capitalism, and the appearance of race. Precisely because slaves possess no inherent relation to value, slavery remains perpetually "stuck in a world of use values even, paradoxically, when slaves function *as* exchange value, because slaves can have *no relation* to value and thus, stand apart from the specific social violences and promises of exchange, unable to partake in practices of freedom."[40] Consequently, it is not only that the disappearance of the slave's body becomes costly due to its speculative value; rather, the slave can only appear as a body of substance on the condition of blackness's incapacity. It is this very incapacity that underwrites the liquidity of the slave and the possibility of value-exchange that measures the slave's worth in gold.

Marriott's ruminations on blackness, slave law, and what he terms blackness's "extravagant expenditure" shed light on this paradox of the slave's value as nothing.[41] Observing a "nonrestricted meaning [in] a categorical shift from duty to surplus . . . [,] an anxiety about work as a system of accumulation and deferral," Marriott notes that this transformation also "involves a displacement from *telos* to *eros*, corpus to jouissance."[42] Similar to Sorentino, he gestures to a counterintuitive image constituted by the nothingness of blackness—a figuration that diverges from LeMenager's illustration of the political economy of slavery in the context of Manifest Destiny. Beyond the paradox in which the slave's speculative value produces a symbolic surplus, blackness's non-value is the catalyst that conjures both the perception (speculation) and the event (production) of that surplus, ultimately collapsing the two. In this way, Marriott's analysis critically shifts away from a generic formulation of contract, labor-production, and exchange to demonstrate that the slave's non-value is instrumental in the financialization of capital. Psychically, the image-form (the wish, fantasies, illusions) of blackness's indefinite work and abjection as a form of pleasure constitutes a libidinal investment inseparable from the economy of the slave. "Turning blackness *into* work,"[43] by actualizing the disappearance of the slave as labor power, reveals how the libidinal investment in the slave is inscribed into the circuits of capital.

In this vein, the "disappearance" of the slave seems to function as a political and metaphysical necessity that precedes economic logic, rather than simply being a contingent effect of the slave's speculative value in a volatile market. Crucially, then, the problem is not solely that the slave fails to appear as a body—a misapprehension that has erroneously led some psychoanalytic thinkers to construe the slave and the worker as interchangeable.[44] The error stems from applying a symptomatic framework that wrongly presupposes the slave is "without a body," an analysis which concludes that the slave "cannot appear as social symptom"[45] within the structures of capitalism.[46] Instead, the necessity of lynching blackness from the possibility of appearances—even in the appearance of the disappearance of the slave—functions to render the antinomies of capitalism's base illegitimate and structurally illegible. Such a mechanism of the representational subsumption of (anti)blackness, though seemingly fitting with the general Marxist description of contradictions that "[arise] out of the antinomies of [capitalism's] base,"[47] operates here not as a symptomatic expression of the base, but as its constitutive, dissimulating blind spot. The resulting foreclosure—the dissimulation of blackness—is essential to the promise that the myth of Manifest Destiny remains vital. The mechanics of this maintenance are found in the structures of exchange that Sibylle Fischer identifies: "The abstraction that makes people, words, and money exchangeable means that none of the units is able to capture the reality of the things exchanged . . . On the basis of this improper system of valuation, the true nature of the slave trade can be obscured completely."[48] Such obscuration masks the necessary absence of the slave which allows the myth of destiny and manifestation to endure, thereby facilitating the dream-work of Manifest Destiny. Put another way, what allows the desire, the wish, of Manifest Destiny to take place is the dialectical necessity of its form, its appearance, which is imbricated with the non-value of the slave, the absence of blackness. Furthermore, this structure demands that the "unknown" across these domains must be preserved to sustain a repetition of an interpretation through which whiteness recuperates a sense of inherent instability.

Blackness need not appear, nor must its "presence" be registered within the scene of the dream, for the myth of Manifest Destiny to maintain its form. Rather, the absence of blackness subsists at the very threshold of the representable; it is incised into the transformative force of the dream-work, folded into every texture and seam of that national imaginary. The Western horizon of Manifest Destiny signaled a space for limitless possibility to exercise "popular sovereignty," lawlessness, and "community"; yet the "disappearance" of the slave—the psychical lynching of blackness's capacity to appear—remained the essential condition for these images of white sovereignty. The ontological ordeal underlying the conversion from the nothingness of blackness to the (dis)appearance of the slave animates the endless permutations of possibility to manifest white destiny in all its forms. In the dream-work of Manifest Destiny, this conversion, "an exchange and alternation between heterogeneous orders . . . establish[es] a reality proper to the image,"[49] even insofar as that image rests on a foundational nothingness. Ultimately, the displacement of blackness and antiblackness is a necessary condition of possibility for formulations of sovereignty and justice to emerge. And yet, this displacement simultaneously establishes the vanishing point through which blackness problematizes a formulation of and for these terms to appear.

At the level of historical discourse, the mirage of this "new dawn," of course, was in no way a transformation of racial liberation, despite the later promises of Reconstruction. Nor did the sectional crisis provide an opportunity to assuage the taut division between slavery and abolition then fracturing the nation during the mid-nineteenth century. Instead, fueled by a persistent desire to retain the institutions and practices of slavery and segregation, the American West provided the fertile grounds for a newly imagined modern democracy that rested on a "people's justice"—a rhetorical stand-in for the laws of white selfhood, an entitlement that founded its most extravagant expression in the speculative liquidation of the slave.

The American West was perceived as a vast holding cell for the nation's "criminals," before and after Reconstruction. Coupled together, vigilantism and migration to the West sketched a fantasy of a divergent justice system: a "cowboy justice" where juridical rule and law enforcement were dictated by "the people" and popular sovereignty. Ergo, even as the American West was idealized as a territory for white lawlessness, it was simultaneously envisioned as a space where punitive measures could be applied to those deemed "criminal" without regulation. Indeed, lynch law frequently pursued executions to "prompt a summary mode of trial and punishment unknown to the law."[50] The uncertainty of normalized rule, thus, was inextricable from the possibility of imagining sovereignty, lawlessness, and justice at the hands of "the people." Yet, it is not merely the "unknown" status of the law that welds fantasy to the desire for sovereignty. As Slavoj Žižek reminds us, "The fundamental level of ideology, however, is not that of an illusion masking the real state of things but that of an (unconscious) fantasy structuring our social reality itself."[51] The repetition of this interpretation—distinguishable from the mere recurrence of a specific antiblack event—requires the rigorous maintenance of an "unknown" referent. By preserving this zone of illegibility, the political and libidinal economies of antiblackness, enmeshed together, ensure that the violent encounter remains open to infinite reinvestment. As such, this cycle of repetition allows whiteness to recuperate its own ontological fragility, transmuting it into the robust image and rhetoric of sovereignty.

Manifest Destiny marked the possibility to reformulate a notion of "sovereignty," namely in the relation between law, the *polis*, and the social body that would encourage migration from the South to the Western states even before the economic devastation that the South experienced as a result of losing the Civil War. "Popular sovereignty" upheld the interests of whiteness and white mobility—formations with a sustained commitment to antiblackness and ways to reinforce the ideologies of white supremacy through the rule of law. During a period of "frontier exchange economy,"[52] the American West represented an undefined space where settlers could purge the racial anxiety that surrounded an anti-abolition sentiment linked to the anticipation of a destroyed national economy.[53] The Southwest fostered the conditions that actively obscured the ambiguity of both anti-slavery and pro-slavery sentiments by privileging the rhetoric of "sovereignty." I argue that the foundational absence of blackness—the (dis)appearance discussed above—fueled a sense of imagined freedom and potential exceptionality in the Western territories in comparison to their Southern and Northeastern counterparts. The seeming absence of blackness figured notions of "sovereignty" and "exceptionality" in "Southern efforts to extend slavery westward [that] were in large part a political ploy to secure additional proslavery representation in Congress to prevent any significant dissolution of the peculiar institution in places where it already existed."[54]

As historian William S. Kiser observes, "Preexisting Mexican laws regulating human bondage were continuously called into question during discussions over slavery in the newly acquired territories. Legislators temporarily mitigated these incendiary issues with the Compromise of 1850, allowing popular sovereignty for New Mexico and the Utah territories and free-soil statehood for California."[55] Further, "although on several occasions they did take up the issue of African American rights and chattel slavery, New Mexico's territorial legislators typically avoided mentioning peonage and captivity during official proceedings."[56] Characterizing this simply as an "avoidance" of captivity, however, elides the structural labor of antiblackness in negotiating the shift from Mexican to American law. Because "Mexico's antislavery provisions had not been automatically repealed when the Southwestern domain shifted to American jurisdiction,"[57] a profound ontological crisis emerged regarding the status of the unfree. The resulting jurisdictional friction served as the primary mechanism for a representational subsumption that sought to strip blackness of any residual legal protection. By rendering Mexican abolitionist precedent "unknown" or inapplicable, the new territories could secure the ground for a white "free-soil" identity predicated on the absolute foreclosure of blackness as a subject.

For historians such as Kiser, the application of law hinges on a taxonomic distinction: Did "a law regulating slavery constitute a 'civil or municipal law' or a 'public or political law'?" As Kiser argues, if the former were true, "then Mexican legislation could not remain in effect beyond the moment of American conquest."[58] Yet, the historical record suggests that the reach of the law functions only insofar as it rests upon its own calculated failure and limitations. Instead of asking, as Kiser does, how the regulation of slavery should be classified, I ask what the repetition of these legal contradictions serves to mask. What does the cycle of seeming oppositions—between chattel slavery and peonage, between rights and captivity, and between the indiscernible presence and absence of law—occlude regarding judgment, reason, or a (non)knowledge of blackness?

That "popular sovereignty" was a way to mediate competing ideologies discloses something about the privileging of white autonomy; namely, it confirms that "the concept of freedom"—as Toni Morrison explains—"did not emerge in a vacuum. Nothing highlighted freedom—if it did not in fact create it—like slavery."[59] Morrison elucidates the stakes of this dependency, noting that "Black slavery enriched the country's creative possibilities. For in that construction of blackness *and* enslavement could be found not only the not-free but also, with the dramatic polarity created by skin color, the projection of the not-me. The result was a playground for the imagination."[60] Within this interplay of the free and the enslaved, the bonds of slavery do more than underscore a set of oppositions; they provide the essential scaffolding for the white self. What is more, in spite of the apparent opposition figured by racial slavery, an imagination stoked by antiblackness frequently adopts the political garb of (white) popular sovereignty to mask the structural necessity of the slave.

A playground for the lawlessness of the white imagination formalizes the site where the rule of law and the caprice of popular sovereignty achieve a violent synthesis. The ostensible enmity between lynch law and the formal jurisprudence here masks a more pervasive symmetry: both systems demand the actualization of slavery, materially through law and at the level of the imaginary where the unfettered desire to repudiate and hold captive blackness continuously recurs. The ambit of statecraft and its emergent carceral apparatus, including the vision of a reformed criminal justice system, in the West mirrors the extralegal mechanics of lynching; the symbolic integrity of the state rests upon a fantasmatic construction of blackness. The imagined presence (or absence) of the slave functions as the negative coordinate allowing for sovereignty to recognize its own possibility and desire for settlement and transformation. In turn, the disarticulation of blackness, its simultaneous deracination and intense libidinal investment, broadcasts a counterimage and distinction in which this image can be made: the acquisition of *terra nullius*. The rule of law does not civilize the state of nature without a master; rather, it asserts itself against the projected lawlessness of nature by anchoring its authority in the ritualized exclusion of blackness.[61]

But if, as I have been arguing, blackness makes necessary a certain set of forms and appearances before the law (our beginning example being "crimes of the blackest hue") yet is still latent to them—the manifest content of Manifest Destiny—then *terra nullius* cannot be reduced to notions of sovereignty, property, possession, and race without repeating the founding gesture in which blackness is lynched. The difference here is not a gap between event and perception, but a structural condition of incommensurability—the space where the interpretation of repetition of a "traumatic deferred interpretation not *of* an event but *as* an event that never took place as such."[62] This formulation, which collapses the event into its own interpretation, captures how the lynching of blackness operates not as a historical crime to be perceived and recovered, but as a foreclosure of the conditions of possibility for appearance and perception themselves. The purported lawlessness of nature—the myth underwriting the seizure of *terra nullius*—is revealed as nothing more than the structural necessity of antiblack violence for the actualization of lawful white sovereignty.

Lynch Law as Claims

In the migration of lynch law toward the Western territories, the interpretation of natural law and evocation of punishment as destined fate ("any alternative to lynching impossible") legitimizes itself by presuming a force (*Gewalt*) that proclaims positive law and justice of the courts irrelevant. I will discuss this dimension of *Gewalt* at length in Chapter 3. For now, I focus on how such reasoning-as-violence secures a *sense* of natural order and rights, fusing the language of destiny with the "sovereignty of the will." This claim is necessitated by the psychic life of antiblackness: a libidinal economy in which black death is instantiated as—to evoke the chapter's opening provocation—*ante legem*. Such violence is prior to the law and the laws of its violence. In this precedence, black death braids together race and reason—not as a secondary effect of racist reasoning, but as its precondition—emerging through the imagined contamination of blackness to beget the sovereign racial grounds for adjudicating the right to kill and to enact the decision to deploy that right. Such preceding violence—the imagined racial mark underpinned by blackness—is foundational not simply to the notion of "the people's sovereignty," but to the sovereign right that determines the boundaries of claims to personhood and the claiming of boundaries for being.

The non-appearance of blackness, the fact that the mark of blackness does *not* appear, is all the more indispensable for the preservation of a "people's will"; its non-appearance speaks of the psychic reality (desires and arbitrary borders) that produces a capacity for reason and volition. As Jacqueline Rose has observed, "It is not solely through will, intent, and reason (all claims of conscious volition) that we fashion and experience our political worlds. Precisely because the very idea of 'claim' is the problem, it can serve as the place where" a particular dialogue between a text and politics "will begin."[63] Rose identifies an aporia in the notion of "claims" that establishes the conditions of possibility for connecting text and politics, and hence also a reading that may have not otherwise taken place. Taking Rose's provocation further, I submit that where a particular dialogue between a text and politics arises, the possibility of a political text is inseparable from the metaphysical and psychical violence that conjures it. As important as it is to see where a dialogue between a text and politics emerges, it is equally critical here to examine how the possible writing, rewriting, and unwriting of that text relies on a kind of erasure. This violence is not a blank space, but the violence of absence that authorizes the text of politics (and the politics of that text) to narrate and claim its own plenitude. "Self-lynching" enacts this process of erasing blackness (and the reason why blackness can never *be*), which animates the signifiers of lynch law—sovereignty, justice, truth, value—and also operates as an inscription in the law to augment itself and its excess.

In this respect, identification with blackness *as* image (as opposed to the image *of* blackness)[64] works "not simply [as] one psychical mechanism among others, but the operation itself whereby"[65] lynch law and sovereignty are instantiated. Marriott, following Frantz Fanon, describes this "in the sense that blackness never stops being lynched in its image, or lynched as image . . . , this is why its vertiginous movement is always a drop toward the void."[66] In light of this pervasive expulsion, the double inscription of (anti)blackness—the simultaneous projection and foreclosure that paradoxically allows blackness "to appear"—emerges as a fundamental necessity of the racial imaginary. The underwriting of state-building mechanisms and the visceral requirements of lawless white civilians meet in this psychical economy, actualizing the political desires and fantasies of the nation-state.

The reach of this operation extends beyond whiteness or the white cultural imagination. Coinciding with Southerners' migration to the West and the Northeast, a parallel gesture emerges within the historical interpretation of racial formation—one that bolstered the pretenses of racial liberalism as an essential feature of the American West's liberal political horizon. Rudolph Lapp's observations illustrate the production of "race," the notable anxiety in perceiving racial blackness, and how such anxiety configures a set of social relations.

> While color distinctions were less abrasive in Mexico, it was still a mark of status to be considered "Mexican" rather than "mulatto" or "Negro." This may explain why Mexican-Californians with some African heritage never alluded to it.
>
> In the early part of the nineteenth century, Californians occasionally showed hostility to those of unmistakable African ancestry. When the French adventurer Bouchard raided the coast of California in 1818, he was driven off, but several of his associates, among them some blacks, were captured. It is reported that one California woman thought they possibly had tails and wanted to burn them alive. Historian Hubert Howe Bancroft believed that the unpopular California governor Manual Victoria was socially ostracized because he was clearly of African ancestry. According to Bancroft, Californians at this time were accustomed to seeing Negroes only in menial capacities.[67]

In this detail of racial formation, historical description gives way to a double exposure: the observation that the "allusion" to blackness is avoided (African heritage is never alluded to among Mexican-Californians)[68] sits alongside the violent interpellation that traffics black people as beasts to be decimated through the inhumane act of burning. Together, these dynamics speak to how the allusions to antiblackness are in effect without reservation yet also without question of how this systemic operation functions. Antiblackness resides within the historical image even while underwriting it. Rei Terada gestures to a similar logic of figuration when she says that "perceiving an object *as* an instance of appearance—in the mode of appearance—comes to be experienced as *postponing* the requirement to endorse its reality."[69] To view antiblackness as simply an object of history is to obscure its role as the force structuring the racial formation and the broader field of racial knowledge. Consequently, this failure of recognition masks how the social construction of these formations serves their own historical recognition. Such misrecognition—a failure that Jared Sexton identifies as that which "endlessly renders the black body image as the 'anchor' of racial knowledge"[70]—confirms antiblackness not as a historical residue, but as the foundational lack that animates and sustains the very capacity for racial knowledge and thought.

Lapp's conceptual premise engages a necessary tension between a historical account of racial division and the meta-exegesis of racial formation that makes the narrativization of such history possible. The structural logic of this tension is discernable in the material events of the period. This tension is brought into sharper relief when Lapp explains that shortly after the new Mexican Republic's constitution abolished racial slavery, California—as its northernmost region—witnessed an increase of "ships with multi-racial crews" arriving on its shores in 1823.[71] Upon first glance, the transition from an explicit policing of blackness at the levels of individual self, law, and politics to the formal abolition of slavery might appear as a complete volte-face—a move from the suppression of racial anxieties about blackness to a performance of racial liberalism aimed at black liberation. While the transition frames racial politics as being at the mercy of law, it also indicates an unconscious wish to relegate blackness, and thus the exercise of desire and power, to the register of law. Just as the power to suppress and ostracize blackness is legislated into a positive representation of abolition, the division between the imaginary and the symbolic is driven by a perpetual desire to maintain blackness as a point of capture.

Crucial contributions to the understudied history of Africans and African Americans in the American West, specifically in California prior to and during the Gold Rush era, have expanded the understanding of the history of black life in continental early North America, challenging a research tradition that has largely centered on the Eastern Seaboard port cities and Southern plantations to the exclusion of the rest of the continent.[72] Such historical scholarship identifies an existing black population in California as early as the sixteenth century during a period of Spanish colonization led by Hernando Cortez, who traveled with three hundred black slaves to the Gulf of California.[73] The settlements that led to the Spanish colonization of Mexico and Baja California also brought an influx of free blacks and slaves, who served in the Spanish Navy and merchant marines.[74] From the first formal Spanish colonial settlements at the turn of the nineteenth century, settler-colonial life exploited the essential labor of black people—whether enslaved or "free"—to underwrite the initial formations of towns and cities across California.

While studies of previously neglected black life in California during this period successfully challenge the misconception that the state was beyond the national "black/white" dichotomy, my interest here pivots toward a structural inquiry. Specifically, I examine how those very misconceptions reflect a fundamental denial of antiblack sentiment and violence—a denial that undergirds the ultimate wish for the state to serve as a repository of white popular sovereignty. California was imagined, and continues to be perceived, as a space uniquely free from the antiblack hostility that was rampant across the nation and integral to the operations of Spanish colonialism in Mexico and Mexico-California. Yet, such impressions were laden with a sovereign desire to efface blackness from the geopolitical and historical representations concerning the space of settler occupation, thus sustaining the material practices of power and domination that subtended them. In effect, this desire realizes the dissimulation of blackness in the psychical register upon the racial grounds of white sovereignty. Such a structure bears the violence that at once secures the right to enjoy property and perpetuates black abjection. Sexton, following Fanon, describes this as follows: "Within the universe of antiblackness, the social and historical forces that materially and symbolically invent the black body also seek to destroy it. The forces that seek to destroy the black body also seek to maintain it, to insist that it be there in its place."[75] Sexton points out that invention and destruction are not diametrically opposed, submitting that invention is a force of destruction, and that, conversely, destruction necessitates invention. This mutual conversion, however, remains largely opaque. The competing and contradictory forces attending the construction, invention, and destruction of "the black body" reinforce our earlier argument: namely, that blackness falls between the orders of *de jure* and *de facto* law. As antiblackness underlies both orders, its operations must be examined against the precedence of positive law. To restate this foundational argument again, we must consider the law of laws—that which "remains invisible and hidden in each law, so one might suppose that it is the law itself, the law that causes the laws to be laws."[76] The structural reach of antiblackness is precipitated by this void—the law within the law that remains imperceptible even as it governs. On this score, Fischer reminds her readers, "No doubt, abolitionism masks as much as it exposes: for every abuse revealed there seems to be an interest concealed or an intention hidden."[77]

As rule of law, the formal abolition of racial slavery in the 1823 constitution staged an opportunistic space of migration for the enslaved and freeborn black Mexicans in California, but it also effectively deflected the reality of burgeoning anti-slavery sentiments.[78] Before California's admission into the Union in 1850, the California Convention in 1849 debated aggressively "to bar all free blacks from entering the state under any circumstances."[79] California was ultimately admitted into the Union as a free state and yet, "disregarding that distinction, lawmakers not only adopted and enforced strict fugitive slave laws, but they passed legislation that ensured that *all* blacks were denied basic civil rights."[80] The denial of basic civil rights was not the only dimension of black dispossession. The enforcement of fugitive slave laws would also become a means to regulate freed slaves and freeborn black people by forcing many of them to "claim" themselves as fugitives as a way to deport them back to the South. If they were not sent to the South on their own dime, "slaves were generally forced to pay large sums for their freedom, and even after payment slave owners often found ingenious ways to keep them in bondage."[81] The legal system offered no recourse due to the Testimony Exclusion Law, passed in 1850 by a California Legislature "dominated by pro-slavery Democratic lawmakers."[82] The statute explicitly stripped black residents of the capacity to defend their personhood or enforce contracts, effectively trapping them in an endless cycle of financial and legal bondage. Specifically, the law rendered it illegal for any "black or mulatto person, or Indian . . . to give evidence in favor of, or against, any white person."[83] Despite entering the Union as a free state in 1850, the California legislature quickly enacted laws—most notably the Fugitive Slave Laws of 1852—that protected slaveholder rights while formally preserving the state's anti-slavery constitution.[84] Masters could thus "hold the slaves who [*sic*] they had brought to California before statehood and take them back to the South. Any enslaved person who resisted this process would be criminalized as a fugitive slave."[85] The synthesis of the Testimony Law with the concurrent enactment of the Fugitive Slave Act exposes a dual legal apparatus that functioned as a *de facto* pro-slavery shield. As such, the state's *de jure* anti-slavery constitutional status was successfully negated through the weaponization of the courts and the reinforcement of black dispossession.

We are reminded once again how the very idea of a claim remains a problem since "all claims of conscious volition" that "fashion . . . our political worlds" decisively obscure "the vertical transmission of cultural inheritance."[86] In this instance, the act of *claiming* a fugitive (whether correctly identified, real, or imagined) points directly toward a calculated political compromise. The legislature's endorsement of such claims, despite the prohibition of black testimony, effectively supported a "moderate" view of slavery and slaveholder rights. While the capacity *to* claim alongside the refusal to grant others the rights to make claims ought to appear as a paradox, the disavowal instead enabled law "to come as close as possible to creating the ownable, enslavable human."[87] As Barbara Johnson observes:

> By not using the word "slavery" in the Constitution, and by revising the text of the original Fugitive Slave Clause to refer to the legality of slavery only at the level of the states, rather than the federal government, the framers built a double intentionality into the very foundation of their law . . . A written text of law can thus contain a double intention, the trace of a compromise between differing opinions . . . The intention can always already be multiple.[88]

The true difficulty lies beyond the buried intentions in law; rather, it requires recognizing how multiplicity and moderacy diffuse the psychic valences of antiblackness. Such diffusion allows the fugitive slave law and testimony exclusions to function seamlessly together as if they are not in conflict with the state's anti-slavery constitution. More pointedly, no such contradiction exists. The appearance of heterogeneous views in the legislature serves to mask the singular, violent antiblack intent that animates all the resulting laws. Saidiya Hartman has written at length about this deception: "The benign representation of the paternal institution in slave law depicted the master-slave relationship as typified by the bonds of affection and thereby transformed relations of violence and domination into those of affinity." She explains further:

> If what is at stake in social fantasy is the construction of a nonantagonistic, organic, and complementary society, then the ability of the South to imagine slavery as a paternal and benign institution and master-slave relations as bound by feelings depended on the specter of the obsequious and threatening slave, for this Manichaean construction undergirded both the necessary violence and the bonds of affection set forth in slave law. As well, this fantasy enabled a vision of whiteness defined primarily by its complementary relation to blackness and by the desire to incorporate and regulate black excess.[89]

Although Hartman is referencing the impossibility of the enslaved to testify in the South, her assessment of law's imagined innocence highlights the strictures preventing the slave from appearing as a legal subject. Any sign of black resistance is read as excess and in need of regulation. Posing a threat to the whiteness of law, blackness is inextricable from shaping the formations of historical consciousness in relation to law as sociopolitical institution and mechanism. At the same time, state desire abstracts the state into the author and authority of reality—a "reality that lends itself to narrative representation [as] the conflict between desire and the law."[90] Such an abstraction dictates who defines the borders between what is imagined and what becomes real for the subject. Consequently, by permitting and shaping the relationship between juridical form and content, the division between absence and presence becomes malleable, bending to the desires of those deemed to be proper subjects.

Within the nation's tenuous political fabric, lynch law established a capacity for policing in multiple registers. This authority was forged through the very critique of federal, state, and local jurisdiction that lynch law embodied, thus maintaining the desire for competence in policing blackness from within and without the representation of law. Such state-building was sustained because it operated as part of modernity's cultural logic, which integrated political pro-slavery campaigns against abolitionism. In this sense, lynch law quickly became a mode of policing par excellence, opening the door for decentralized and overlapping practices of control. The ascendancy of lynch law on the heels of California's Gold Rush was a means to not only fill a void, but actively animated and renewed policing practices that appeared, at least superficially, to be disintegrating. The banner of "popular justice"—conceived as the people's collective means of policing—encompassed, for example, the segregation and surveillance of gold fields specifically designated for black miners.[91] Such instances demonstrate how the generative nature of lynch law appealed to the collective imagination of the nation by synchronizing internal and external policing strategies. California, as a horizon for expansion, proved idyllic in that segregation and policing were legitimized through institutional sanctions without requiring immediate formalization. Accordingly, the nascent liberal criminal justice system in the American West did not combat lynch law but rather mirrored and codified its violent logic, incorporating underlying principles of racial abjection to secure white popular sovereignty. Thus, the lawless modes of segregation and policing reinforced the racial imaginary, ensuring that blackness—conceived as the apogee of criminality—marked the boundary of who should and could be policed.

Even in its unwritten form, as Ida B. Wells-Barnett reminds us, lynch law is capable of politically representing the highest terms of the state—sovereignty, people's justice, truth.[92] What lynch law "claims" in terms of sovereignty, will, and justice marks only the initial contours of the problem which antiblackness endures. Lynch law operates to imagine and create boundaries outside the normalized rule of law, an operation that is preceded by a judgment condemning blackness before lynch law is even constituted. Residing in a state of (non-)being that resides *before* the law, blackness mirrors the structure of lynch law, which always presents itself as *ante legem* to galvanize sovereignty beyond the constraints of positive law. What we are presented with is neither a problem of legal representations or interpretations nor simply a matter of establishing constitutional rights. Instead, the crisis resides at the threshold of these distinctions where a prior judgment has already condemned blackness as irredeemable.

At the level of constitutional discourse, law reveals its negative relation to slavery with stark clarity—most notably in the Thirteenth Amendment, which establishes the convict labor lease system of involuntary servitude.

This provision confirms that constitutional law does not conceal its antagonism to blackness. Nor does it hide the fact that the exclusion of the slave is foundational to law's mythic character and its naming of personhood and rights. Black death is written into the text of law as a social and civic death.[93] Yet, does this provide us with enough to conjecture that the law is fundamentally antagonistic toward blackness, or that there is an antiblack antagonism *in* law? In raising this question, I am attempting to emphasize that antiblackness operates less as an external force—a phenomenon in relation to the law—than as a structural element at work within, toward, and of the law itself, preceding and exceeding its constitutional iterations. Such a shift brings to the fore a recursive *mode* of questioning, rather than an alternative set of inquiries: How do these multiple antagonisms cohere in the function of antiblackness? How might they, at the same time, speak against one another? And, ultimately, what do these tensions reveal about "self-lynching"? In posing these questions, I seek neither definitive nor conclusive answers. Nevertheless, these inquiries highlight the core problem of reducing antiblackness to limited readings and interpretations that rely solely on the representations of positive law. Such a reduction often manifests in isolating antiblackness to the Thirteenth Amendment as the supposed example of law's negative relation to slavery. Consequently, this negative relation must be understood not as a mere concession, but as driven by antiblackness as the generative condition for the law's own structure and its capacity to define personhood and the self.

More than this, the difficulty of answering such questions stems from the indiscernibility of how blackness is arrested, even imprisoned, within and as a consequence of various modalities of law. Such opacity leads directly to Jacques Derrida's concept of the laws of law: "what remains invisible and hidden in each law, so one might suppose that it is the law itself, the law that causes these laws to be laws, the being-law of these laws."[94] The recognition or misrecognition of antiblackness at the register of law's letter necessitates the possibility of law's representation and its law-preserving violence. The problematic of law here remains at the level of representation, which lynch law simultaneously dismisses and embraces without hesitation. Such contradiction—this seeming diremption—directs us to ask: What other laws are at work, or how they are put to work, in order to maintain the explanatory power of lynch law as an assertion of sovereignty and white sovereign truth?

Take, for instance, the deference given to lynch law as a sovereign truth—marshaling not only the people's judiciary but also serving as a collective signifier of whiteness. Lynch law magnified the precarity of constitutional rights following the abolition of slavery. In doing so, it demonstrated that the political value of tolerance—conceived as the capacity to extend fundamental rights and civil liberties from the Constitution—can be wielded as a political tool. This tool is used in the staging of racial liberalism in constitutional forms.[95] The Three-Fifths Compromise itself provides a historical precedent for such perverse logic, deployed as a symbol of political tolerance to reconcile anti-slavery sentiment with pro-slavery political power. This framing enabled the conceptual coexistence of anti-slavery positions with pro-lynching practices.[96] Put more plainly, one could advocate for abolition while also standing up for white sovereignty. To that end, mob violence often took precedence over the formal abolition of slavery, exposing the limits of constitutional "tolerance."[97] Violence functioned here as the active expression of Northerners' residual and ongoing pro-slavery sentiments, thus asserting white sovereignty as a greater moral and civic obligation superior to constitutional adherence. In this light, lynch law was not merely an affront to abolition, nor did it simply enervate the formal institutionalization of abolition. Counterintuitively, the practice was energized and invigorated by its opposition, in order to articulate and represent whiteness as a value system with antiblackness as its structural propellant. The deference to lynch law signals a psychic investment in whiteness, not merely as a sign, but as a sign of mastery. This underlying commitment remains masked, however, by the public peddling of tolerance as a political value and tool of constitutional politics employed primarily to assuage racial guilt. Such psychic investments in whiteness anchor a discursive framework that both denies the significance of "race" and disavows its interiorized violence toward blackness. The issue here displaces a mere moral-political dilemma; rather, the expression of racial guilt is structurally subsumed by the operative affirmation and imperative of (white) superiority. Tolerance, even in its benign appearances of love or benevolence, results from some formulation of guilt—a process that detours and represses the underlying aggressive impulse to annihilate difference. D. W. Winnicott distinguishes legal guilt, specific to crime, from moral guilt in "[reference] to inner reality." He explains that "there is gradual building up towards this point [that] involves a gradual recognition of the difference between fact and fantasy."[98] In this sense, lynch law, as an expression of the people's sovereignty, doesn't outperform tolerance as an index of racial guilt and as a political constitutional tool. Rather, lynch law emerges as an imagined reparative gesture to the inner realities of racial anxiety and aggression that spawn guilt in the first instance.

In this way, lynching from the nineteenth through the turn of the twentieth century can be understood as both a response to and a manifestation of the ubiquitous symptom of the nation's libidinal attachment to racial slavery—a desire for its technologies and regime to develop and thrive. For those Southerners who upheld lynch law as the people's sovereignty, the denouncement of positive law intervenes to provide meaning and discourse to lynching as unwritten law. But if the racial politics of representation governing the normalized rule did not differ significantly from lynch law, then why was the latter embraced as *truth*? The conviction of laws shifts from positive law to the extrajudicial precisely because the mythic power of lynch law was understood to uphold a form of sovereignty that positive law could neither capture nor represent. While it is true that the extrajudicial and extralegal use of excessive violence allowed for the precedence of one order over another, this functional shift only partially explains the phenomenon. We must look further into the nature of violence that permits judgment and reason to accompany lynch law so effortlessly—a logic that distills lynch law as both natural law and a divine right of whiteness. As the *ante legem* condition of the order of law(s), black death marks the site of an originary violence through which blackness is suspended and put to death, establishing the possibility for law, both written and unspoken, to appear and operate.

I submit that lynch law and positive law not only mirrored one another in this sense; they also fortified their coherence as legal practices through an active and necessary misrecognition of blackness. Safeguarded by the rhetoric of law and sovereignty, such misrecognition sustains their representational possibilities. Here, the force of one's imagined *de facto* rights gives way to a collective sovereignty that supersedes legal and civic rights, thus generating the dubious "problem" of claims. Specifically, this force naturalizes the coercion subtending the rhetorical utility of law and sovereignty, productively turning them into customs. Violence alone does not conjure the sense, appearance, and entitlement of law and sovereignty. Force and custom together make coherent the meaning and knowledge of lynch law as a type of truth to be recognized.

Timothy Bahti examines the notion of governance—or policing—within historical formations by tracing the correspondence between meaning and knowledge. He describes how varying criteria of judgment interact to "de-absolutize" one measure of judgment against another, thus, "still [holding] the absolute as a benchmark" while "preserving all the distinctions between good history, bad history, and what is not history at all."[99] In this prelude to G.W.F. Hegel's model of historical truth, Bahti illustrates for us "the manner of a law-governed connection"[100] between historical knowledge and meaning—a relation that sustains the bond between explanatory power and necessity. For Bahti, claims regarding historical truth rest upon this correspondence and a consensus on what constitutes the boundaries and discourse, a structure he characterizes as "a circle, to be sure."[101] This ouroboros of consensus determines which practices of correspondence are deemed effective or existent. Within this closed circuit, the historical narrative that generates the possibility of white sovereignty relies upon the necessary abnegation of blackness to secure its explanatory power, illustrating how consensus dictates whose existence is admitted into the circle and whose abjection is required to draw the line. Hence, correspondence functions as an interiorized mode of policing. The strength of this policing lies not only in the alignment of meaning and knowledge, but in the violent unmaking of a self that must anchor any self-understanding of history. In this sense, the very possibility of historical truth is predicated upon a "self-lynching"—a foundational, recursive act that eliminates blackness to the coherence of the historical "I." Through this elimination, the law-governed connection between meaning and knowledge is consummated as a performance of white sovereign truth.

The law-governed connection that establishes a self-understanding of history shares with lynch law a singular, necessary feature: the unmaking of a self to facilitate the dialectic of recognition and misrecognition. There is, in other words, an internal and recursive lynching—a violence that remains out of view—whereby a self is necessarily displaced to allow the structures of history and law to cohere as recognized truth. Such a displacement explains why the use of force is inextricable from lynch law's assertions and representations of sovereignty as truth. The foundational premise is the suspension of *a* self—an internal, structural displacement necessary to name the entitled, claiming subject. Because such violence causes the self to vanish, a representative form must emerge to refashion that disappearance and render it structurally legible. Derrida limns that "the tension of force itself" coincides with the way in which "*form* fascinates when one no longer has the force to understand force from within itself. That is, to create."[102] Ergo, when force is internalized as something other than law or violence, it remains structurally essential. Such fascination with form—here, the static appearance of a coherent, self-justifying system through the order of law—arises precisely at the moment when the originary force of its creation is disavowed and interiorized. Formalizing the laws of law in this manner allows the representations of lynch law to articulate their own logic as sovereign truth. Within this gambit of law, truth, and self, whiteness is not only maintained by a consensus of what is considered knowledge and meaning, but is also established negatively by blackness—that which can never be the bearer of truth nor witness to its absolute abolition. Therefore, *ante legem* is not simply about the positioning of black death or whiteness in relation to the law. Rather, it is about how the negativity of blackness enables, positions, and functions before the law, allowing the law to operate under a perceived limit. This threshold of legitimacy maintains the myth of law's neutrality while simultaneously demanding the constant, structural operation of antiblackness.

Moreover, such a limit is less a matter of the norm, or the codes by which the legal order abides, than a question of how the law adjudicates an impasse, an uncertainty, or a rupture. It concerns the process through which that judgment is subsequently submitted as truth. Monique David-Ménard's analysis questions "a certain renouncement called autonomy, but one relative, in its truth, to certain organizations of desire that need to render the objects of desire interchangeable before the renouncement of an object may take place. Then it becomes the truth of a fantasy, perpetually tied to the type of transformation of drives it allows, and not the truth of a concept."[103] The "truth" of legal judgment and the "truth" of fantasy thus overlap, mutually informing one another. This convergence, however, obscures the reality of a concept in favor of the vicissitudes of desire. Within the racial state, this obscuration allows the desire for white sovereign coherence to dictate law's judgment, overriding the objective reality of equality or justice. The law's judgment is revealed as something other than a declaration of objective truth; it functions instead as a mechanism for the political and psycho-affective maintenance of racial sovereignty.

As the limit of positive law yields the possibility of lynch law, the resulting dynamic elucidates the psychic investments that drive fantasies of sovereignty and truth indexed by whiteness. Because lynch law was imagined to realize the dreams of popular sovereignty and westward expansion, those dreams were most acutely threatened by the negativity of blackness, thus making lynch law a necessity for blackness's ongoing suppression and repression. The mechanism through which lynch law and law work negatively from blackness is precisely what also suspends blackness from notions of self, truth, sovereignty, and claims.

In many respects, "lynch law" was exercised within the framework of a national dream-work to attain popular sovereignty: the pathologizing of blackness as criminal made clear the bond between the formation of white civic life and a logic of defense that pivoted on the reinforced operations of antiblackness. Within the racial imaginary of the nation-state—particularly during the state-building of California—antiblackness played a more insidious role precisely because it could never come into appearance. The suppression embodies a paradox that fundamentally situates antiblackness: it signaled a wide range of possibilities for expansion, sovereignty, and law at the level of representation, and simultaneously telegraphed the potential for a psychical conversion from fantasy to reality. White sovereignty, as a cultural and sociopolitical expression of the state's racial imaginary, was a direct outcome of how racial slavery and blackness were policed *without* the police. In this sense, California served as an ideal screen for staging its liberal exceptionalism through its very practices of lawlessness.

Having opened with the example of "crimes of the blackest hue," this chapter has questioned the casting of an ontological judgment of blackness that produces the illusory signs and signifiers of (anti)blackness. Such processes and their ontological and structural implications directed us to explore lynch law in order to understand how it is guided and driven as a psychical operation. The explicit appearance of blackness or antiblackness, as I have argued, is not sufficient to determine whether they inform the material practices of lynch law and its representation of law, sovereignty, and truth; rather, the supposed *reason* behind lynching rested on, and worked toward and from, an abstraction of (anti)blackness. In this respect, the psychical operations of antiblackness underlying the violence of lynch law signal a perpetual and persistent operation of displacement that structurally prevents blackness from being. This structural displacement, which operates as a castration, enables a specific set of appearances to emerge within politics and knowledge, allowing lynch law to enter into meaning through the dissimulation of (anti)blackness. The circular psychical movement is, in itself, a lynching that castrates blackness by suspending its very possibility of becoming a self. Our genealogy of translation has tracked how the foundational void of blackness enables a specific set of appearances in the material, economic, and juridical domains, making the internalized complex of lynching and policing essential to the racial imaginary of the nation-state. The psychical operations, in which antiblackness undercuts representative forms, are interdependent with the correspondence between meaning and knowledge—an interiorized mode of policing that manifests in the violent making and unmaking of a self. Ultimately, this complex of lynching and policing blackness is indelible to the racial imaginary and development of the nation-state and state-building. It is particularly evident in the context of Manifest Destiny, where westward expansion—meant to emblematize the people's will—was sustained by an essential antiblack dream-work.

The idealization of California as a liberal and lawless frontier was not in contradiction with the nation's broader racial imaginary; it invigorated the nation's social and psychic ties to slavery and segregation—a bond held together through an impossible undoing. Legislative sanctions, such as fugitive slave laws, testimony exclusions laws, and attempts to bar free blacks from the territory, indicate how its operations of segregation and exclusion invited the practices and political values of lynching. The entry of lynch law into California, in turn, established the groundwork for multiple permutations of policing driven by the nation's preexisting antiblack desire. Because California was ostensibly external to the political division of North and South, it presented itself as the perfect screen for white justice, a space where the rule of law could be suspended for the supposed sovereign good of "the people" through the rituals of lawless violence.

Lynch law, as a movement of "people's sovereignty," did not create the American West *ex nihilo*. Rather, under "the sign of a lasting sovereign power,"[104] the West enabled—even fortified—lynch law, securing its psychical economy against the displacement of blackness that sustained it. The following chapter extends this examination of lynch law as a psychical economy and a mode of sovereignty predicated on the recursive lynching of a self. We shall ruminate further on how the critical difference of "self-lynching"—which constitutes law from within and without—becomes essential to the image of sovereignty and sovereignty of the image.

Two
At the Edge of Presence
Antiblackness and the Image of "Self-Lynching"

In the first chapter, we established that the psychical operations of lynching and policing are required for the myth of legal neutrality to cohere. We demonstrated that this latent process creates a "difference of self-lynching"—the necessary unmaking of blackness as a self—which constitutes the rule of law from within and without, thereby enabling its assertions of white sovereign truth. Having established this premise, this chapter turns to the juridical and aesthetic image that figures lynch law and its *afterlife*. By examining two seemingly disparate instances, I demonstrate how "self-lynching" as a transitional phenomenon facilitates the erasure and displacement of blackness necessary for the image to make a claim about an imaginary self. We begin this examination with a historical media report that lays bare this perverse dynamic: a seemingly unremarkable newspaper article that illustrates how the policing of blackness functions as an image of sovereign truth.

"Life's a problem." The pithy statement stands alone as a singular paragraph and the second sentence of an easily overlooked newspaper article at the turn of the twentieth century (Figure 1). The sentence refers to Hilliard Denton, a twenty-eight-year-old African American man. The article describes the San Francisco police "rescuing" Denton from a mob of stevedores intent on lynching him for the theft of a package of cheese—an act committed out of hunger. Though the theft was unrelated to the stevedores, the mob pursued Denton and subjected him to both physical and psychological torture.

> Stevedores chased him six blocks, caught him, tied a rope 'round his neck and gave every indication holding an immediate necktie party. [Shortly thereafter,] they beat and kicked their captive . . . [He] was kicked and beaten so badly before the officers could carry him to a waiting ambulance that he was nearly senseless. A rope eighteen feet long dangled from his neck and was removed by the police.

After "rescuing" Denton, the police charged him with petty theft, and Denton spent the night in the city jail. The municipal judge was seen as merciful, giving him "a chance" by mandating him to sixty days of a suspended sentence, after which Denton could then be "free." Denton, however, recognized the hollow nature of this freedom and replied to the judge: "It's all the same to you, boss—I'd rather stay here. Those boys may be waiting outside with the rope again." To this, the judge directed the bailiff: "If there's no crowd waiting, put this man on a streetcar and see that he keeps on going." When asked which streetcar Denton preferred, he asked in response, "Which one goes furthest from those boys?" The newspaper article frames this forced departure from the beginning by noting: "Somewhere out in the sub-

Man Rescued From Lynch Mob Is Set Free by Judge

SAN FRANCISCO, Jan. 22.—Somewhere out in the suburbs, far from crowds of dockside stevedores, Hilliard Denton, 28, Negro, is sitting and puzzling.

Life's a problem.

Yesterday, desperate with hunger, he stole a box of cheese from in front of a warehouse in Battery street.

Stevedores chased him six blocks, caught him, tied a rope 'round his neck and gave every indication of holding an immediate necktie party.

Police rescued Denton; he spent the night in the city jail, charged with petty theft.

"Why did ...

If there's no crowd waiting, put this man on a street car and see that he keeps on going." Judge Steiger instructed a bailiff.

"Which car, buddy?" the bailiff asked.

"Which one goes furthest from those boys?" Denton countered.

Figure 1. Partial headline and text from *The Oakland Tribune*, January 22, 1931, documenting the attempted lynching of Hilliard Denton. Source: *Oakland Tribune.*

urbs far from crowds of dockside stevedores. Hilliard Denton, 28, Negro, is sitting and puzzling. Life's a problem."

Wittingly or unwittingly, the short article indicates "an indefinite sentence"[1] that Denton faces and cannot escape. Whether inside or out of the holding cell, in the city or in the suburbs, the threat of lynching remained an everlasting sentence that made his life conditional—an inescapable psychic encounter with an unbound toll where life is, indeed, a problem without respite. The headline, "Man Rescued from Lynch Mob Is Set Free By Judge," compels us to ask: What definition of "rescue" is at play here, and from what structural forces was Denton truly being "rescued"? If the headline frames his release as a deliverance, it masks how his "freedom" was already undermined by the state's own role in positing lynch law as a legitimate extension of legal order. Rather than securing his freedom, the state and its repressive forces maintain a façade of white innocence that attempts to veil any racial anxieties around blackness.

Media coverage of experiences such as Denton's was rare unless they were circulated by the black press or black anti-lynching organizations such as the NAACP or black women's clubs. In effect, this scarcity tells us something about media representation and whiteness. That is, antiblack violence was so deeply naturalized and routinized that it seldom warranted any coverage in the mainstream press. Regarding the violence that subtends "editorial comments and strategic publishing protocols" of lynch law, Jacqueline Goldsby notes:

> Not unlike the lynching postcards (which sought to codify the event into a portable "view"), wire news accounts of lynching diminished the violence to a point of inconsequence. Often lining the margin of an inside page, these bulletin accounts figured lynching as but a small detail, a routine occurrence in the course of the everyday. As filler for a blank space on the news page, the story then served as its own kind of grave, a place to bury and cover over what would otherwise be an empty spot.[2]

Considered inconsequential and marginal, the image of a space that can cover the attempted lynching of Denton is an anticipated grave. And still, this "empty spot" reserves a barren space which only black death can fill and to which it will return in the writing of future passages. The possibility of such writing together with this empty space, then, tells us that there is a judgment that condemns blackness as and to death—a judgment that precedes the signification of lynching in its antiblackness. This spatial marker and the possibility of future writing are not posed as origins of a pre-judgment, but as structural indices that reveal its operation. But insofar as this judgment might come into view through the traces of lynching, it exposes the structural necessity of the "self-lynching" of blackness, the perpetual movement of blackness's effacement and foreclosure from the symbolic order, rather than pointing toward a readable origin that precedes all traces. In other words, the "empty space" shows itself as the material evidence of this ontological violence: the *real* breaking through into symbolic law built on an unsymbolizable act of racial sacrifice. The pre-judgment can, thus, be better understood as the affirmative violence of this *real* dictating that blackness must function as the site of unspeakable terror. In this respect, the "empty space" and the "possibility of writing" are traumatic traces that index the ontological commitment to black death required for (white) sovereignty to assume the posture of "truth" and stability. By the same token, the "self-lynching" of blackness—the double movement where the violence of the *real* is written into the symbolic conditions for sovereignty—is the mechanism that writes antiblackness as reality. If antiblackness actively writes lynching as law, sovereignty, and truth, what does this reveal about the psychical representatives, their drives and splits, that animate this *afterlife*?

If our previous chapter demonstrated how lynch law, in its significations of sovereignty, truth, and justice, extends an ontological judgment of condemnation as a reality, then this chapter focuses on the juridical and aesthetic image that figures lynch law and its *afterlife*. Drawing from the preceding analysis, we will examine two specific instances that show how antiblackness underlies the image of the historical memory of lynching. In the first section, I will analyze the media representation of and the extrajuridical and political response to the lynching of two white men, an event that is commonly misconceived as the origin of the Californian anti-lynching statute. In the second section, I focus on the work of contemporary artist Ken Gonzales-Day, who reimagines archival photographs of lynchings through his digital practice of the image. While the two instances are seemingly disparate, I place them together to elaborate my earlier conceptualization of "self-lynching" as a transitional phenomenon. Such a perverse dynamic facilitates the erasure and displacement of blackness—often from subject to object—which precedes and recurs in the image. In each instance, blackness is necessarily displaced for the image to make a claim about an imaginary self. In this way, we see how these images complicate notions of sovereignty of and for the image as they actively extend slavery's *afterlife*.

The image and lynch law come together to conjure a legal object, not just by producing extrajudicial representability, but by manufacturing a representability of "sovereignty of the people"—a political banner used to assert lynch law. As image and lynch law thus work together in the name of sovereignty, the notion of "real presence" becomes instrumental in the racial rhetoric of sovereignty, centering the very language that might be deracinated. *Real presence*—the impression an image makes, often defying common sense and normative semiotics—implicitly plays a role in the historical memory, cultural production, and rituals of lynching, avowing not only the extralegal but also theological and political value of the antiblack reasoning that underlies lynching. Upholding an image of sovereignty (whether as the sovereignty of the people to mean whiteness or the sovereignty of the body to mean nonblackness) strives to master a logic of law and justice, writing and image, but only as a way to defer and deflect blackness from the representational frames of the image. Both statecraft and the psychical economy of lynching are thus interdependently linked to the notion and affect of real presence as they come together to repress blackness under the sign and gesture of mastery. I argue that lynch law and the image work together through the "self-lynching" of blackness. Together, they also mirror the collapse between the juridical and aesthetic in producing so-called realities and the truth of a self, furthering the scales and turns of antiblackness that bolster what Patricia Hill Collins might call the "matrix of domination."[3]

The question of what might be latent in the racial representation of sovereignty leads me to consider how antiblackness operates in the image and writing of sovereignty itself—threaded into its machinations and laws beyond representation. To be sure, the objective is not "to see" or redeem blackness as a presence, nor is it to render blackness visible. Rather, we can better understand how the contemporary "felony lynching" arrests are in fact uncanny, not because these distorted uses are happening for the first time, but because they mark a return and recurrence of the lynching of blackness. We will return to this notion of the uncanny in Chapter 5. For now, let us ruminate on this recurrence: a figuration that is, itself, a lynching of blackness within and of the image.

Many assume that California either exemplifies a continuing liberal racial exceptionalism—in which such abuses did not occur—or that it was "exceptional" within the historical context of lynching in the United States. This insistence on California's difference typically claims that because its vigilante justice targeted victims across the color line, it was, therefore, distinct from the racial antiblack terror seen in the rest of the country.[4] Yet, by interrogating what is construed as blackness's non-presence in the material operations of statecraft, I submit that antiblackness remains indelible to the racial and cultural imagination of the nation-state. It fundamentally shapes the horizons of the liberal imaginary, such as in California, as part of slavery and lynching's *afterlife*. A key element here is the visual iconography of that *afterlife*, which persists, seen or unseen, in various juridical and aesthetic contexts.

In this chapter, the logic of displacement continues to be fundamental to "self-lynching," which animates the possibilities of representational forms and historical memory. As the term "felony lynching" magnifies the *afterlife* of racial slavery and segregation, it reaffirms policing, its technologies, and exclusionary practices—demonstrating the persistence of antiblack violence into the present (Chapter 3). As such, "self-lynching" connects to the notion of *afterlife* in its capacity to represent something ostensibly hidden within the sphere of the living and among the profane structures of representation.[5] It reveals that antiblackness is, in fact, not hidden,[6] but overwritten or even ghosted by representation—a process that complicates how black life as life (or *afterlife*) might be understood. In turn, the historical, juridical, or aesthetic image evinces that its resistance to blackness is enacted not merely in the content of a given appearance, but in the structure of appearance itself. Representation functions as an abstraction built upon the absence of blackness; blackness thus persists as a powerful negativity that is, paradoxically, captured by or entered into the image's logic of appearance only through its own exclusion.

Lynching Blackness as a Self and the Image of Sovereignty

The *re-membered* history of the penal code, to evoke Toni Morrison's maxim, shows that antiblackness not only frames how one comes to understand the historical image of lynching, but also how that image is necessarily distorted and relegated to the margins or interstices of history.[7] This *re-membered* history and its deracination play a fundamental role in the re-presentation of the anti-lynching statute's origins. The lynching of two white men, John Holmes and Thomas Thurmond, is often positioned as the catalyst for California's anti-lynching legislation, displacing the black activists and organizers whose responses to antiblack lynchings regionally and nationally coincided with the changes in the penal code. While, at first blush, the lynching of two white men might not appear as a racial (or for that matter, antiblack) issue, the treatment of Holmes and Thurmond's lynching as a positive expression of popular sovereignty makes clear how antiblackness begets the affirmation of whiteness. So, one must ask: Why does *this* image serve as the historical pivot that anchors the myth of anti-lynching legislation? How does the desire to position whiteness as the "exception" to lynching play a role in re-membering the history of the statute? Furthermore, what does it mean to re-member whiteness in the image of sovereignty? The affirmation of whiteness does not simply tell us about the relationship between a perceived truth and an image conjured by myth. It also informs us how blackness of the *real* makes such representation possible, thinkable, and speakable—only for (anti)blackness to recur against the foreclosure of the visible, circling the desires that animate the image.

Indeed, while lynchings at the turn of the twentieth century occurred across the racial divide, the lynching of Holmes and Thurmond left an ineradicable mark on the historical memory of the American West, serving to solidify and fortify the logic of state security. Thurmond and Holmes were held on charges of the abduction, extortion, and murder of Brooke Hart, the son of Alex Hart, an affluent and influential merchant in San Jose. On a Wednesday in late November of 1933, Holmes and Thurmond were greeted by a sea of reporters and a group of men, both colleagues of Hart and strangers, at San Francisco City Prison as they were supposed to be transferred to the Santa Clara County Jail in the city of San Jose. What began as the "Santa Clara University lynching," plotted by acquaintances of Hart, quickly transformed into a public invitation to gather the wider citizenry to participate in the suspects' removal from the state's custodial protection. Rather than awaiting a juridical verdict, the mob sought to circumvent the uncertainty of a trial, substituting the legal process with the immediate "truth" of a public execution. Soon, thousands of people converged from across the Bay Area

Figure 2. Crowd gathering at the lynching of Thomas Harold Thurmond and John M. Holmes, San Jose, California, November 29, 1933. Source: Alton H. Blackington Photograph Collection, Robert S. Cox Special Collections and University Archives Research Center, UMass Amherst Libraries.

to participate in or witness the lynching of Holmes and Thurmond; the jail ceased to function as a site of law and custody, becoming, instead, a threshold for the mob's sovereign violence.[8]

As Figure 2 illustrates, members of the crowd gathered anything from the event. Here, the image documents members of the crowd peeling the bark of trees, a practice of souvenir collection consistent with lynching rituals. While not visible in this specific frame, other archival images of the Holmes and Thurmond lynching depict spectators scavenging for sticks and shredded pieces of clothing from the victims. Based on the framing of this image, we can also infer that this image was captured for a postcard—a common mode of cultural production that was part and parcel of lynching rituals. In the image, we see a crowd of white citizens, some smiling and looking up at the lynching while others stare directly into the lens of the camera. Notably, the crowd occupies almost the entirety of the image, as opposed to the hanged body, which was typically at the center of images featuring antiblack lynchings. This distinction suggests that when the gaze of the white spectator faces the camera rather than the lynching victim, there is an identification of the spectator with the aggressor. In contrast, a scenario where the crowd is facing the lynched body and looking away from the camera suggests an aggressive identification with racialized subjects, implying that the spectators see themselves as the aggressed.[9] Goldsby has outlined this as "a particular kind of 'scopic aggression' [that] rages in lynching photographs, thwarting any such sympathetic identification between the viewer and the black (dead) subject."[10] An aggression driven by "white scopic pleasure," as David Marriott also tells us in his exposition on blackness and lynching images, emphasizes, echoing Richard Wright, that "the law is white."[11] I place the perception of what becomes real in the immateriality of the image alongside what lynching photographs tell us about the scopic field of the image (its wishes, anxieties, pleasures, and desires), because together they show how the law conforms to the status quo of whiteness, and not simply in a *de jure* scope. Racial law works together with media technology to draw racial meaning from the image of lynching and the narratives that it wishes to assemble; media, in turn, also corroborates the law's processes, effects, and desires.

The San Jose lynching remains the definitive reference point as the inaugural event that would shape the 1933 California penal code and its legal

HANGING OF 2 LESSON TO U.S., GOVERNOR SAYS

Mob Batters Way Into California Jail, Seizes Kidnapper-Slayers.

Figure 3. Archival clipping of newspaper headline illustrating media condonation of the 1933 San Jose lynching. Source: National Association for the Advancement of Colored People (NAACP) anti-lynching papers with the Newspapers and Microforms Library, Doe Library, University of California, Berkeley.

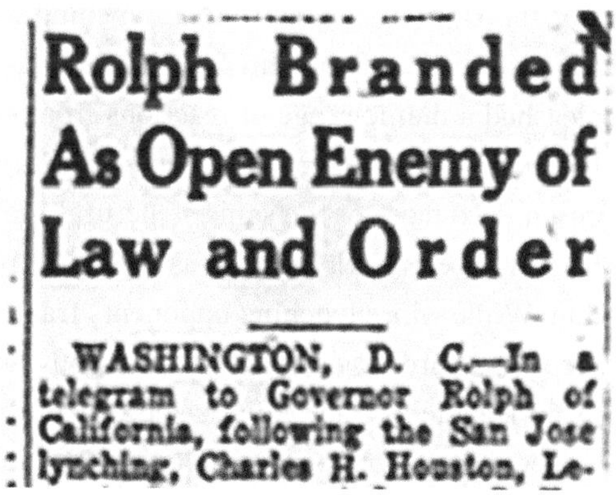

Rolph Branded As Open Enemy of Law and Order

WASHINGTON, D. C.—In a telegram to Governor Rolph of California, following the San Jose lynching, Charles H. Houston, Le-

Figure 4. Archival clipping of newspaper headlines framing the Thurmond and Holmes lynching as a matter of "law and order." Source: National Association for the Advancement of Colored People (NAACP) anti-lynching papers with the Newspapers and Microforms Library, Doe Library, University of California, Berkeley.

PARDON READY FOR ANY HELD ON WEST COAST

Governor of California Calls Execution 'Fine Lesson to Nation'

WOULD TURN OTHERS INTO SIMILAR FATE

San Jose, Calif., Nov. 27—(AP)—Frank approval from Governor

Rolph Decides to Pardon Any Lyncher Held

Continued from Page One

was only natural that, peaceful and law-abiding as they are, they should rise and mete out swift justice to these two murderers and kidnappers," the Governor said.

"They were probably reminded of the heritage of justice by the vigilantes in the early days of San Francisco's history. And the pioneer blood in their veins caused them, in the height of their feeling, to avenge the murder and kidnapping.

"The Sheriff and law enforcement officers of that community did all they could to preserve order and uphold due respect for the law. They did their duty as far as it was possible, but the might of the people was determined to serve notice to the world that kidnapping and murder will not be tolerated in California."

The Governor's statement earlier in the day brought a deluge of messages from all parts of the country, while the Daily Express of London

Killer Hugs Officers In Joy Over Escape

San Jose, Calif., Nov. 27—(AP)—In a surprise move, authorities today rushed Anthony Serpa, convicted of manslaughter and for a time last night in danger of being lynched, here from San Francisco, took him before a Judge, got him a one-to-ten-year sentence, and hurried him off to San Quentin Penitentiary.

Serpa, convicted of slaying a ranch foreman, was taken to San Francisco last night, after some members of the lynching mob sought him.

Serpa was wrapped in a big coat of Deputy Sheriff McCaffrey and hustled out a side door, where the two mingled with the crowd, walked five blocks to an automobile and drove to San Francisco.

Trembling and hysterical, Serpa rushed through the protecting

ings. He said his duty was to prosecute any person against whom charges were filed, but added he did not expect any charges due to the difficulty of identifying the members of the mob.

Prison Official, Mrs. Pinchot Attack Statement of Rolph

The statement of Governor Rolph, of California, upholding the lynching of two kidnappers by San Jose citizens is "perfectly awful," in the opinion of Dr. Louis N. Robinson, newly appointed trustee of the Eastern Penitentiary.

"The Governor's declaration," said Dr. Robinson last night, "will simply encourage further lynching and lawlessness in the future. It seems to me that his stand will serve to discourage the enforcement authorities of that State.

Figure 5. Headlines from the *Philadelphia Public Ledger*, November 1933, reporting on Governor Rolph's promise to pardon any participants in the San Jose lynching. Source: *Philadelphia Public Ledger*; Image courtesy of the National Association for the Advancement of Colored People (NAACP) Records, Library of Congress.

definition of "the taking by means of a riot of any person from the lawful custody of any peace officer." Governor James "Sunny Jim" Rolph's notorious endorsement of the Holmes and Thurmond lynching received nationwide attention; his description of the San Jose lynching as "a fine lesson to the nation" unleashed a manic range of reactions from both white pro-lynching advocates and white lynching opponents (Figures 3 and 4). Yet these groups represent two faces of the same structural problem, both obscuring the insidious nature of antiblackness as the fundamental principle underlying lynching. While white lynching opponents framed the San Jose lynching as a symbol of a threat against the criminal justice system, legal institutions, and American democracy, Rolph's approval of the lynching validated the state as an example of "popular sovereignty" and "community justice," effectively signaling to the rest of the nation the continued legitimacy of lynch law practices. By condoning the seizure of "justice" by and for (white) citizens in the American West, "vigilante justice" was reframed as exceptionally liberal. This framing, however, served a compound purpose: it deflected the language of racial violence while denying any internalization of antiblackness. The ostensible absence of black victims or antiblackness in this specific scene allowed for the weaponization of a colorblind rhetoric to justify putting the law into the hands of "the people." However, as the following media responses across the nation show, the representation of colorblind lawlessness was both driven by seemingly past principles from the South and by the intention to draw California as a liberal horizon.

A *New York Times* article from Atlanta, Georgia (Figure 6) outlines some of these responses: "And when Rolph's praise of lynching was printed, sentiments in line with the following overheard utterances indicate the reaction of certain groups: 'Let's send all the n***** to California.' 'There ought to be more lynchings.' 'Those Westerners are learning how the South handles 'em.'" Fantasies of the state are revealed by what these reactions do *not* say just as much as by what they *do* say. More specifically, the responses illuminate the ideology of a racial state system which understands the state to be the guardian of whiteness. As Amy Wood has explained, the images of and media responses to the Thurmond and Holmes lynching "made this conception of lynching, one that obscured race and assuaged white Americans' sense of guilt and collective responsibility, *visually evident*—their circulation accentuated that some victims of lynching were white."[12] Read as "visually

THE NEW YORK TIMES, SUNDAY, DECEMBER 3, 1933

ROLPH'S LYNCHING PRAISE SHOCKS SOUTH, CALIFORNIA OPINION BACKS THE GOVERNOR

WORK OF YEARS UNDONE

Effort of South to Prevent Lynching Gets a Setback.

FIGHT A THANKLESS TASK

Association of 15,000 Women Sends Western Governor Telegram of Protest.

By JULIAN HARRIS.

ATLANTA, Ga., Nov. 29.—

PUBLIC SHOWS APPROVAL

Showers Executive With Telegrams Commending San Jose Stand.

BUT PRESS IS CRITICAL

Bar Association Also Sees It as a Menace to Public Security.

By IDWAL JONES.

SAN FRANCISCO, Calif., Nov. 29.—

two prisoners by a San José mob. In one utterance, Rolph has set back for years the efforts of the South to prevent lynchings.

It is impossible to estimate the havoc wrought in this section by the incendiary utterances of the California Executive, who is, by his own confession, an accessory to the lynchings, before and after the fact. For Rolph, by his refusal to prevent the lynching and his promise to pardon any or all of the murderers who may be connected for participation in mob action, has given to lynching the accolade of authority.

The fight against lynching ... continues to be a difficult and thankless task in the South. The sinister element of race prejudice is a handy basis for justification when a Negro, innocent or guilty, is hanged by a lawless group. And when Rolph's praise of lynching was printed, sentiments in line with the following overheard utterances indicate the reaction of certain groups: "California's my address from now on." "Let's send all the niggers to California." "There ought to be a lot more lynchings." "Those Westerners are learning how the South handles 'em." "That California man oughter be President."

Southern Women Protest

Comparisons are odious, but it should be said of the South that its leaders have fought fearlessly to extirpate the spirit of lynching. And the Governors of Southern States have not only never praised lynchers but have usually attempted to prevent lynchings. Within the

MISSOURI LYNCHING BRINGS AN INQUIRY

Gov. Park Condemns It and Instructs Attorney General to Prosecute.

SHERIFF IS UNDER PROBE

Gave Up Negro Prisoner to Save Others Innocent of the Crime.

By LOUIS LA COSS.

Editorial Correspondence, THE NEW YORK TIMES

ST. LOUIS, Mo., Nov. 29.—Within forty-eight hours after a mob in San José, Calif., had lynched two confessed kidnappers and murderers, a mob of 7,000 battered down the doors of the jail at St. Joseph, Mo., hauled Lloyd Warren, 19-year-old Negro who had admitted attacking a white girl, to a tree in the public square and hanged his body at the end of a rope.

If the action of Governor Rolph of California in condoning the lynchers of his State with a promise to pardon all convicted of the crime caused the Missourians to believe that their own Governor

Figure 6. Composite image of the *New York Times* headline and magnified excerpts from November 30, 1933, documenting Southern reactions to Governor Rolph's endorsement of the San Jose lynching. Source: Composite image by author. Original headlines and text from *The New York Times*, November 30, 1933. National Association for the Advancement of Colored People (NAACP) anti-lynching papers with the Newspapers and Microforms Library, Doe Library, University of California, Berkeley.

evident" *or* as visual evidence, the threat to white life transformed lynching into a "problem" for the state to resolve, whereas lynching as antiblack terror was overlooked and even normalized. If these utterances disclose an immediate relation between state and citizenry—that is, the way a response is elicited by the threat to whiteness or white life—they also signal a larger psychical complex through which such a symptomatic exchange can take place. Such symptomatic speech elucidates how a desired recognition is at work against the concealment of a black *imago*, an "unconscious prototypical figure" as a "way of apprehending others" and as the residue that enables this acquisition of a particular imaginary.[13]

Another headline from *The Washington Tribune*, "Lynching of Two Calif. White Men Arouses Nation" (December 7, 1933), puts this dynamic into sharper focus (Figure 7). The double entendre does not simply speak crudely to the sexual politics of lynching, which are driven by a racialization of sexuality that psychosocially constructs black criminality. More fundamentally, the pun avows whiteness as the arbiter of state security and the inherent pleasures in safeguarding whiteness. Henceforth, the headline presents a more complex historical image of sexuality and racial difference. It showed not only that lynchings took place in California and "that some victims of lynching were white"—"facts," Wood observes, "that certainly startled those who otherwise dismissed lynching as a Southern problem of race hatred."[14] Rather, the desire for whiteness in and of the image establishes a racial sexual complex that attempts to rectify the image of whiteness through ways that ultimately cannot conceal the antiblackness

BEST NEWS OF THE NATION'S CAPITAL THE WASHINGTON TRIBUNE, THURSDAY, DECEMBER 7, 1933 ELEVEN

Lynching of Two Calif. White Men Arouses Nation

Senators Make Statements that They Favor Anti-Lynch Law

Senator Costigan Tells N.A.A.C.P. He Will Introduce New Federal Anti-lynching Bill in Congress in January; United Support Asked

Rolph Statement, and Revolt on Eastern Shore of Maryland Show Only Federal Law Will Stop Mobs, Says Association

VA. LONGSHOREM'N FIGHT SHIPPERS' CANTRACT BREACH

Code Commissioner Told Ship Owners' Use of Crews Violates Pact

Abyssinia Grants Julian

Federal News Notes

by Laurence J. W. Hayes

Figure 7. Headline from *The Washington Tribune*, December 7, 1933: "Lynching of Two Calif. White Men Arouses Nation." Source: *The Washington Tribune*; Image courtesy of the National Association for the Advancement of Colored People (NAACP) Records, Library of Congress.

operating in the background of historical memory and its representation. The headline, thus, betokens a wish for white people to be seen as both victims and saviors of lawlessness, demonstrating how such a desire avowedly erects a semblance of the nation-state. The rhetoric of arousal places the sexual nature and politics of lynching at the center; however, it does so in this instance only by centering whiteness. The connotation of this message becomes overdetermined by the various accompanying images of the lynching. In this way, the centering of whiteness banishes blackness to the *real*, where the *jouissance* of white sovereignty serves as the symbolic mask for that exclusion.

Wood's insightful research on the Holmes and Thurmond lynching highlights the disproportionate attention afforded to the event, a consequence of the socially sanctioned culture of displaying whiteness. For instance, it was only after local papers and souvenir-makers circulated photographs of the hanged naked bodies that the police confiscated them on the grounds of "indecency," prompting newspapers to retract them. Even after the images of the Holmes and Thurmond lynching were officially banned, they continued to circulate in an underground economy as bootleg images, souvenirs, or postcards, often inscribed with Governor Rolph's notorious applause for the San Jose lynch mob.[15] Such artifacts both censored and exaggerated the sexuality of the displayed bodies, demonstrating how the state's attempt at "decency" invariably facilitated a more intimate, illicit mode of consumption.

> *The San Jose Mercury News* . . . announced to its readers, with smug self congratulation, that although it would publish no pictures from the lynching, it had not been "scooped." It simply had chosen, in "good taste," not to print the "gruesome and horrible pictures" so as not to shock "children and sensitive women." Yet, while it found the photographs of the lynching "gruesome and horrible," the paper's editorial on the lynching refrained from condemning the mob, deeming them a "vigilante committee" that has simply "demanded what they and the general public believed to be justice."[16]

In contrast, Wood describes a different example in which the sexuality of Holmes and Thurmond is heightened through a technical manipulation that could only be carried out on an image of two white men (Figure 8):

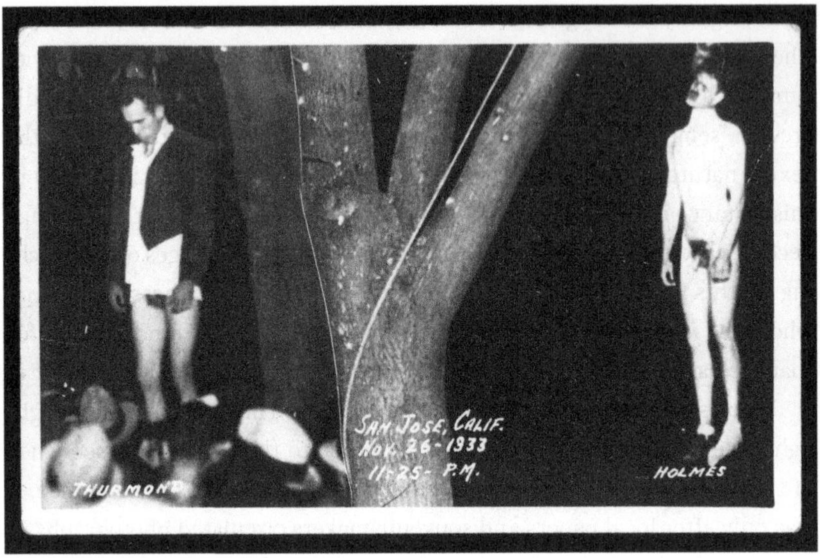

Figure 8. Composite archival photograph of the bodies of Thomas Thurmond and John M. Holmes, San Jose, 1933. The image illustrates the visual construction of the lynching spectacle for circulation. Source: Visual Materials from the NAACP Records, Library of Congress, Prints and Photographs Division. Title: [Thurmond, nude from waist down, and Holmes, nude, hanging from tree after being lynched, San Jose, Calif.] LC-USZ62-84470.

> For one postcard, a photographer manipulated the image to elongate Holmes's penis and make it appear semi-erect, a salacious alteration that would never have been made to a photograph of a black man's lynched body—to the contrary . . . black men's genitalia invariably were covered up for the camera.[17]

Given that photography was still a relatively recent invention, the technical manipulation to alter the length of Holmes's penis must have required considerable effort. The effort to modify the body indicates an underlying drive to telegraph the sign of the white phallus as the arbiter of law. With Holmes's body and enlarged penis facing frontward, the viewer is confronted with the promise of the white phallus to signify even in death. The resulting *jouissance* is perfected through the exercise and exhibition of a law rendered as irrevocably paternal and white.

The act of "[displaying] oneself in order to be looked at," Freud tells us, is always an inversion where "looking precedes being looked at."[18] In the act of scopophilia, the sexual pleasure derived from the object stems from looking at one's own body. The exchange, in other words, serves also as an analogy between the parts of one's own body; the exchange serves as an analogy between the parts of one's own and someone else's body.[19] The elicitation to look at Holmes's enlarged penis is, therefore, less about the person and body being lynched than it is about the possibility of enjoying the violence transmitted through the power of the sign—the white phallus. Yet, the power of the sign, its law and transmission, is irreducible to the image of whiteness. As Wood notes above, the possibility of such an explicit display stands in stark contradistinction to the historical censorship of any signs of black men's sexuality.[20] Dora Apel has also explained that castration as inherent in the "eroticized sadism of the victimizer" addresses "not just black masculinity but also white masculinity, which exists only in relation to it."[21] She explains further that "as a violent and perverse homoerotic exchange, castration reveals the common white obsession with the black penis and a displaced desire to 'consume' the body of the Other."[22] The historical censorship of any signs of black men's sexuality and the violent physical mutilation executed during lynching are not merely parallel acts; they are manifestations of a structural castration. In this sense, lynching "is constituted by symbolic indebtedness."[23] This symbolic indebtedness, in turn, reinforces the white phallus as both real and authentic, wielding a sovereign authority over the scopic field. By censoring the black penis, concealment is put directly into view, thus indicating an active dissolution of black sexual difference in the image and within the imaginary. Like the shadow cast by a ring—darkening the space that narrows into a hole—the avowed censor further displaces black sexual difference in the image, even as black sexuality remains the structural element that constitutes the very image. The displacement of black sexual difference—and sex and desire more generally—underscores an even greater investment in the sign of the white phallus; its concealment, subsequently, secures whiteness as the sign of power and power within the structure of the image.

Given the archival silence of antiblack violence in California leading up to the 1933 penal code—and the way Rolph's comments on the Holmes and Thurmond lynching monopolized nationwide attention—the common misconception regarding the statute's origin is perhaps inevitable.[24] Specifically, the California penal code is often erroneously seen as the state's attempt to criminalize the seizure of a person from law enforcement *in response* to the Holmes and Thurmond lynching. But in fact, the California penal code was introduced earlier that year, passing the State Assembly unanimously on March 31 and being authorized into law on May 16, 1933.[25] Far from a reaction to white "vigilantism," the bill was driven by the persistent advocacy of Delilah Beasley, a writer for *The Oakland Tribune* at the time. She requested that William F. Knowland, who would become the primary sponsor of the legislation, introduce the bill in the California legislature.[26] As part of her anti-lynching efforts, Beasley mobilized a network of institutional witnesses, drafting urgent petitions to the NAACP to counteract the state's dismissal of antiblack terror as a "joke." Her work meticulously documented the local presence of the KKK, the state's complicity, and the inadequate response from both San Francisco and Oakland city councils, forcing a recognition of the antiblackness that the official archive and historical memory sought to repress. As one example, she writes to the National Association for the Advancement of Colored People (NAACP) Field Secretary William Pickens:

> Jan. 26, 1931
>
> Dear Pickens,
> Shall [I] send you full particulars to-night, in the mean time do you think you could [advise] the branches around San Francisco districts to look into such cases as the enclosed clippings? They have thus far treated the incident as a joke, unless [by] my protesting to day they look into it.
>
> I would appreciate you [sending] me a letter to hand to Messrs. Knowland, and Levy, editor and managing [editor] of the *Tribune*, thanking them for their courage . . . in allowing me to publish in full these resolutions . . . I am asking this because as you know this state especially this part was a hot bed for the K.K.K., and because of a conversation I held with Mr. Knowland of several hours duration pleading for my race he threw [all] his strength toward [crushing] the organization . . .
>
> Hastily,
> Delilah Beasley[27]

The institutional response from Pickens confirms the circulation of Beasley's collected evidence—the "clippings" of antiblack lynching incidents that the law had hitherto refused to see. By dismissing these terror formations as a "joke"—the affective twin to the applause of Governor Rolph the state—recruits laughter as a scopic weapon. Such derisive vision maintains the (non-)presence of blackness within the symbolic order to consolidate the *jouissance* of whiteness that thrives on the excision of blackness. In reply to Beasley, Pickens writes:

> January 29, 1931
>
> My dear Mrs. Beasley:
> Thanks for the clippings. I am turning them over to Mr. Seligmann, our Publicity Director. Most certainly I agree with you that incidents of this kind should be investigated by our nearest branches, and proper protest should be made . . . I am passing your clippings onto Mr. Seligmann.
> Very truly yours,
> [William Pickens] Field Secretary[28]

Beasley's committed efforts to document antiblack lynching in the state and inform both the public and authorities were critical and persistent. Yet when William F. Knowland was interviewed by *The Oakland Tribune* about the law's origins, he mistakenly framed the legislation as a direct response to the Holmes and Thurmond lynching. He (mis)remembers that "we wrote up this statute to cover a situation of this kind, [the San Jose lynching], and that's the background of the legislation that was passed and became law."[29] As legal historian Michael J. Nolan observes: "In terms of the execution of the anti-lynching legislation, the San Jose lynching was archetypal, and Knowland's reference to it is a clear indication of the narrow legislative intent behind the law's enactment."[30] That the Holmes and Thurmond lynching was archetypal but *not* the *event* in the image of historical memory indicates a foreclosure in plain sight. Knowland's reference to the San Jose lynching as the *background* for the law demonstrates how the image of "whiteness"—which that case brought to the fore—eclipsed any racial justice imperative behind the legislation. What passes for the image of truth and desire here is critically about a deracination underwriting the image as much as it is a question of what is hidden and revealed by such legislation.

Knowland recalls Beasley's critical influence only as an afterthought. In a move demonstrating a clear "racial" strategy, he sought out Frederick Roberts—California's first black assemblyman—to cosponsor the bill. Knowland's stated goal was that Roberts's participation would create "the clear implication to have a special interest to black constituents," simply because "he was black."[31] While the critical roles of Beasley and Roberts should not be underestimated, Knowland's recollection—with its particular focus on the Holmes and Thurmond lynching—shines a light on how lynching functions at the level of the imaginary as an expiation of white innocence, only to cast a shadow over the black lives involved. Blackness is forced to haunt from within the very image of origins it authors. The racialization of blackness is inextricable from the formation of lynching and lynch law in the state's imaginary, and this inextricability is located not in a misrepresentation of the origins, but in the displacement of blackness as what Barbara Johnson calls "the primal self-difference of origins."[32] The displacement of Beasley and Roberts in the historical memory and re-presentation of the statute telescopes a larger metaphysical structure: blackness conjures the very conditions of possibility for the being and relationality of non-black subjects. Here, the archive enacts what Frank Wilderson and Patrice Douglass have described as "the violence of presence"—a violence "that enables black (non-)being"[33] and "[gives] rise to the philosophical contemplation of metaphysics and the thick description of human relations."[34] A violence that makes the *irreal* presence of blackness appear *real* is coextensive with the violence of the image re-presenting the law's origins. That is, the re-presentation of origins is not fundamentally about imagined origins themselves, nor their source; rather, this re-presentation points to a violence that simultaneously escapes the image and allows for its appearance. This violence ghosted by the image also holds blackness in custody for the preservation of whiteness.

The violence that makes the presence of blackness real asserts from a structural vantage that white privilege cannot be interrogated solely through the lens of race relations. Instead, this violence forces us to ask how antiblackness constitutes the condition for the possibility of symbolic authority and state violence. Such unconscious, irredeemably violent erasure and expenditure at once highlights and enfolds "self-lynching's" *afterlife*—a survival that directly informs the final set of images in this chapter.

"Real Presence" and Sovereignty of the Image

As we have observed, the materialization of "race" and the way it comes to matter in the image do not simply hinge on the exclusion of blackness. Instead, blackness structurally places pressure on the assumed dichotomies between absence and presence, materiality and immateriality. By haunting the frames of the image of lynching and law, blackness coheres and gives plenitude to a racial logic of erasure and expenditure, a logic through which the desire animating the historical memory and image of Thurmond and Holmes's lynching evinces a colorblindness undergirded by antiblackness. In seemingly direct contrast, artist Ken Gonzales-Day asks the viewer "to see" race and the racialized body in artworks that aim to re-imagine and restore a historicity to the image of lynching. Yet, the perversion of "self-lynching" that governs the state's memory reappears in Gonzales-Day's aesthetic judgment and artistic production. These images reveal that, within the continuum of slavery and lynching's *afterlife*, what qualifies black life *as* life must be suspended.

Negotiating the boundary between art and documentary, photographer Ken Gonzales-Day aims to re-situate the historical image of lynching via contemporary art and digital tools in his series, *Erased Lynchings*. He describes his meticulous process of editing archival materials and historical images:

> By erasing the victim's bodies, I sought to create a visual experience that would force the viewer to see the "absence" as a presence and direct the viewer's focus on the crowd and in doing so, to foreground the racism and bias that was foundational to many of these acts of collective violence, which have increasingly come to be seen as central to understanding race and difference in America.[35]

Let us keep in mind the word "force," and what it "foregrounds." The relation between the two will allow us to approach the following key question about lynching and the juridical limits of representation.

For Gonzales-Day, an immediate identification operates between the artistic images he creates and the sequence of historically produced ones: "A solitary figure on a solitary journey, I have documented the empty space that lies between the historically unseen body of the lynch victim and my own unseen body."[36] What might be this empty space that Gonzales-Day feels so compelled to document, the space between the unseen body and his own? Furthermore, what, for the artist, is this space that "lies" between a collective misrecognition and self-recognition?

Through his series *Erased Lynchings* and his accompanying book, *Lynching in the West*, Gonzales-Day suggests a new mode of viewing. He asserts that the viewer, informed by empirical data itemizing deaths across racial and ethnic lines, can turn to the digitized image of the landscape where a lynching once occurred and "see" a body that is absent, yet nonetheless reminiscent of the artist. The newly digitized image performs a gesture similar to a veil being lifted, while functioning as a mirror to the artist's own body. This purported gesture, however, is achieved only through the obliteration of the lynching victim's body compounded with the expungement of blackness. The twofold wish of the image rests on a double obliteration: one "sees" a body, namely a racialized body only by being compelled *not* to see blackness.

Even though Gonzales-Day's wish for the restoration of the racialized body seeks to invoke a sense of *real presence* in the image, the effort only lends itself to the question of what one sees in the absence of the dominant sign of the body. Indeed, the desire to project and capture in the image a definitive "racial body" appears to reproduce the continuity of lynch law by adopting its specific scopic economy—one where blackness is the essential expenditure for the production of the image and any "recognizable" subject. The act of making the body appear only through the imposition of limits reiterates the terms of its original structural erasure. Here, "self-lynching" functions as a psychical dismemberment: blackness must be suspended for there to be a recognition of a "self." In brief, what we are presented with is not a body, but the foregrounding of a judgment as to what should be seen but can never be witnessed—a decision on what must remain unseen so that the "racialized subject" can appear.

Gonzales-Day's desire to restore the body by creating a presence from an absence might remind us of "Freud's challenge to the visible . . . to the 'blindness of the seeing'"[37]—a method to interrogate social control through the lens of unconscious figures, drives, and representatives. Here, I apply a similar pressure by asking what is happening at the level of the unconscious against what Jacqueline Rose has limned as "a fully social classification relying on empirical evidence as its rationale."[38] At stake is how the body is both "racialized" and "seen" through a purported empirical truth that actively masks the artist's didactic foreclosure of blackness. The imagined yet "seen" racialized body, thus, emerges through what Rizvana Bradley terms an impossible inscription: blackness as "a problem *of* and *for* 'the body'" that maintains antiblack metaphysical violence against "those who have never been able to claim a proprietary right over the body."[39]

For example, in "The Wonder Gaze," Gonzales-Day reproduced a photograph of the Holmes and Thurmond lynching with their bodies erased from the frame (Figure 9). Whether reproducing the 1933 archival image or reoccupying its specific location, the work anchors its "erasure" in the physical epicenter of the San Jose spectacle. The choice of the St. James Park photograph is telling: by erasing the white bodies of Holmes and Thurmond from the very site where their death was staged as "white" justice, the artist paradoxically utilizes the coordinates of their specific execution to map a generalized racial absence.

The technical production of these images discloses the formalized mechanics of this erasure. Gonzales-Day digitally enhances the tonal contrast to create an illusion of exceptional depth in the background. The entirety of the landscape has also been removed to bring the lynching into singular

Figure 9. Ken Gonzales-Day, "The Wonder Gaze (St. James Park)," 2006. From the *Erased Lynching* series. The work centers on the site of the 1933 San Jose lynching, focusing on the spectators' gaze while the victims' bodies are absent. Source: Courtesy of the artist and Luis De Jesus Los Angeles. © Ken Gonzales-Day.

focus. The background is a complete negative space—a monochrome blackness. Blackness here operates through the subtraction of space and depth, grounding the figures, the tree, the imagined and erased body, and the sociocultural characteristics of the lynching ritual. We, as the viewers, see the backs of spectators whose gazes are directed at either the tree or the dark void that forms the background. The digitally enhanced contrast blurs the few faces in the crowd that look toward the camera, leaving no detail of their expressions. The lower half of the image illustrates the sociality and "culture" that the ritual of lynching promises—a practice of "community-building" and expression of "community justice" that unified citizens including local city officials, families, children, and reporters, often prompting the closure of schools and businesses to encourage a larger gathering. Observers are looking out into the backdrop, away from the central space where the lynching occurred. Closer to the tree, a small group of faceless spectators gaze up to where the bodies of Holmes and Thurmond once hung, peering infinitely into the background—as if the pleasure of losing oneself into the darkness compensates for the loss of the very object the gaze originally sought to consume: the ethical demand of the absent, "racialized" body. The image coalesces around the visual effect of thus continuous space but also a pervasive unknowingness. Such effect is achieved through the use of negativity (monochrome blackness) that dominates not only the background but also the majority of the foregrounded space. That space, it could be argued, is the space of judgment, the space in which the image offers itself as the equivalent of that judgment and its enduring *afterlife*.

A facilitated gaze upon a gaze, the spectator enters the emptiness of Gonzales-Day's digitized image, which is framed by the artist's reminder that the representation and historical memory of lynching have been dominated by the lynching of African Americans in the United States. He guides the spectator not only to look past the historical focus on black victims (or, for that matter, blackness), but also to deny a confrontation with the absence of the black body itself. This dual shift will fill the viewers' imagination with a different "racial body," a disavowal that both reproduces antiblackness and eclipses any understanding of the antiblackness inherent in lynching. Given that these strictures reformulate not just the historical memory of lynching but also the image of that memory, the erased and yet imagined body in Gonzales-Day's "The Wonder Gaze" rests on a peculiar countertransference between him and the spectator. Essentially, this transference extends between Gonzales-Day and the same institutions that docket these images, the archive, law court, and the art gallery.

In other words, "race" and the lynching victim's body become vehicles that activate the spectator's imaginary with a deracialized memory and landscape of lynching. These vehicles also manage the spectator's own racial anxieties—Lacan's "sum of the prejudices, passions, perplexities"[40]—thus undermining the dialectical process that might otherwise force a confrontation with the image's structural violence. Such an imagined body, ironically, takes for granted the historicity of "race" it seems to challenge, thus reinscribing the operation of power that Evelyn Higginbotham terms the "the meta-language of race." As Higginbotham observes: "Perceived as 'natural' and 'appropriate,' such racial categories are strategically necessary for the functioning of power in countless institutional and ideological forms, both explicit and subtle."[41] Or put another way by Jared Sexton: "What is taken to be black is taken for granted, openly available to all. That is a matter of virtually unrepresentable power, but it is also a structural impossibility to forestall the dissemination of signs, for better or worse."[42]

The evocation of blackness's (non-)meaning also registers at the level of language, where it is shored up as a possible symbolic intervention that must be repressed. This necessary repression is perhaps why it is both fitting and impossible for blackness to be anywhere other than in the photograph's backdrop. The foreclosure of blackness—as the ontological precondition and structural logic of antiblackness—gives rise and cohesion to the imagined racial body, historical memory, and image while the force of antiblackness is reproduced and materialized by the rituals of lynching and the racial logic of print technology. Put another way, the logic of foreclosure necessitates the creation of these rituals to reify that logic. Thus, lynching and print technology function not as the source of foreclosure, but as the material manifestations and social technologies that re-confirm and execute antiblack violence, pointing to the ways in which black death remains *ante legem*. In this way, the rituals of lynching and the racial logic of print technology coalesce as coterminous forces at their peak and in their operations of racial terror.

To be sure, the point here is not an attempt to "see" or integrate blackness, nor to itemize the number of black deaths as a way of countering what Gonzales-Day views as a "racial bias" that ostensibly privileges blackness in the historical memory of lynching. Still, this assumed "privilege" raises a crucial question: What exactly does this privilege hold? In place of this perceived advantage, we observe a denegation—a double erasure of blackness—central to Gonzales-Day's impulse to work with an empirical record and a racial logic. This mechanism supports not only the animation of an imagined racialized body, but also the reification of normative coordinates for image, space, and belonging. Ergo, in mirroring the historical image and remembering of the Thurmond and Holmes lynching, "self-lynching" acts as a form of psychical legislation and claim to an imaginary self—a process that overwrites the same conditions foregrounding its own representational possibilities.

The overwriting of the image formalizes a psychic reproduction of antiblack violence, securing the nonblack "self" through the disappearance of the phobogenic object. The digital (and rhetorical) elision not only prohibits and obscures blackness as possessing a body; it organizes the visual field around blackness as a constitutive absence. By disregarding blackness in this way to facilitate a "racialized" scene, Gonzales-Day reifies what Hartman posits as "the construction of black bodies as phobogenic objects . . . [attesting] to the power of the performative to produce the very subject which it appears to express."[43] As she explains further, even when blackness does not appear, "the seeming obstinacy or the 'givenness' of 'blackness' registers the 'fixing' of the body by terror and dominance and the way in which that fixing has been constitutive."[44] Such a fixing ensures that blackness structures the materialization of a particular psychical content of antiblackness, sustaining the representational power and capacity of the racial image, not least in the image of the racial body.

In a similar vein, Erin Gray explains, "Antiblack violence and removal was not merely imagined as a simple casting *out*. Historians of lynching and lynching's extant visual archive tell us that the violence was celebrated, brought home, and otherwise made familiar through ravening metaphors."[45] Importantly, Hartman's and Gray's critical reflections also help us to consider how blackness can never consent to its own capture within the image as a custodial apparatus. Blackness, in a nonsovereign position, cannot circumvent the violence of *real presence*, even insofar as that position gives rise to articulations of sovereignty. In this regard, blackness (and antiblackness) remain impossibly concealed, invulnerable to the artist's digital scrutiny.

There is, after all, nowhere to hide: the very "givenness" that Gonzales-Day attempts to displace is precisely what "fixes" the image.

Gonzales-Day's "Shadowlands" further articulates the futility of attempting to displace the "givenness" through digital intervention. By enlarging what appears to be the filmic negative of a photographic image, the artist again digitally removes the lynched body from the image, foregrounding instead a liminal stage of the photographic process (Figure 10). The isolation of the negative performs a specific promise associated with this stage of the medium: that the negative preserves a sharper, more transparent reality than the final print. Displaying the negative as an autonomous image implies a preoccupation with the mythic authority of photography in which the incomprehensible in an apparent system of signs now becomes legible, visible. Here, what cannot be seen or has been obscured in the final photograph metaphorically and literally "comes to light." Yet, in this attempt to recuperate the latent image, what is recovered is not the seeming presence or

Figure 10. Ken Gonzales-Day, "Shadowlands," 2006. From the *Erased Lynching* series, installation view at the Minnesota Museum of American Art. Source: Courtesy of Minnesota Museum of American Art, photo by Rik Sferra. © Ken Gonzales-Day.

absence of a "racial" subject, but the structural permanence of the violence itself.

As in "The Wonder Gaze," the negativity of blackness functions here as an organizing principle that frames the image's racial visual politics and internal laws of reading. While the negative technically offers a higher degree of granular detail—indeed, one sees more detail in the negative—such framing allows the law of judgment governing the representation to manifest as both *image* and *event*. Yet, if Gonzales-Day employs the negative to expose what may be hidden in the print, a fundamental contradiction emerges: Why digitally remove the body from the image? Why seek the magnified legibility of the negative only to excise the figure from the frame?

The answer might lie in the compulsion to resolve the image's structural incoherence. The artist's implicit insistence that a "racial" body can be recovered where blackness cannot constitutes a denegation—one designed to establish what Roland Barthes has alluded to as the coherence of signs within the image.[46] In this schema, the recuperation of loss and the desire to see a body become strictly conditional. Black death is assumed to be relinquished by discursive formations of meaning and representation to recover the historical memory of multiracial lynching, but only in the sense that "multiracial" stands in as a proxy for the non-black racial body. That is, the signs of "race" become necessarily consolidated via a shared system of racial difference. Consequently, what becomes racially encoded is an inversion of colorblind logic: the image permits the visibility of a racial spectrum only by facilitating the prohibition of blackness. The expungement, in other words, does not differ from the technocratic management of excluding or distorting blackness in original lynching rituals and their media documentation—a continuity of exclusion that persists even in the *re-membering* of the Holmes and Thurmond lynching as an image of historical memory.

In his book, *Lynching in the West*, which serves as both a historical monograph and an artist statement, Gonzales-Day outlines his methodological approach: "The lynching of African Americans has long shaped the discussion of lynching in this country, and as noted in the introduction, I was able to document eight cases in California, six more than were previously recorded by either the NAACP or the Tuskegee Institute Archive." My concern, again, is not the numeration of black death despite the artist's stated objective to "count the dead."[47] By itemizing lynchings across racial lines, Gonzales-Day attempts to decouple multiracial lynching in the American West from lynching's racial terror in the South. For him, documenting lynching as it crosses racial lines exposes a bias that goes unacknowledged in the national discourse surrounding the region's regime of terror:

> The presence of whites, or Anglos, in the national statistics has not diminished the impact of lynching on African American history. Asians, American Indians, and Latinos of Mexican and Latin American descent were lynched in the West, yet no one has acknowledged that racial bias may be as integral to the study of Western lynching as it has been to the study of lynching nationwide. The historical erasure has been heightened by the fact that lynching has become conflated with white racism against blacks. This observation is not intended to diminish the significance of lynching to the history of African Americans; it instead attempts to acknowledge that the history of lynching has touched other racial and racialized communities in other historical moments.[48]

Part of Gonzales-Day's objective is, thus, to counter such misconceptions—specifically that lynching is exclusively "conflated with white racism against blacks"—by quantifying the number of deaths resulting from lynching violence and summary executions. On his account, illustrating a death toll that is largely non-black, but also non-white, serves to disrupt this perceived historical conflation. Yet, by submitting this empirical account to accompany the photograph, in which the spectator is asked to see a particularized body, Gonzales-Day re-casts a racial logic that wields the categories of race as instruments of disciplinary power, virtually foreclosing blackness from its frames. What the artist qualifies as "racial bias" thus functions as a disavowal of his own: a framework where "multiracial" and "racial violence" are defined by, and become conditional upon, the exclusion of (anti)blackness. In this schema, racial bias is only recognized insofar as it fails to incorporate the racial divide that remains predicated on the absence of blackness.

The visual and suggestive cues of Gonzales-Day's works initiate an engagement less concerned with the artist's intent to avoid pathologizing the racialized body in the imaginary, and more with the problematic way in which he leverages black death to resolve the image's structural incoherence. Thus, the disavowal—which rests on garnering dead bodies while foreclosing black death as a way into the image—reinscribes the politics of witnessing (or the inaccessibility thereof) within the unethical spectacle of lynching that Gonzales-Day attempts to rectify. As statistics, the quantification of dead bodies serves to qualify the scale of racialized violence; in doing so, it reproduces what Denise Ferreira da Silva has described as "signifiers of the horizon of death," where one's racialized existence functions "as an effect of the tools of raciality."[49] This effect, da Silva tells us, is at work when "the state acts only in the name of its own preservation."[50]

Such statist(ical) preservation is precisely what Gonzales-Day's method attempts to navigate, yet ultimately reproduces through visual technology. When the artist resituates the lynching photograph to signify racial mourning and racial violence, the signs of "race" necessarily become consolidated via a particularized system of racial difference, as "visual technologies and racial taxonomy fashion each other."[51] For the digital lynching photograph to function as an effective simulacrum—at once an archival document and a letter of mourning—the image stems from a double effacement: the obliteration of an obliteration of blackness. This "double effacement" is not a finite count of two erasures, but is a structurally operative re-doubling, a split between two distinct levels of necessary erasure. The first is the ontological foreclosure of blackness from the possibility of representation, the symbolic order; the second is the archival and social oblation of the visible trace of that initial foreclosure. The latter movement renders the subsequent violence (the lynching ritual) legible as a moral, rather than structural, necessity. Unlike the general structure of iterability—the principle that any mark must be repeatable to be legible—this specific structural repetition, or "self-lynching" of the image, maintains antiblackness in its endless re-doubling to permanently cohere the sign of the racial body, a sign under which blackness is positioned as inherently without meaning.

Thus, just as the lynching photograph depicts the desecration of the black body, the image also attests to lynch law's submission to (white) desire—a desire that both avows such obliteration and, through this communal affirmation, assumes the force of law. This obliteration is subsequently reproduced through the mediated circulation of the lynching image itself. As both sign and component of a sign-system, the image naturalizes lynch law by disavowing black (dis)appearance and death.[52] Law and visual media work together here to reinforce what race and technology scholar Ruha Benjamin describes as "the faith in photography's power to picture the truth,"[53] reminding the viewer of a certitude born of a desire that has no other recourse than its violent and murderous effects.

Even insofar as Gonzales-Day states that his photographic series aims "to help viewers to engage a critical approach to *whiteness*, by drawing their attention to what is missing, absent, and erased to raise awareness of this [racial] history,"[54] this methodology remains flawed. What becomes present or visible in the image rests on the deracination of the lynching photograph's violent history and its function within mass media. Yet what also becomes marginalized is the black history of responses to such media—a history that not only aimed to dismantle the assumption that *whiteness* is neutral or innocent, but also challenged whiteness's purported immunity to the terrorizing effects of the image and its technology.

The efficacy of Gonzales-Day's work, particularly his digital manipulation of the filmic representation of the lynching ritual, rests on an epistemic premise that ultimately advances visual technologies as projectors of racial truth. In his critique of the link between race and technology, Marriott observes the ruses of the "power" attributed to technology as a means of eliciting racial consciousness. He writes:

> That is, the question of technology is always about the *racial* limit that technology attempts to eradicate. But in this case, as they say, even paranoia has technical racist prostheses. Or perhaps we would say that denying the paranoia of technical life doesn't make those racially "real fears" go away.[55]

The unconscious wish for race-free technology only reifies race by eliding and disavowing the racism internal to those paranoic fears. While technology is often thought to produce discursive formations and objects through processes of racialization, the dynamics that underlie racialization and intensify a racial limit *within* technology are seldom considered. The libidinal investment coterminous with a "racist incapacity,"[56] then, is not solely about the fantasmatic technical effect of subjection faced by the subject of racial technology, nor about becoming a virtual-technical object; it is also about what gives value to the wish for racial technology as a means for redemption and restoration. When we view the digitized photographic image in Gonzales-Day's *Erased Lynchings* series then, there remains a question: How, and to what effect, does the racial limit internal to technology facilitate the proposed body that Gonzales-Day evokes in the viewer's imagination? This question concerns the way the work enables or forces one to witness an internalized racist incapacity—the incapacity that prevents one from seeing the "real presence" of black social death on screen, as image, as art, and as white law.

It is through black death that white self-identification can pursue an *idée* of superiority "that the living self will try to equal."[57] Though Gonzales-Day's images position "real presence" as distinct from a theological one, they both rely upon the notion that an immaterial essence extends beyond what is visually present. In a theological sense, "real presence" refers to the way a material element—such as the Eucharist—is believed to contain an actual, spiritual essence that transcends its physical form. This assumed immateriality operates as an indexical gesture toward the absent. The "primal scene" that engenders this theological notion derives from the example of Christ's empty grave, which, as media theorist Sigrid Weigel notes, "gives rise to the specific Christian desire for images."[58] There is, in short, an attempt to put into relation something outside the scope of human vision into the perceptible field. In this primal scene, it is not the body that elicits the idea of resurrection and the joining of mortality and immortality; rather, it is the *absence* of the corpse that gives rise to a desire for images through abstraction.[59] "Indeed," Weigel writes, it is "*death*, but not *the dead*, [that] lies at the origin of the idea of the image being a double."[60] On this view, Gonzales-Day's "erased" image functions as a secularized empty grave: by vanishing the corpse, the artist facilitates a desire for a "redemptive" history that can only be imagined (and imaged) once the material evidence of antiblackness is removed.

In the rituals of lynching, black death is the axis that makes connections possible between positive law and sovereignty, the citizen and the socially dead, desire and images. To that end, the lynching of the black body was not just a powerful symbolic gesture essential to image-production; it was mutually interdependent with the justification of extrajudicial murder and punishment. The obliteration of blackness served as a kind of "shadow and phantom image [*eidolon*]"[61] linking disparate domains: the divine and human, the alive and socially dead, body and incorporeality. As Wood tells us, lynching "became a divinely sanctioned retribution for black 'sin,' sin that threatened not only white authority but white purity and virtue"[62]—an act that "psychically restored a sense of communal purity and social order."[63] The photographs, postcards, and printed media preceding and extending the rituals of lynching telegraphed these modes of retribution, expiation, and psychical restoration. The image of lynching transmitted a notion of "real presence"—of a higher and unified power consisting of white communal solidarity and its union with divine law—through the obliteration of the black body. The affect of "real contact," too, was widely circulated, shared, and "revealed" through the haptic—the physical touch—of the media material. These artifacts of lynching are not simply products of modernity; rather, they evince the libidinal investment of lynching's cultural logic, providing what Goldsby describes as the "deepest pleasures from those that disavow an exact coherence with the real world."[64]

In Gonzales-Day's works, I have explored the problematic of *real presence* as it mirrors the cultural logic of lynching rituals. This psychical dynamic of "self-lynching" underscores racialized notions of the presence/absence dichotomy where *real presence* reinforces a sense of *real contact*—the theological belief that one is in touch with a divine power and law. In this context, presence—standing in for white communion and a proximity to divinity—allows the spectator to perform a ritual of ablution, a symbolic exculpation from the extrajudicial murder of black people, as death follows the moral imperative of blackness's banishment and execration. Just as lynching rituals "gave visual form to white supremacist beliefs," they enabled acts of "witnessing conferred truth"—acts of pure conviction that rest upon the perception of blackness as the damned. Moreover, the antiblack fantasy of *real presence* also makes clear an investment and idealization of an aesthetic—a materialization of the immaterial—through which blackness can only return as something demonic or negatively bound. More significantly, such antiblack fantasies not only marshal a sense of real presence that parallels the establishment of a self and belonging within the conventions of white lynching rituals; these fantasies of negation, which entail the desire for blackness's erasure, become tolerable, even naturalized, in the formulation of the image. The image-form is thus indispensable; the desire for the image of black death consolidates the wish for the absence of the black body. It is the black corpse that is then utilized to fix that absence as a sign, mobilizing the expression of sovereignty and signaling the truth, grace, and virtue of the (whiteness of the) human.

These are the stakes of blackness's negativity in the representations of sovereignty and the sovereignty of the image; that is, blackness's negativity defines their very structures and possibilities, what is deemed ethical and ontologically sound. Perhaps this is why black feminist thinker Sarah Haley observes that "the parameters of subjection technologized through the carceral state reached far beyond 'its announced material boundaries and juridical limits,'"[65] since the carceral state rests not on state-sanctioned violence alone, but on the ways in which desired images of white life as "truth" provide an inscription for its politics. Such systems of carceral power and lawless lynching function to explain not only the power of these images but also the desire for them—a desire maintained even through the myriad conversions the image's materiality undergoes. What does not change, in other words, is the aggressive identification and the staging of desire for black death that gives rise to the ubiquitous images of whiteness, and the mediums through which they can sustain their power.

Real presence is intimately bound to the libidinal investment in blackness, only for blackness to be legislated to and from nothingness. The concept of "self-lynching" is fundamental to the images that I have discussed because they demonstrate the simultaneous investment in and negation of blackness, whereby a convergence of aesthetic and psychic domains shapes "realities" of the self. The dissolution of the two—the aesthetic and the psychic—as driven by antiblackness forms the link between the two sets of images, the historical and the contemporary erasure, even in their seeming disparity. The tension between the elision of the specific history of lynching black subjects and the void of blackness within representation opens itself as a site of an inevitable unfolding. To pursue the claim of historical effacement—the deracination of a particular history of antiblack violence—is to realize that this very act of erasure must negate itself as a claim, insofar as its analysis leads inexorably to the structural conclusion that the issue is the antiblackness of representation as such—a derealization and disavowal whose object is unclear and uncertain because it is ontological. Such a structural preclusion, in turn, finds its necessary archival and legal manifestation in historical effacement. The desire of an imagined self demands and procures the investment of the image as truth, but the transition from desire to demand—between an imaginary self and its projection in the image—rests on the arrest of blackness whose moment of custody is indeterminate and unlocatable. And so, the stakes of antiblackness in the image of "self-lynching" leave us with a question: Where does the custody of blackness begin and end? This question forces us to interrogate the structures of racial representation which, in turn, beget a kind of seeing that is in service of its own antiblack desire. Thus, at the edge of *real presence*, one might reevaluate that desire as a revelation of how antiblackness belies the lynching and projection of a self in the deadly judgment of certain images.

Three

Untranslatability, Resistance

The Afterlife *of "Self-Lynching"*

As established in the previous chapter, contemporary racial representation, even in its attempt at critique, cannot escape the structural demands of anti-blackness. The racial limit—whether internal to the image, technology, or in the historical memory of lynching—is sustained by the libidinal investment in black death. Through the mechanism of "self-lynching," this investment enables the images of whiteness and sovereignty to cohere. By paralleling the psychic function of "real presence" with the theological tradition that procures an image from absence, I have shown how the image-form is indispensable for consolidating the desire for blackness's erasure into a "fixed sign" that defines the category of the "human" or "person." These intersecting systems of carceral power and the image of sovereignty reveal that the issue is not simply one of *misrepresentation*, but of a constitutive arrest of blackness—a moment of custody that remains permanently indeterminate.

Such a foundational ambiguity leaves us with the critical question of where the custody of blackness begin and ends, but also provides the necessary critique of any political project that advocates for abolition at the level of the symbolic—or for that matter, the imaginary. The wager to move beyond abolition, the abolition of the *real*, is the limit that also compels us to move beyond the image's material function into its survival *as* an *afterlife* through language. This chapter mobilizes the case studies of *People v. Jones* and *People v. Anthony J.* to demonstrate how the legal apparatus actively structures a "self-lynching" through the seizure of custody and volition to reinforce blackness's position as perpetually nonsovereign. It takes up the notion that blackness is fundamentally untranslatable, and explores how this condition, echoing Walter Benjamin's concept of "afterlife," challenges the very notion of meaning, equivalence, and sovereign transference in the continued life of the image and writing of "self-lynching."

On the night of June 30, 1969, Reginald Jones attempted to intervene in the arrest of Mercy Roaches Sandoval, an eighteen-year-old who was intoxicated in public.[1] Sandoval was breaking glass bottles in the parking lot of a restaurant when two Santa Ana police officers on routine car patrol arrested Sandoval for being drunk in public. As the police officers led Sandoval to the patrol vehicle, Jones asked the police what they were doing. When the officers replied that they were arresting Sandoval, Jones decided to intervene on Sandoval's behalf. He told the officers that an informal agreement had been reached between the citizenry and the chief of police, that they would be allowed to take care of their own problems around the restaurant. When the officers did not respond to his plea, Jones yelled, "Don't let the fucking pigs take him away!" The crowd threw rocks and bottles at the car to prevent the officers from leaving. Jones and another man were able to reach into the back seat of the patrol car and free Sandoval. The police officers left the parking lot as the crowd gathered to celebrate Sandoval's release. There was no further pursuit of Sandoval after the patrol car was targeted by the crowd. The next day at his place of work, however, Jones was arrested on the charges of lynching and incitement to riot.

The *Jones* case was the first to interpret the term "lynching" from the 1933 California Penal Code §405(a),(b), which was established as an anti lynching statute in its original legislative intent, and defined as the "taking of a person from the lawful custody of a peace officer." The court decision in the *Jones* case would later inform the interpretation of another case in 1999, that of *The People v. Anthony J.*, in which the court found the defendant guilty of having "aided and abetted his own lynching."[2] The interpretation of these two court cases has had significant repercussions for both the legal and common understanding of the word "lynching." This chapter explores how these legal distortions obscure the antiblack violence and racial terror that accompany the historical memory and sociocultural and ritualistic practices of lynching.

Such interpretations eventually sanctioned racist and antiblack police practices against racialized subjects protesting in the Black Lives Matter and the Occupy Wall Street Movements. In this regard, subsequent interpretations highlight the intention of the original authors, as Erin Gray submits, "to bolster law enforcement, and to protect the right of the state to define the boundaries of rational and legitimate violence."[3] The state's weaponization of its own anti-lynching statute reveals that legal criteria are used to define rioting and vigilante violence as illegal and illegitimate. Crucially, this mirrors the ways in which the state justifies its use of racialized state violence and punishment, allowing the opacity of legal terms and conditions to function in defense of the statute's validity.[4]

In what follows, I interrogate the question of resistance (*to* blackness and *of* blackness) in the context of *Jones*, the first recorded juridical interpretation of California's anti-lynching statute. By examining how the courts and the police translate this statute, I explore the nature of blackness's untranslatability and the manifold resistances inherent in language and law. The untranslatability of blackness girds a violence of reason and partial truth that sustains a juridical imaginary persisting both within and out of the courtroom.

The Legal History of "Self-Lynching"

The structural analysis of untranslatability finds its clearest manifestation in the legal history of the anti-lynching statute and its subsequent distortion. In the context of the legal history of "self-lynching," the roles of defense and resistance are complicated by the dissimulation of antiblackness that underscores its legislation, conceptual plentitude, and persistence in(to) the present. The first two court cases to interpret and translate "anti-lynching" as "lynching thyself"[5] do not simply raise questions regarding juridical personhood; they also illuminate the production of a plurality of subjects at the expense of blackness as a non-self. This phenomenon hinges on the instrumentalization of lynching rhetoric by the court to refigure the defiance of authority—a maneuver that violently severs the term "lynching" from its strong, historical association with antiblack terror. The resulting neutralization of the historical reality of antiblack lynching in the legal field constitutes a fundamental fiction. Ultimately, these court cases reveal that the law's capacity to preserve itself depends entirely upon this constitutive maneuver: the legal subject can only be stabilized through the violent production of blackness as the non-self—a "self-lynching" achieved through the displacement of antiblack violence.

More than half a century after California introduced anti-lynching legislation in 1933, the statute was weaponized to validate racist police practices against racialized subjects. In recent years, the "felony lynching" charge was applied to nonviolent Black Lives Matter protesters who resisted arrest, whether their own or that of fellow demonstrators. Such legal distortion, however, represents no radical break from the past, but rather a structural return to the logic of antiblack terror inherent in the statute's pre-history. As discussed in Chapters 1 and 2, practices of white vigilantism under the banner of "frontier justice" and popular sovereignty mark not only this penal code's pre-history, but also "the re-racialisation of whiteness as the intensification of anti-blackness."[6] Historically, white lynch mobs presented their collective violence as an authority residing beyond the normalized rule of law. The extraordinary and unusual translation of the law from "anti-lynching" to "lynching" thus mirrors the mob's historical practice of inflicting deadly force beyond institutional juridical limits—an antiblack imaginary that perceives racialized subjects as always already "lynching themselves."

The first reported application of the 1933 anti-lynching statute occurred forty years after its enactment, in the 1970s. The significant temporal gap between the anti-lynching statute's enactment and its first reported use indicates the breakdown of juridical strictures to admit the case—a failure that fundamentally disregarded the law's original intent, the prevention of targeted extrajudicial violence against racialized subjects. This jurisdictional failure and temporal deferral created the condition for the statute's weaponization. Indeed, it allowed a novel, extralegal interpretation of "lynching" to emerge precisely because the law failed to account for how antiblack violence had already been routinized and naturalized as a quotidian practice.[7] The forty-year gap further signals that the decision to apply the statute was fundamentally arbitrary, compelling us to ask how lynching's legibility—or more accurately illegibility—has been constructed in the eyes of the law.[8]

While the *Jones* case fleetingly acknowledged the historical context of lynch law (both state- and nationwide), it ultimately remained a matter of passing mention. The history of lynching's racial terror was, thus, fundamentally excluded from the interpretation of §405(a),(b). The defendant was charged under the penal code with the felony of rescuing a prisoner, "not in order to do him harm, but to help him escape." In his defense, Jones raised the following issues pertaining to the lynching statute: that it was unconstitutionally vague and that the trial court erred in not instructing the jury *sua sponte* (Latin for "of one's own will" or meaning "one's own volition") on the specific elements of lynching and incitement to riot.[9] In sum, Jones rightly identified a critical linguistic fracture; he argued that his defense depended on the discrepancy between the statutory and dictionary definitions of the term "lynching." The former effectively effaced the historical memory of racial terror and black death inherent in the latter.

At the time of Jones's trial, there had been no *reported* cases of lynching as extrajuridical antiblack violence since the implementation of the antilynching law. Such an absence, however, is not a testament to lynching's non-occurrence, nor does it signal a simply mistranslated meaning or lost legislative intent. Rather, this silence highlights the structural imperative of law and its apparatuses (the courthouse, archive, and news media) to foreclose antiblack violence from being inscribed as a legible case. The violence remains untranslatable not because its meaning is being distorted, but because blackness, as the *n'est pas*—the structural nothingness of blackness—is always already incommensurable with the logic of (legal) signification. A foundational untranslatability prevents the violence from being accounted for as a referent or a precedent, and structurally portends, as a consequence, the original legislative intent—designed explicitly as an antidiscrimination measure—to be lost in the later applications and interpretations of the statute, precisely because the law can only recognize violence *within* its own language.[10]

The court in the case of *Jones* favored the interpretation that Jones's words constituted an attack on "lawful custody," strikingly characterizing his words to the police as "a lit torch." In this view, Jones's words were understood as an assault on "lawful custody" itself—the state of "physically holding or controlling a person or piece of property." While the term "lawful custody" was tacitly assumed to be self-evident, Jones argued that the court should have used its *sua sponte* (its own motion) authority to instruct the jury on the specific elements of lynching. As was described in the court documents, "the defendant claims *sua sponte* instructions were required, since without any specific advisement, the jury was unable to make any determination on the issue of lawful custody." Although this defense was a legal necessity, such a strategy should not be mistaken for an assumption that a jury is neutral or exempt from the reach of antiblackness. To appeal to the jury is to appeal to a feature of popular sovereignty—a concept, as we discussed in Chapter 1, driven by antiblackness. As a representative of "the people," the jury does not stand apart from state violence; rather, it serves to legitimate the violence of antiblackness internal to the state's representational authority. The court's refusal to instruct the jury on the definition of "lawful custody" was, therefore, less a judicial error than a structural operation: it ensured that the abstraction of the term could remain tacit and unexamined. Both "lynching" and "lawful custody" were abstracted from their sociohistorical and cultural contexts of racial terror, with the latter being sustained by the disavowal inherent in its "self-evident" presumption.

The failure to instruct the jury meant that "lynching" was effectively severed from its sociohistorical and cultural context of racial terror. Such a judicial move inverted the statute's original legislative intent: while the law was designated to protect the potential victim from the criminal activity of the mob, the court's interpretation reframed the captive as the primary threat to "lawful custody." This disparity in definition—where "lynching" was narrowed in scope while "custody" remained an unexamined "self-evidence"—rendered Jones's defense an impossibility. The structural imbalance here dictates the translation of not only the legal person under scrutiny but also the nature of willful action. By reading Jones's words as "a lit torch," the court obfuscates the determination of his actual intent while simultaneously replacing his sense of self with a caricature of an insurgent threat.[11] Jones's observation that the court and jury lacked a basic understanding of lynching underscores the fundamental displacement of the statute's original anti-lynching intent. The displacement only further perpetuates the dissimulation of antiblackness: it ensures that indefinite custody is integral to the *afterlife* of black death, as an impossible self before the law.

Because custody is neither circumscribed nor granted lawful specificity in the context of the arrests, it functions as something other than a predetermined legal category. Indeed, custody as a component of "self-lynching" requires further interrogation. From the state legal vantage, custody is central to the penal code's definition of lynching, as it delineates both the transgression that supposedly warrants the arrest—"the taking from the lawful custody of a peace officer"—and the hierarchy of those who judge versus those who are the objects of that judgment. More critically, this construction of custody serves to articulate and maintain sovereign police violence while establishing the racialized grounds on which such violence is legitimized and performed. Yet, what becomes custodial, and who the subjects and the objects of custody are, remains perilously unclear. If "lawful custody" historically refers to protecting a captive from a lynch mob, then the felony occurs when an outside agent *seizes* the captive *from* the state's protection. The "felony lynching," or "self-lynching" cases, by contrast, perversely redefine the captive *as* the lynching agent, thus obliterating the state's responsibility to protect and substituting it with a duty to secure compliance. In this inversion, the prisoner morphs into the agent of their own lynching. Under these conditions, the ambiguity of what operates as "custody" or who is "custodial" mirrors the narrow discrepancy between extralegal and unlawful violence—a confusion weaponized to then determine how actors and criminal activity are positioned outside the law. Custody is necessarily misaligned with notions of protection; it functions instead as immediate imprisonment—a mode of capture and captivity that precedes the moment of arrest. The significance of this pre-lawful arrest is the psychical state that holds it: a white desire whose intensity amplifies its own antiblackness, maintaining black death before and as the law.

The *Jones* case brings into sharp focus the impossibility of supplying evidence to testify against one's lynching—whether that evidence seeks to defend actions taken against lawful custody or to contest the charge of "self-lynching." According to the court and law enforcement, Jones's words were the instrument that incited a riot and constituted the attempt to remove a person from custody. The court, in designating Jones's words as "a lit torch," was forced to assign will and agency to his speech act in order to secure a finding of guilt and criminal intent. Such an assignment of criminal agency stood in direct contradiction to the court's maintenance of the jury's will-lessness (or unreflective interpretation) regarding the terms "lynching" and "lawful custody." The court's refusal to instruct the jury *sua sponte* ensured that the violence of antiblackness structuring "lawful custody" remained tacit and unexamined. Through the contradiction of assigning an imagined agency to the defendant while demanding will-less abstraction from the judiciary, a structural merging of agent and act occurs. Here, the "agent" of lynching (Jones, in the court's eyes) and the "act" of lynching (the person being taken from custody) become indistinguishable. This collapse forecloses the possibility of resistance, making the (projected) body's capture and captivity the necessary precursor to the moment of arrest and the ultimate ground of "lawful custody." That merging is mirrored by the way custody and death fade into one another—a fading that clearly echoes the history of lynching and the horrors of a constant oscillation between life and death, a movement that takes place not by chance, but because it descends from beyond the juridical scope. And yet, the oscillation, though constant, finds no expression in law.

In other words, what might constitute historical proof of lynching's unwritten law of antiblackness evanesces, as it can never satisfy the demands for evidence in a court. In this system of jurisdiction, as Frank Wilderson has explained, "Black people cannot bear witness to the coherence of prior plenitude because their 'loss' is overwhelming and irreparable . . . and with desire for redress that must be channeled through the conceptual frameworks and cognitive maps which crowd them out as subjects."[12] Wilderson highlights the paradox wherein the interdiction of blackness, at the levels of subjectivity and desire, serves to stabilize the juridical framework. In this light, the case for lynching always already exceeds the juridical scope of judgment insofar as antiblackness as racial law predetermines and qualifies blackness as a crime. Had the court in the *Jones* case instructed the jury *sua sponte*, it might have registered the structural absence of evidence—or, more fundamentally, the way antiblackness, before the law, shapes one term as self-evident and another as infinitely open for interpretation. Instead, the jury affirmed Jones's conviction.

The translation of "anti-lynching" into "self-lynching" signals a deeper problematic involving testimony and the legal archive, a problematic rooted in the fact that testimony relies on translation indexical to the human subject. While it might beg the question about who the self is in the legal interpretation of lynching, attempting to answer such inquiry leads to a dead end, for both the question and response rest on an investment in the due process of law and its possible reform, as if any change in the representation of legal categories and forms could radically alter the relationship between the *n'est pas* of blackness and *Gewalt*—a constitutive (non)relation that will become the subject of discussion momentarily. For now, we can understand that any translation emerging from this relation precludes blackness from ever being and becoming a self. In this way, the translation from "anti-lynching" to "self-lynching" requires an interrogation of the historical image of lynching and testimony, telescoping the ways in which blackness marks an absence in the symbolic structure of law that scripts memory and truth—a site in which blackness is never fugitive, but fundamentally untranslatable in its non-being.

We can thus identify a fundamental misrecognition in the shift between different registers of language and signifying systems intrinsic to the process of translation itself. Here, racist myth and white sovereign truth converge, with antiblackness at the very heart of their *archē*, whether asserted by law or by "the people's justice/sovereignty"—a convergence predicated upon black social and civic death. The problem is not about an error *in* translation, which might then be corrected to provide for better legal representation in and outside of law's own antiblack practices of misreading and interpretation, but about that which remains uncertain within the conventions of translation itself—the process of conversion and discernment of truth and justice in which antiblackness has no analogy.[13]

If we consider Sigmund Freud's notion that translation is a form of repression, we can infer that blackness is displaced in the process of translation and representation because it is anticipated as a possible disturbance—a threat to the material being translated.[14] Translation, in other words, labors to avoid terms and signs that would destabilize its own coherence. Antiblackness undergirds this order of signification, operating as both its immanent logic and its constitutive limit. It is through this repression that the untranslatability of blackness produces the possibility of translation and legal interpretation; it provides the void upon which the law exerts its force. Therein, blackness inhabits an irreconcilable oscillation between law-preserving and law-making violence—a site where the state simultaneously enacts its authority and recreates its own necessity.

Blackness's untranslatability also precedes and conflicts with the possibility of bearing witness, insofar as testimony is fundamentally predicated upon human presence. In this context, the time lapses between the archival housing of antiblack lynching and its emergence as a "wrong" decision or legal misinterpretation cannot be attributed to the evidence itself, but rather to the conditions of terms and order of events upon which the decision rests, and the signifying structure through which any legal decision is formulated. Blackness's untranslatability avers an irreconcilability with the ordering of order itself, an abyss that precedes and exceeds the diachrony and synchrony of language, and the order and sense of *de jure* and *de facto* law. There is always already a radical difference through which signification proceeds, and its originary point remains as a trace.[15] However, I want to submit that the untranslatability of this radical difference is all the more complex, even lethal, when the law's desire to simultaneously claim blackness and prohibit its entry into an organizational structure functions to prosecute and judge blackness, *and* make its defense impossible.

The *Jones* case interprets the anti-lynching statute via a translation from anti-lynching to "self-lynching." These problems of translation return us to an original non-origin in which blackness does not translate as having personhood or rights in and beyond the law. As Jacques Derrida has described in another register and as Emily Apter reminds her readers, that which remains untranslated preserves the "sectional life" of a sentence, "where indefiniteness meets infinitude,"[16] and the semblance of language draws from an open abyss. The untranslatability of blackness, its unbearability of a truth, marks the *archē* of an impossible trace that cannot be recorded. The "indefiniteness" of blackness is nonetheless acquiesced in the moment of judgment, decision, and decipherability, reproducing a grammar of violence not just as an event of antiblack murder but also as an a priori indictment, a type of foreclosure, in which blackness has no possible plea as defense. In this sense, we can conceive the interpellation of law and blackness as a nonconsensual bind, which involves a conversion from the untranslatability of blackness to blackness as an imagined legal subject, a process to which blackness never consents yet which confirms the vanishing of blackness in the bolstering of state defense.

The case of *The People v. Anthony J.*, the second court trial that applied the anti-lynching statute twenty years after the *Jones* case, concretizes this point in its stark interpretation of the defendant as a subject who intended to lynch himself. Anthony, a teenager attending a community vigil in San Francisco, was sought by the police with an arrest warrant for auto theft. Interrupting the vigil for Anthony's recently deceased friend, three police officers pursued his arrest as community members endeavored to persuade the police that their timing was inappropriate. However, the police persisted in targeting Anthony and called for backup. The number of involved police officers was clearly disproportionate, and attendees of the vigil urged them to halt the sudden and unnecessary surge of force. According to the prosecution, Anthony fought against his arrest when the crowd of mourners attempted to set him free. In his defense, Anthony explains that he never asked the crowd to free him and that he only began yelling when the police threatened his mother. The crowd responded to Anthony's plea for help as he was being escorted to the officer's patrol vehicle. Anthony, still handcuffed, was able to run away. When he was found, he was charged as a juvenile for resisting arrest, aggravated assault on an officer, and "self-lynching."

Similar to the *Jones* case, the *Anthony J.* case disregarded the original legislative intent and the historical and racial context of the anti-lynching statute. The core question confronting the court transcended a simple interpretation of "lynching" according to its common or legal definition. The case arrived before the court to resolve the question of whether one could voluntarily lynch oneself under the statute's conditions by protesting against being held in lawful custody by a peace officer. This transformation refashioned "self-lynching" from "taking a person from lawful custody" to an act of "defense and resisting arrest," as well as from "harming a prisoner" to "willfully obstructing being taken into custody," thereby accenting the structural conditions that enable the law to recast the self as a potential agent of lawlessness in its own mirage.

The court's interpretation of lynching rested not only on an abstraction of lynching violence, but conversely enabled the process of legal transformation wherein the prisoner who is held captive is refashioned as a self against the custody of a peace officer. In the *Anthony J.* case, the court shifted its focus to the assumed nature of justice that emanates from the grounds of the juridical subject rather than the will of the subject. Such a shift was only possible by referencing the previous *Jones* case, which affirmed "that the Legislature is free to define and punish offenses as it sees fit (subject to the prohibition against cruel and unusual punishment), and may choose to define a word in a way that varies from its traditional meaning."[17] The reasoning in the *Jones* case, according to which the principle of *sua sponte* can be invoked as a privilege of the court to act "of its own volition" but denied to the custodial subject, becomes essential in *Anthony J.* While the reasoning appears to read the will of the defendant's actions, filtering them through this lens overdetermines Anthony's actions before the justice of the courts and rule of law. The application of this principle to Anthony's interference with his own arrest results in his behavior being construed as a criminal act. In the eyes of the law, Anthony J. is perceived as a criminal figure, a subject who in and for his sense of self attempted to disrupt the custody of law enforcement. What, then, is the structural economy created by refashioning the custodial subject's volition into a criminal self? That is, how and why does the case of *Anthony J.* serve as a pivotal "quilting point" that stabilizes the legal structure, and what is the logic that allows translation and resistance to function simultaneously despite the perceived errancy of blackness? On the one hand, we might see the court's interpretation of the law as a bad-faith reading, a reading that stems from what is imagined as justice and how justice is to be staged, a reading that is ostensibly both spontaneous and synchronous, both in its eminence and immanence. On the other hand, the interpretation does not pretend to perform otherwise—the law functions as the court's own racial authority, able to perform within the strictures of the racial state system and to disavow the racist conditions of (im)possibilities that it inscribes.

Derivative of law's antiblackness, these racist conditions and violent inscriptions point to both law's positive operation under the apparent horizon of justice and the limit where blackness is imagined as nothing other than law's captive, bound antagonistically to the real. This is illustrated in what Keramet Reiter has conceptualized as a "legitimacy paradox."[18] Anthony J. uses the law and asserts his rights accordingly to protect himself and his mother against the encroachment of the police, only to be targeted by the law as a criminal subject of his own making without the possibility of defense. The instantaneous transformation (at once legal, yet also an act of the law's spiritualized rituals) has been described by Saidiya Hartman as the nexus of the "impossibility of self-possession." This impossibility, Hartman explains, dictates that "the slave's very condition of being or social existence is defined as a state of determinate negation. . . . Thus the fashioning of the subject must necessarily take place in violation of the law, and consequently, will, criminality, and punishment are inextricably linked."[19]

Extending Hartman's argument, we might say that the essence within—a transversal effect that underlies this constellation—telescopes the exclusion of blackness on two levels. First, it magnifies the relationality between "the first person" (the grammatical "I") and "the constitutional person" (the subject of rights) itself,[20] both positions that exclude blackness by their very definitions and the processes of becoming involved in these respective positionalities. The volition of the first person is reinterpreted and distorted *against* the subject, thus presenting an agency that is not his own. It is at this juncture that the law relegates and instrumentalizes the racialized subject as if submitting him to his own subjugation and punishment. Second, this punishment draws its penal character from the exploitative nature of antiblack lynching, in which it specifically conscripts the dissimulation of blackness as part of its extrajudicial practice of violence and murder. The illusion that Anthony J. submits to his own subjection echoes Hartman's elaboration of the slave as *always already* in an impossible position of self-possession. The dissimulation of antiblackness only consolidates the orchestration of power and authority under a pretense of liberalism in the law.

Following Hartman's analysis even further, we can understand that the arms of the law have staged scenes of riot and so-called disturbance through the crowd in both the *Jones* case and *Anthony J.* case. In doing so, the extent to which the conceptual malleability of lawful custody and sovereign will are defined and executed by the police also enables the conflation of resistance *against* police violence and "unlawful" violence. With this in mind, we can consider the riot, the collective protest against the abuse of police power, as an expression of opposition to the way in which the crowd is imagined by law (*Recht*) and also interpreted based on a legal position (*Rechtslage*).[21] Riot in both cases is therefore not only an active resistance against state violence, but also a critique of state law and police violence, that is, the ways in which the state instrumentalizes the police as arm of the state to foster lawmaking and law-preserving capabilities. Delio Vásquez has pointed to how the

> conflation of *Blackness* with *crime* has a complex and varying history in the US, taking different shapes and access across time periods depending on that period's particular economic, political, and cultural arrangement of white supremacy. . . . [including] later in efforts by politicians starting in 1965 to depoliticize the urban riots of civil rights movements by connecting them to a concept of "criminal deviance" with original roots in nineteenth-century Europe.[22]

What is critical in the unquestioned (mis)translation of blackness as crime is the deracination that takes place internally yet moves laterally across the institutional arrangements of antiblackness to sustain a political meaning of white supremacy. If we see, over the course of time, how such pronouncements of "law and order" can occur even when, or perhaps because, antiblackness spreads through the operations of statecraft in plain speech and sight, then we can also infer that such operations and arrangements rely on an untranslatability of blackness and as such must be maintained.

From *Ursache* to *Afterlife*: The Untranslatability of Blackness and the Law-Making Void

Translation and untranslatability, language and claims: what is at stake is not simply a matter of the signs of language and its representation, on which legal and judicial interpretations rely, but also the traumatic and racialized effects that come with the repetition of such interpretations. These judgments rely upon the deferral of racist reasoning, which operates by simultaneously condoning and obscuring policing practices of racial targeting and subjection, and in turn weaponizes language to justify and fortify the securitization and sanction of state violence. As I have discussed, blackness's untranslatability precedes and exceeds the orders of law, whether *de facto* or *de jure*, echoing a violence (*Gewalt*) that, as Walter Benjamin observes, is irreducible to a material or physical violence. Insofar as it manifests as a force situated conceptually "well before the historical differentiation between *potestas* and *violentia*, between legitimate and illegitimate violence,"[23] this violence is not solely a tool of the state, but the ground upon which the state is posited. Analyzing the nuances of Benjamin's notion of violence, Sigrid Weigel notes that *Gewalt* is also defined as:

> neither physical *violence* nor institutional *power* but rather *as a reason* (*Ursache*) that "intervenes in ethical relations." . . . In other words, Benjamin is interested less in the exertion of physical or political violence and more in the way *a reason* intervenes in law and justice, which is to say the procedure of justification or legitimation. To be more precise: the focus is on the transformation of a reason into *violence* by way of its *intervention* in the concepts of law and justice.[24]

It is vital to stress this translation of *Ursache* as "a reason," even though it also carries the meaning of "cause."[25] Notwithstanding the conceptual correspondence between "reason" and "cause," for example in the work of G. W. F. Hegel, Benjamin's use of *Ursache* within his critique of *Gewalt,* concerning its presentation (*Darstellung*) of law (*Recht*) and justice (*Gerechtigkeit*), points toward a justificatory logic rather than simply a mechanistic one. As Julia Ng informs us:

> Indeed, Benjamin calls law-positing a function as well as character of "*Gewalt.*" What this law is that is supposed to be the direct object of this positing, though, appears already in the very opening sentence of the essay . . . The "and" between *Recht* and *Gerechtigkeit* in this sentence does not conjoin them, however, as their etymologies might suggest they be. Rather as the rest of the opening paragraph takes as clear and self-evident, the end is a disjunction: "*Recht*" *or* "*Gerechtigkeit,*" law *or* justice. In fact, the disjunction is so radical that "*Recht*" *or* "*Gerechtigkeit*" entail for Benjamin wholly differentiated spheres, namely that of justified means and that of just ends.[26]

Ng's important observation of this disjunction between law and justice reminds us that the law-making character of *Gewalt* is inextricable from its appearance. The disjuncture internal to justice proper (*Gerechtigkeit*) simultaneously indicates a fundamental oxymoron: the claim that law is "just" requires the violent conflation of law's necessity with law's structural impossibility—a contradictory unity that precedes its linguistic meaning. The oxymoron—the idea of a "just law"—collapses upon the structural examination into the concept of justified violence. Through Benjamin's "Critique of Violence," and as seen in the two court cases, we can understand that the oxymoron exists because the legal system's concept of justice inherently contains two opposing yet inseparable elements: law's claim to a true, universal justice (*Gerechtigkeit*) and an originary foundation in violence (*Gewalt*).

The concept of *Ursache*—which translates as both reason or cause—exposes a critical disjunction in the translation of justice (*Gerechtigkeit*) during the act of law-making. Insofar as *Ursache* is concerned, its meaning is not limited to the violence of law-positing (the initial, transformative act of setting law), but extends to the violence of law-preserving (the subsequent, stabilizing maintenance of that law). Said another way, the duality of *Ursache* (reason *or* cause) casts light on the violence of reason that underlies the appearance of law as force (*Gewalt*). This occurs not only through the transformation from reason into violence, as Weigel suggests, but also through the way its justification (reason/cause) is issued from what it is not—the contingency and extralegal void that the law must perpetually conceal. The violence of *Ursache*, therefore, is this: the law is understood not only through the violence that transforms it into appearance (law-positing), but through its unceasing labor to translate the extralegal void into a justificatory ground, thus asserting a mastery over the very contingency it works to elide.

The violence of *Ursache*—a justification drawn from the law's own concealment—provides the necessary framework for understanding the structural violence of blackness's untranslatability. At this critical juncture, the extralegal void is revealed to be the violence of translating blackness into the *afterlife* of "self-lynching": a "life" that is not life as such, but the perpetuity of the non-being and nothingness of blackness. As the *Jones* and *Anthony J.* cases demonstrate, this untranslatability grounds the violence in radical difference itself, rather than in a specific transformative act. Reconsidering the appearance of violence in this counterintuitive way—that is, not solely through the relations of law-positing violence—positions the disjuncture at the level of law (or the "law of laws"), as opposed to the level of statutes. While statutes are mutable rules subject to amendment within the material symbolic order, the radical difference of (anti)blackness is lodged in the law's structural authority; antiblack violence constitutes the legal system itself, regardless of any statute's specific content. This fundamental division between law *or* justice highlights the core problem of untranslatability: if the relationship between these two concepts cannot be translated, then the language of law is always already fractured.

It is specifically in this transformation from a reason into violence that we see—prior to the institutional arrangements and operations of law across its legitimate and illegitimate applications—both the reflection that "there is inherent in all such violence a lawmaking character"[27] and a critique of the language of law and justice. The moment a reason transforms into violence (*Gewalt*) constitutes an intervention that destabilizes the conceptual difference of law and justice. Such an intervention reveals that the production of both is underscored by a foundational force—the force required for any juridical decision to administer their appearances. When a juridical decision is materialized, it claims to resolve a call for justice. Yet, this finality enacts a fundamental disavowal of its own contingent foundation. Its claim to necessity obscures the specific, non-universal conditions from which its authority emerged. As Benjamin notes, these juridical decisions appear "however, apodictically,"[28] despite their reliance on a contingent process. The sustained relation between force (*Gewalt*) and law—and the enduring life as the *afterlife* of language (*Fortleben*) maintained through translation—share a common fulcrum: the threat of a transformative conversion of a reason into violence that would disrupt the positive forms of law and language. As Benjamin identifies, *Fortleben* is not a neutral process of survival. Rather, the enduring life of language (*Fortleben*) persists due to a structural imperative in the work of art and language; that is, it survives only by perpetually displacing the force (*Gewalt*) that grounds its positive forms. For our meditations, this suggests that *afterlife* (in the sense of survival through language) is the process through which antiblack violence is sustained in the present structure of law and language. It is precisely at this point of displacement that blackness's untranslatability intervenes here, not as a challenge outside of language, but as the irreducible limit that constitutes the language's capacity to endure, survive, continue.

Thus, the survival of positive forms of law and language is perpetually grounded in the structural inability to translate blackness, making untranslatability the condition of the translatable itself. This structural paradox—where the untranslatability of blackness is the condition of possibility—presents the specter of an apparent and constant threat. Such a theoretical elaboration on untranslatability and the structural threat that it poses to *Fortleben* (law's enduring life as *afterlife*) reflects back on the law's response through its own language and evaluative criterion regarding the two court cases that interpreted the California anti-lynching penal code. From this vantage, we can recognize that "self-lynching" was constituted not only as a legal fiction, but as an essential component of the law's imaginary life.

In the historical memory of lynching and in its *afterlife*, (anti)blackness comes to index an impossible position in relation to language, meaning, and potential lexical conversions. This impasse in language underlines what David Marriott's theorization of blackness's *n'est pas*: what blackness appears to be, when forced into any mode of representation, is precisely what blackness is not.[29] The relation—if such a term can even apply—between the *n'est pas* of blackness and *Gewalt* requires further theorizing, as violence is inseparable from the *afterlife* that perpetually shapes violence's representations, translations, and appearance in law. Provisionally, however, we can say that blackness is always already positioned to relinquish a type of meaning to the dominant orders of history and time, being and testimony; while at the same time blackness might be imbued and overdetermined with (non-) meaning.

Blackness's untranslatability also suggests a resistance of resistance—that is, blackness resists the very language that grants whiteness the power to define and award the terms of proper (or legitimate) resistance. In this light, the untranslatability of blackness guarantees that something must remain—not a fragment awaiting redemption, but an unredeemed claim, a conceptual surplus, that refuses to be fully captured by the vision and framing that the whiteness of law and language imposes upon its terms and conditions.

All that said, is the untranslatability of blackness, itself, an imprecise notion? The violence that underlies the transformation of *Ursache* into *Gewalt* injects itself into law, enabling law's justification or legitimation. Critically, the imprecision lies not in the critique of untranslatability, but in the structural instability of law's own language and its failure to reconcile *Recht* (positive law) and *Gerechtigkeit* (justice). As Marriott notes, "the *n'est pas* does not constitute a concept; it is the dark *invisable* of reason—for it is not *determinable* or *meaningful*."[30] Placing these concerns together might make the untranslatability of blackness appear oxymoronic; I argue, however, that it is, indeed, a structural imperative. The *n'est pas* of blackness, always already incommensurable with any conceptual aim of law and justice, enacts an untranslatability that serves as the condition which necessitates the transformation of *Ursache* (reason) into *Gewalt* (violence). Law must violently transform a reason into force because it encounters the absolute limit of blackness—a structural void that cannot be dialectically mediated or contained by stable meaning. The translation (or transformation) that occurs is the translation of violence into legitimation, where blackness remains the untranslated excess that makes this violent translation necessary. The untranslatability of blackness, thus, does not speak to a failure of meaning to be conveyed, but to the inherent inability of blackness to be assimilated into the economy of meaning-making at all. The distinction between what is translatable and what is untranslatable is therefore the structural difference between signification and the non-relational ground. Blackness is not determined by what is translatable nor redeemable within the law's terms; rather, the entire economy of translatability (and the transformation of reason into law) is structurally determined by the antiblack necessity of its untranslatability.

The question remains, however: How does this incommensurability place blackness into, and as, an abyss? This placement—which I argue is homologous with untranslatability as the constitutive location of blackness's non-being—not only reveals the structural limits of the language of law and the laws of language, but also facilitates what Paul de Man describes in the technical sense as a *mise en abyme* regarding the untranslatability of a text.[31] The abyss, in other words, functions as the ontological necessity for the *mise en abyme* to operate as its textual symptom—a structural vertigo that appears when the text of law attempts to account for its own unrepresentable ground. At the same time, the *mise en abyme* structure, as a textual figure, cannot fully comprehend the radical, non-determinable difference of the *n'est pas* (as a privation of meaning); instead, it serves as the essential symptom that reveals the structure's necessary failure. In this respect, the untranslatability of blackness structures the formation of the text even as it is concurrently obscured, or ghosted, right before the reader's eyes. The simultaneous processes of structuring and obscuring reflect the self-referential ghosting inherent in the *mise en abyme*. The stakes of an absent reading extend beyond the misrecognition of positive law or attendant legal interpretations; they compel a reading that rests on the misrecognition of blackness's untranslatability as a necessity, even as this very necessity secures the text's materialization and survival as *afterlife* (*Fortleben*). Thus, the misrecognition is not an error in judgment, but is a constitutive gesture that produces the text's continuation under the conditions of antiblackness. That is, the text's survival is paradoxically locked in by transforming blackness's *n'est pas*—its indeterminate non-meaning—into the foundational stability necessary for inscription and narrative continuity.

Thus, the untranslatability of blackness poses questions that concern language, law, and resistance—not merely questions of status and function, but of difference and kind and impossibility. What, exactly, might resist the political demands and meanings posed by law? And how is the untranslatability of blackness essential to what law deems to be justice? Untranslatability highlights a fundamental impulse to overcome an already existing internal resistance—a condition perceived as an imagined threat to the coherence of language. In turn, this impulse generates the desire for plenitude, a drive to transform perceived symptoms of difference into something perceptible, tangible, diagnosable, interpretable. Within this framework, the untranslatable "is rather what one keeps on (not) translating."[32] Persistently "untranslatable," blackness is therefore positioned as a threat and must be contained within the carceral confines of language. Such containment operates in direct relation to the whiteness of the law, which sustains antiblackness from within and without. It is this structural persistence that simultaneously undergirds both the desire for meaning and desire's collapse into, and as, law.

Indeed, the relation between translation and transience signals a central paradox: blackness's untranslatability configures an *afterlife*—a continued (non-)life of antiblackness maintained through the inability to translate it. In Benjamin's conceptualization of translation, he notes that "translation is a mode."[33] Deceptively simple, this "mode," a manifestation of the immanent nature of being, requires that "one must go back to the original, for that contains the law governing the translation: its translatability."[34] For Benjamin then, "a translation issues from the original—not so much from its life as from its afterlife. . . . Their translation marks their stage of continued life."[35] But how does translation persist if the incommensurability of blackness makes it untranslatable, and if this failure compels the juridical transformation of *Ursache* (reason) into *Gewalt* (violence)? Following Benjamin, translation can take place in spite of, if not always with, a type of errancy. In other words, some part of the original must be mistranslated or untranslated to a degree. Translation and "translation issues" emerge, therefore, "not so much from its life as from its afterlife."[36] Barbara Johnson highlights something similar when she explains:

> What translation allows us to see is also a fantasy language uniting the two works, as if all translations were falls away from some original language that fleetingly becomes visible. But nothing proves that this is not another back-formation from the difficulties of translation. We are so used to the model of wholeness falling into multiplicity that we read the effect of the effect as if it were a cause.[37]

Such a process of translation involves an operation of fantasy, which reconciles different orders (whether of language, time, being) through the revisions of positive law. Translation, in this particular relation between the fantasy of wholeness and the fall into multiplicity, attempts to recover and maintain that which is irrecuperable while "[enhancing] the belief that there is an origin"[38] and still moving forward for the purposes of interpretation and evidence. It also, as Johnson points out, involves a type of reading whereby translation appears to fulfill the fantasy of wholeness and unifying disparities in language. Such an illusory aim becomes both teleological and defensive since fantasy functions as a way of coping with what appears alien(ating) to language. Or as Johnson reminds her readers via Benjamin, "Translation, he writes, is 'a somewhat provisional way of coming to grips with the foreignness of languages.'"[39] Placing together Benjamin's notion of translation as *afterlife* and Johnson's idea of translation as a fantasy of language, the moments of decision that translation can afford reveal how they also furnish the ensuing legislative nature that conceals an undergirding irreconcilability. Translation acts as a mask, and it is through its visage that words and law appear. In the cases of the "riots" described above, we have observed such an irreconcilability, something fundamentally antiblack in the law where an antagonism between blackness and lawful custody takes place. It is in this split, this irredeemable fracture—that constitutes the space situated in and outside of the interpretation that takes place in the courtroom—that we explore further the materialization of "self-lynching" and the nonsovereignty of blackness.

Beyond Reform: The Impossible Translation of the Drive's Circuit

Symptomatic of the desire to foreclose blackness, the impossible position of self-possession reflects the wider strictures of representation, meaning, and interpretation in and of law. And yet, the *desire* for the foreclosure of blackness to become the exception of, only to affirm everything else—not just in law but in language, critique, and, so too, in writing and interpretation—cannot simply remain an assertion, nor can it be conceived at the level of the symbolic. Hartman's historical argument also reveals a negation of legal personhood at the level of politics and rights, statute and legal discourse. This negation has been taken up by Afro-Pessimism as a libidinal economy of antiblackness—a term no doubt informed by Jean-François Lyotard.[40] However, that conception remains largely at the level of the imaginary, leaving the question of how such desire at the level of representation (*Vorstellung*) actually manifests, particularly in the face of—or perhaps because of—racial doubt. We are left, then, with the question of drive and the nature of its force—a question that cannot be reconciled by moral and racial judgment, though it is often met with both. The drive, of course, is never straightforward. But the attempt to ruminate on the impossibility of the *real* raises, nonetheless, important questions of whether it is the drive itself that is antiblack, an antiblack drive, or a drive motivated, undergirded, by antiblackness.

These questions allow us to think about the blackness of the *real*, and why black (un)freedom, though symbolically at stake in the register of law, continuously arrives as a missed encounter. Alenka Zupančič offers an efficacious exposition of such stakes when she reminds her readers of the importance to delimit an analysis of desire by interrogating the "dimension of desire, which circles around the real *qua* impossible."[41] Within this framework, "the question of desire does not so much lose its central place as cease to be considered the endpoint of analysis."[42] This Lacanian orientation of the *real*, to which Zupančič signals here, directs us toward the drive in ways that are importantly irreducible to its stated aim. Thus, manifestations of violence and racial terror underpinned by antiblackness cannot be limited to, nor simply construed, at the level of the symbolic. We must ask—following Frantz Fanon's sociogenic critique—whether the *real* is a neutral void or inextricably tethered to the indistinguishable material and psychic imposition of antiblackness. We will discuss the distinction between a Lacanian and Fanonian *real* momentarily. At this point in our analysis, blackness's encounter with law must always appear under the jurisdiction of Cheryl Harris's well-known maxim of "whiteness as property," but in ways that might be taken for granted as *de facto* in both representation and analysis.[43]

I reference Harris's landmark work, "Whiteness as Property," to gesture toward the problematic of black exclusion, or more pointedly to ask where the exclusion resides. Harris illustrates for her readers that "whiteness" and "property"—as features and concepts of the law—"share a common premise";[44] that is, "a conceptual nucleus—the right to exclude."[45] In this vein, Harris sees the relational subjection of blackness that stems from slavery as enabling this right. Yet, such a frame remains constrained by the logic of property rights, which only accounts for what the law *possesses* rather than what the law *is*. To think beyond the status of the object, one must confront the antiblack structural *necessity* as the law's foundational impulse. On this view, blackness is not simply an object of exclusion but the condition of the law's self-generated violence—the juridical necessity that compels the "self-lynching" of blackness through which the foreclosure of the being of blackness enacts the law's foreclosure of the possible subjecthood of blackness. Further, if the "right to exclude" rests entirely upon the exclusion of blackness, one must ask: Can whiteness ever truly be "inalienable"? Harris frames the inalienability of whiteness—defined as the impossibility of separating the right from its holder—as paradoxically related to its alienability, its market value.[46] She explains, "The inalienability of whiteness should not preclude the consideration of whiteness as property. Paradoxically, its alienability may be more indicative of its perceived enhanced value, rather than its disqualification as property."[47] Yet, this paradox only further exposes the structural limits of property law. Since the "value" of whiteness is not self-sustaining, it requires a stable horizon against which its worth can be denominated—a horizon provided by an underlying deprivation. The only truly inalienable and nonnegotiable term is the structural necessity of blackness's foreclosure here, which serves as the permanent, unmovable foundation that produces the property status and value of whiteness. As a consequence, Harris's property-based framing cannot adequately address the following circularity: Without whiteness or the law, is there a sense of property? And without property, can there be whiteness as property?

These concerns might raise the question of how natural right is theorized or taken up in the notion of "whiteness as property," but it also could be argued that the question of natural right (and natural law) remains absent even insofar as Harris unpacks the abstraction of "property and expectations."[48] As legal theorist Brenna Bhandar has outlined, Harris's understanding is heavily shaped by the Benthamite and Lockean traditions.[49] In my reading, Harris situates natural right closer to the domain of custom, which allows her to rhetorically ask "whose custom?"[50] The rhetorical turn away from the formulation of natural right, and the attribution of the role of natural law to "a *custom*—of valorizing whiteness,"[51] leads Harris to critique how the operation of American law reinforced property as a reinscription of the protection of whiteness. Yet, this critique also assumes a form of sovereignty—one that Harris suggests Native Americans can theoretically experience.[52] At this juncture, Harris's argument reaches its apex: the "right to exclude" is essential to the property of whiteness. While sovereignty (or its lack) in respect to blackness is not Harris's primary question, it comes into sharp relief when juxtaposed with Native American landownership. Even if the inalienability of whiteness reinforces sovereignty according to a European and (settler-)colonial conception, the status of the human also influenced the judgment of who was afforded the juridical privileges of lawful protection in court. As Alexander Weheliye has observed in regard to interpretations of *habeas corpus* specifically in the context of the Supreme Court ruling of the Dred Scott case, "the Supreme Court invalidated Dred Scott's habeas corpus, since as an escaped slave, Scott could not be a legal person."[53] Weheliye notes further that the court's justification "to withdraw Dred Scott's legal right to ownership of the self" stood in stark asymmetry to the possibility of the legal position of Native Americans regarding U.S. citizenship and personhood:

> While slaves were not accorded the status of being humans that belonged to a different nation, Indians could theoretically overcome their lawful foreignness, but only if they renounced previous forms of personhood and citizenship. Hence, the tabula rasa of whiteness—which all groups but blacks can access—serves as the prerequisite for the law's magical transubstantiation of a thing to be possessed into a property-owning subject.[54]

The lack of consideration regarding the nonsovereignty of blackness allows Harris to fortify the notion of whiteness as property through the restricted lens of property law. Such a framing assumes that all non-white relations to property were evenly established, even though the right to exclusion falls on the side of whiteness as property. As I have argued in Chapters 1 and 2, aspirations to whiteness and the deflection of (anti)blackness were not limited to racialized white subjects and were, therefore, not simply an identarian problematic. In many ways, the subjection of blackness was simultaneously reinforced by and necessitated for the racial imaginary of the nation-state and the construction of statecraft. Similarly, the slave's impossible position of black ownership—in particular at the level of self-ownership—troubles the possibility of sovereignty as it rests on the incapacity of blackness. And while Harris explains property "to be a right, not a thing, characterized as metaphysical, not physical,"[55] her analysis of property revolves around and arrives at this notion of legal right, prioritizing a reading of positive law. Harris's critical intervention lies in showing that whiteness unequivocally functions like a title or a deed. However, by using the language of property, even when she describes its phenomenon as "metaphysical," she remains within the realm of possessive individualism—a "right" held by a subject. The focus on the metaphysical appearance of whiteness creates a deceptive gap; it highlights how whiteness manifests as a protected expectation while obscuring what it actually is: a structural imposition. Under this formulation, the ostensibly abstract forms of whiteness become reducible to what Benjamin limns as guaranteed ends.[56] Under the sign of legal positivism, the law is construed as a guarantor of property status—a conceptual ruse that collapses the structural violence of the *real* into the identitarian limits of legal personhood. By prioritizing the *possession* of the right over the *imposition* of the drive, the law's foundational violence is disavowed and appears, instead, as a neutral mechanism of title and tenure.

To this effect, the implication of Harris's critique of whiteness as property ultimately puts forward a reformist response to law—one that remains beholden to a thin materialism. Such an approach, which centers on the redistribution or manipulation of property rights, risks sustaining the transcendence of property it seems to dismantle. As I argue in Chapter 6, such exchange—whether at the legal or commodity level—is not only structurally inadequate for addressing antiblackness but actively reifies its violence. The problem rests on treating property as a self-contained, abstract right positioned at the level of exchange. By the same token, the real abstraction of property—to echo Alfred Sohn-Rethel from our introduction—functions to mask the social relations from which it emerges. Peculiarly, this focus on the mechanics of property relations disengages the legal form from concrete social relations, relations that find their grounding in antiblackness. As a result, Harris's analysis confines itself to the material register of exclusion, failing to address the originary violence that constitutes property as a category. The focus on abstract rights, thus, engenders a belief in the possibility of reinterpreting and rewriting the language of the law. Yet, as I have argued in this chapter and elsewhere in the book, the reform of law, marshaled through the advocacy for alternative representation, not only capitulates to the law; it also fortifies the fundamental structure of antiblackness internal to it.

Representing, rewriting, and reforming the language of the law through its own terms brings us back to two important concerns of this chapter: the untranslatability of blackness and the locus of its exclusion. These concerns also return us to the (il)logic of the drives. While property law remains a critical historical site for understanding what shapes the conditions of lawfulness, both within and without the law, there must be further consideration of how such violence operates beyond the scope of property law at the level of the symbolic. For as I have outlined, the *n'est pas* of blackness cannot be contained or accounted for by legal categories such as "property," "rights," or "representation." It is this structural void, necessary for law's symbolic operation, that requires us to analyze the mechanism of the drive. The drive, as Lacan reminds us, reveals not just its aim toward satisfaction, but also shows the absence that marks the enclosure of a field in which the object is situated and where symbolic violence manifests—"the void around which desire turns."[57]

For Jared Sexton, "a critical appreciation of such analytic concepts is vital,"[58] for it allows one "to probe the peculiar intricacies of anti-blackness as a way to locate its singular movement over and above the many family resemblances."[59] His discernment of the drive and the object of desire draws upon the foundational pairing of these terms in the work of Calvin Warren, as they are applied to construe "the global drive" of antiblackness—a pathology defined by "the destructive repetition and surplus enjoyment of this repetition."[60] Sexton explains:

> The drive, then, is in no ways impossible, though its object is strictly unattainable and therefore impossible in that limited sense. But it is the very nature of the drive to miss its object precisely in order to repeat its circuitous route, in order to maintain itself. It does not seek to destroy its object, its aim being to preserve its object in perpetuity. Were it to destroy the object, or to attain it in any real sense, whether aggressively or amorously, it would succeed only in extinguishing itself. The *drive* faces the risk of extinction, not the object, which as Warren rightly notes is fantasmatic and unreal. The violence against the black body is, however, all too real. How to square *this* circle?[61]

Sexton illuminates how the conflation between the concepts of drive and object—where both are limned as "impossible"—runs the risk of disavowing the reification one seeks to critique. The conceptual distinction regarding the "impossibility" of the drive versus the "impossibility" of the object guides my own argument here: the symptomatic expression at the level of positive law cannot be reduced to, or analyzed solely through, its representations. The failure lies much deeper; even the law's explicit language concerning the exclusion and the dispossession of blackness only reveals the symptom and not the structural drive that sustains it. Distinguishing between the drive—insistent and repetitive—and the object—impossible and fantasmatic—clarifies that the law's violence is, in fact, not impossible, but profoundly efficient. It is only the law's "reasoning," such as the object of property, that is impossible.

To analyze this structural drive, we turn to Marriott's critical elaboration on the distinction between the Fanonian and Lacanian *real*, which is key to grasping the singularity of such violence. Marriott informs us that:

> whereas for Lacan the *réel* is at the foundation of the subject, in Fanon's usage the *réel* is also *imposed*, and denotes a being confronted with a violence that makes the *réel* indistinguishable from *réalité*, and thus the experience of a certain violence of constraint, guardedness, inhibition, and indebtedness—as if what cannot be escaped is the *réel* of being constrained by the epidermal violence of culture.[62]

Theorizing blackness through the *real* and the drive—a force without an object, which stems from the void that surrounds desire—complicates how we think about the objects of law before they appear symbolically in social and civic death. Extending Marriott's critique further, the distinction is critical: the Lacanian *réel* names a structural impossibility inherent to the subject, while the Fanonian *réel* names a structural imposition—the epidermal violence experienced as the direct, inescapable constraint of antiblackness on one's being and the psyche that makes reality and the *real* indistinguishable for blackness. This contrast allows us to relate the question of "whether it is the drive itself that is antiblack, an antiblack drive, or a drive motivated, undergirded, by antiblackness" to the speculative observation offered by the Fanonian *réel*. While the drive, as a universal mechanism, is not antiblack in its essence, the Fanonian *réel* suggests that if the imposed structure of reality is underscored by antiblackness, then the symbolic field—the enclosure around the Lacanian *réel*—is always already constructed by that violence. The drive is thus structurally determined and motivated by antiblackness because its circuit, its repetition, and its unattainable object (*objet petit a*) are sustained only through the perpetual foreclosure of blackness as a condition of law.

The circuit of the drive, perpetually missing its unattainable object (*objet a*) to maintain its own repetition, necessitates a conceptual outlet. In a Lacanian sense, the drive operates in the service of desire—the (universal) lack constituted by the subject's entrance into the symbolic order. But as we have explored, if the Fanonian *réel* troubles that very lack through the imposition of antiblack violence, then the drive must be structurally determined by antiblackness to secure the symbolic order itself, making the violence both singular and necessary. In turn, the Fanonian *réel* challenges the universality of the Lacanian construction of desire, as a structural lack, in respect to the black subject. At this disjuncture, where the conversion from desire into a reason begins, I am not referring to pure or natural reason. On the contrary, I am attempting to accent a contingent, particular reason—a justified impulse or libidinal alibi, such as the construction of "lawful custody," that emerges from the void of the drive. The transformation from this unconscious impulse into a legitimate legal claim returns us to our meditation on *Gewalt*: the movement where a reason assumes the appearance of violence as a law-making force. In this conversion, the psychic life of the law is sustained through the endurance of language as a consequence of translation. Henceforth, the antinomy between natural law (pure reason) and positive law (particular reason) is rehearsed and contained; for the law must violently transform its contingent origin—the drive's necessity as a reason—into the self-evident, legitimate force of *Gewalt* to disavow its own antiblack foundation.

The gratuity of the violence prior to its symbolic appearance thus necessitates the untranslatability of blackness and the violence that traffics it into representation; this process cannot be without the law itself—a violence internal to the law's own appearance. The drive then not only outlines such a limit, but also gestures to its violent repetition in the inscription of law—persisting in spite of blackness's untranslatability and the appearance of its exclusion. The transformation of contingent reason into lawmaking force (*Gewalt*) and the necessity of blackness's untranslatability establish that the structural imperative of antiblackness—fundamental to the drive's repetition and symbolic demands—lies far beyond the remedial reach of legal reform or the representation of property rights that Harris champions. To more concretely analyze how the drive dictates the juridical representation and interpretation of "self-lynching," we now turn to the function of *l'entre-je*—the interstitial space where the law figures the resistance of blackness as its most looming threat.

In Between-I's

Blackness as an apparent but enduring absence in the scenes of "lynching" arrests allows us to understand the ways in which antiblackness persists in spite of its imperceptible appearance. From within and without, antiblackness signals the psychical level of a structural problematic in which policing and psychosis are tied together. In its redefining of a self that doubles to lynch itself, the *Anthony J.* case illustrates how a perversion regarding the ends of the self operates as a psychical structure. Through an excessive mode of projecting the Other, the dissolution of the imaginary takes over in processes of identification. The *Anthony J.* case reflects what is being established at the level of meaning-making through an imagined subject, the illusory image of the Other. Said differently, the supposed Other in *Anthony J.*, the self that the law imagines as a threat to the custody of police enforcement because it is seen as acting against itself, is made possible through an imagined body that is not present. In the context of Anthony J.'s arrest, the imagined self is not a double at the level of fantasy, through which the Other intrudes; rather, the self appears very much as a *real*-in-reality, the *real* immanent to reality, obstructing its own arrest. Because this reality of an imagined self is seen as a legitimate course of events in the eyes of the law, the definition of lynching also is reinstantiated and naturalized as something other than racial terror and black death. To engage with how these (racial) figurations and the history of terror become displaced and seemingly irrelevant, I turn to Jacques Lacan's early introduction of *l'entre-je* (between-I) as a function of the imaginary in the structure of psychosis.

In his early investigations on psychosis, Lacan identifies the state of psychosis as the intermixing of subjects conjured at the level of the imaginary yet granted status in reality. As I have argued, the question is not *who* constitutes the imagined self in "self-lynching," but how the relentless persistence of the drive necessitates the invention of such a figure to sustain the law's symbolic coherence. With this in mind, Lacan's discussion of *l'entre-je* helps us to see the problem presented by *Anthony J.* in terms of the destructiveness of the court's racial imaginary, for it is the space of this imaginary that enables the translation of "lynching" as "self-lynching" and the omission of the history of antiblack violence that led to the original statute. Lacan asks not what the delusion affirms, but why the fantasy exists: "at the full tilt upon the domain of intersubjectivity, where the whole problem is to know why it's fantasized."[63] Reflecting on the structural problematic of how the subject "handles" the signifier (its aims, its meanings), Lacan explains that the intersubjective dimension of the subject is in fact "capable of using the signifier;" he adds, "not so as to inform you, but precisely to lure you." The "lure" follows the "use of the between-I [*l'entre-je*],"[64] the inmixing of subjects at one's expense in the mechanisms of defense—speaking nonsense, projecting one's fantasies. It is one's relation to the imaginary as *real*-in-reality that allows the illusory image to be signified. As Denise Ferreira da Silva explains, the imaginary is a "writing of the mind in outer determination, that is, always already before, in a relationship, contenting with 'others,' a version of the self-determined 'I' that necessarily signifies 'other'-wise."[65] It is "a mechanism of imaginary compensation,"[66] a paradoxical economy of excess and deficit—an engine running on empty, yet driven by an unstoppable force. For the subject, "at the heart of psychoses there is a dead end,"[67] but not because one encounters a limit in meaning-making. Quite the opposite. Meaning-making becomes necessarily endless as "an attempt at restitution, at compensation."[68] Thus, with the quintessential dimension of the psychotic structure that is the foreclosure, or exclusion, of the Other, "the bearer of the signifier," the imaginary relation labors relentlessly to supply an image that affirms the space between the subject and vision of the Other. In this interstitial space, Lacan locates the between-I phenomena "at the level of the little other."[69]

Why does this matter in the case of *Anthony J.* and the context of the defendant's arrest? An unexceptional articulation of the self, the Other, or image, for that matter, would suggest that a more ethical interpretation could lead to a different outcome or perhaps prevent the arrest entirely. However, based on the structural imperative of antiblackness that underlies the drive, we argue that the arrest of blackness would remain as a psychic structural necessity. Even the most robust ethical reading of these concepts, if divorced from an understanding of the antiblack necessity of the law, will still lead to the same result: the perpetual subjection and ambiguous custody of blackness to the juridical decision.

The perpetual subjection and custody of blackness to the juridical decision remains necessary because *l'entre-je*—the little other that falls between the positionalities of the subject and the Other—actively sustains the process of identification. The mode of identification that is actively sustained, thus, illustrates the impossibility of finding a presumably better image or an ethical interpretation. This is not so much because the positionalities of the subject and the Other take precedence, but more so due to the space *in-between I's*—that is, what falls between I's—which cannot be seen. The disparity between the "first person I" and the "constitutional person" is only a surface reflection. Beneath it lies a structure where the imaginary animates the subject and its many I's. In her incisive critique of Lacanian ontology, Axelle Karera makes clear why such lines of flight must be questioned and what the illusions of such ontology can afford. She writes:

> For, when one considers Lacan's ongoing critique of ontology in these seminars, *l' être qui fuit* [the feeling being][70] connotes neither a temporary nor a redeemable loss. What Lacan is pointing to is ontology's illusion *(leurre)*—a kind of necessary metaphysical swindle—with which the possibility of a self-possessed and voluntarist being-in-command is assumed as the very truth of being.[71]

When we place these two concerns together—the fantasmatic domain that anchors the terms of persons and I's, and the ontological machinations of an illusory self-possessed being that (so Karera notes) neither flight nor fleeing can recuperate—we can see that there is always a desirable *other* image to be upheld by this interstitial space of *l'entre-je*. And yet, because this mirage of being, the image that coalesces fantasmatically to project an alternative self, rests on a libidinal and ontological knotting, it also brings into sharp relief how this staging, of the two in one, makes law's attempts to rectify the dispossession of a self untenable.

Ergo, we can infer that the hydraulics of the imaginary mobilize the actors, the arrest, and state of policing as part of assembling the law's scopic field. More importantly, what falls between I's cannot be seen but leaves its impression on the symbolic practices of policing and the state. In the context of Anthony J.'s case, the application of *l'entre-je* is essential not for identifying a delusional subject, but for diagnosing the psychotic structure of the state's legal fantasy. The concept maps onto two necessary, fabricated imaginary subject positions required by the law to perform its violent act of displacement. The first "I" is the subject of authority—law enforcement or the court—which claims rational command and acts as the supposed guarantor of positive law—the symbolic order. The second "I" is the imagined self-defying subject—the legal fiction projected onto Anthony J. that sees him as acting against his own self-interests, thereby translating his defiance into "lynching thyself." *L'entre-je*—the interstitial space separating these two positions—is where the state's delusion is established, allowing the structural foreclosure of the *n'est pas* of blackness to be actively displaced from the law's foundation. If Lacan's conceptualization points to a perplexity concerning the signifier for the psychotic, then the state's judicial parlance—mediated by law enforcement and the court—serves to preserve the order of this phenomenon as actual experience. This mapping clarifies the translation of "lynching" as "self-lynching" not as simply an error in the interpretation of the anti-lynching statutes, but as the structural imperative through which the state psychically maintains its authority by forcing the untranslatability of blackness into a manageable, self-destructive legal image. The point is thus not about the imagined other to the Other, but about this interstitial space (*l'entre-je*) which is structurally underlined by the *n'est pas* of blackness.

At the same time, this triangulation between the police, the court, and Anthony J. also reveals a latent presence that remains foreclosed, yet conjures the semblance of this translation of "self-lynching." Here, the structural presence being excluded is the Fanonian *réel*, which, unlike the Lacanian *real*, cannot be foreclosed as the definitive rejection of a fundamental signifier that later returns to the *real*. What we see, instead, is blackness—of the Fanonian *réel*—as a non-referential presence (or a non-presence) that puts referentiality into crisis. This *réel* nonetheless closes the field that categorizes subjects: racialized criminals, law enforcement, and the court. The law that governs this triangulation is what Lacan describes in his explication of delusion in the psychotic structure: "The course of a genesis that starts from elements perhaps immanent to (*gros de*) this construction, but which in their original form present themselves as closed or even enigmatic."[72] In the history of lynching, the element of racial antiblack terror, immanent in the construction of lynching, necessarily vanishes from the scene of the arrest and the interpretation of the court. Such structural disappearance complicates the Lacanian *l'entre-je* by furnishing the space between the I's with the singularity of antiblackness and the violence that subtends the non-being of blackness. However, this Fanonian reading departs from a standard Lacanian analysis by treating *l'entre-je* not merely as an empty space that sustains identification, but as an actively furnished void determined by the structural imperative of antiblack terror. Thus, even when blackness is absent from the explicit terms of the arrest—whether in the racialized perception of the defendant or in the court's dismissal of racialized identity—the Fanonian *réel* insists that blackness remains perpetually under custody, arrested, and psychically lynched by the law's necessity. How, then, does this *réel* manifest its necessity in the juridical event, leading the court to conclude that the defendant is responsible for his own subjection? The court's invention of "self-lynching" reveals not a failure of legal reasoning, but the successful realization of a psychotic structural necessity. By furnishing the void of *l'entre-je* with the history of antiblack terror it refuses to name, the law performs a final, metaphysical sleight of hand: it translates the structural impossibility of black being into a "self-inflicted" death, reaffirming that even in the absence of a mob, the law remains the sovereign architect of the lynching and the *réel* of lynching itself.

On this score, the state appears to ask and answer its own questions in *Anthony J.*: why the defendant would risk his own rights in the hands of law enforcement—the designated arbiter of protection—and why he would do this at his own expense. Maintaining the image of Anthony J. as a criminal perpetrator of and onto himself, the court also upholds the reality and psychical structure in which Anthony J. lynches himself solely on the procedure of evidence and the interpretation of the material evidence presented. Yet, this reading—reduced to the law's own evidentiary parameters—withholds the truths it claims to seek.[73] That is, it is an interpretation that seeks only its own reflection as "evidence tells us everything but how to read it. Beyond its evidence, in other words, there is no other reality, nothing—except the principle that guides our reading of it."[74] In the dissolution of blackness, the law stays within the mirage of its own desire: blackness as the cause of another Other hanging itself before the law. The prohibition of the historical memory and racial terror of lynching magnifies how the Fanonian *réel* manifests its necessity: it forces its own structural absence to guarantee the law's interpretation. Via the elision of blackness, the prohibition becomes the source of power and meaning, and it gives power to meaning (not just meaning to power) as a "crisis of meaning,"[75] in which "lynching" and the self receive a perverse type of plenitude. In this sense, real justice has yet to arrive. The court does not turn away from the racial state system but holds a mirror up to it, reflecting a self that is projected entirely through the racist imagination of the state.

At stake in both the *Jones* case and the *Anthony J.* cases is how an apparent gap between time and the unconscious antiblack identifications short-circuits to manifest the law's most guarded and repressed antagonisms. Translation from "anti-lynching" to "lynching" is deemed a *relevant* translation—even as it deviates from the statute's original legislative intent—not because it is the *right* translation, but because the untranslatability of blackness enables the law to exercise segregative practices as its right. Anti-lynching translates into lynching because it is "the most possible" of translations—a suspension of meaning that thrives on the withholding knowledge. *How* one reads this originary disturbance, and the resistance to it, is crucial for translation's successional formations.

In this regard, blackness falls between the orders of material representation and testimony, before and beyond the orders of *de jure* and *de facto* law, resonating with what Marriott has observed as the "unnamable *n'est pas*" of blackness: "the basic dissymmetry between the *me* and *not-me*, explained by disavowal, [that] opens onto a more vertiginous absence between the *I* and the *it*, and this absence cannot simply be represented by disalienation."[76] Marriott elucidates that this descent into which blackness falls is a kind of immanence wherein blackness's untranslatability signals a non-being without term and against an indexical measure between a law-preserving and law-destroying violence, between mythic and divine power. Marriott's intervention is crucial for the philosophy of law and beyond as it forces us to reflect on the disparities between the embodiment or discursivity of truth and the inscription of evidence, between testimony and traumatic event, between presence and absence in the legal archive—disparities which remain features of the human and sovereign subject. As I have argued, the two court cases bring into view the relational dependency through which the image of time and the historical memory of lynching violence work together to limit a certain conception of the person—that is, personhood as human—and constitute veracity even "as a particular cut-out segment of reality."[77] If testimony—as an event and as an image representative of its time and a time that has ostensibly passed—can only be translated through representations reinforced by law's imaginary (as a self, a prisoner, the lynching victim, the lynch mob), then we can understand the veil of time not as something that has passed. Rather, the distortion of time by law is driven by the ways in which blackness is ungraspable, always in conflict with any normative representation. At the same time, the untranslatability of blackness proves a resistance to what is deemed resistance proper. And for this reason, the untranslatability of blackness unsettles not only a juridical conviction of justice based on law's own terms and evaluative criteria, an a priori judgment that drives its legal and positive forms; it illumines that the language of resistance is but a rope of sand without blackness to project its illusory stability.

This chapter has sought to move beyond critiques of representation and reform, by ruminating on the untranslatability of blackness—the *n'est pas*—to uncover law's most violent antagonisms. By mapping the psychotic structure of *l'entre-je* onto the legal fiction and psychical mechanism of "self-lynching," illustrated in the *Jones* and *Anthony J.* cases, I have contended that the transformation of *Ursache* into *Gewalt* is a structural imperative necessitated by blackness's non-being. The untranslatability of blackness, therefore, makes clear that the exclusion of blackness is not a contingent or a remediable failure in the writing and interpretation of law, but the law's enduring *afterlife (Fortleben)*. In view of this, the *afterlife* of slavery and lynching is revealed not as a haunting historical residue, but as the apparatus of a reason—a state of custody that persists through the law's refusal to translate blackness as anything other than a site of self-destruction. The structural difference between signification and this non-relational ground remains a persistent challenge to any politics of abolition, inasmuch as it poses the question of how (or if) thought can proceed *beyond* abolition while operating within the law's symbolic constraints. The broader implications of the violence that anchors this structural difference—and the question of how thought might proceed from this irreducible limit—will be the focus of the chapters that follow.

Four

"High-Tech Lynching"

Irony, Sexual Difference, and Toni Morrison's "Metaphor of Itself"

The carceral confines of language, as we have discussed in the previous chapter, are exposed by the way language becomes resistant to the perceived threat of blackness, indicating blackness's untranslatability—a resistance of resistance. In turn, we saw that, in its untranslatability, blackness reveals a radical immanence, a resistance that cannot be penetrated, grasped, nor (made) fugitive in positive forms of representation. Because the law's foundational language is structured by (anti)blackness, any attempt at resistance is immediately caught in a paradox. By defining blackness solely through its absence and exclusion—as a category constituted by what the normative subject *is not*—the law sustains its own coherence. A structural relationship emerges that imposes an ontological double bind upon blackness. On the one hand, blackness is convicted of what it is not; on the other, it faces a perverse obligation of "annulling [oneself] as black, which is in fact impossible."[1]

In what follows, we examine a performative instance of such annulment by way of metaphor. Our example will be Toni Morrison's critical study on Clarence Thomas's use of the phrase "high-tech lynching," in which blackness is summoned to animate a metaphor of lynching. In offering a close reading of Morrison's observations, I propose that metaphor as a racial trope is problematic not solely through its representational logic, but through an identification with the image of such racial representation that reinforces a process of disavowal. But as I will argue, Morrison's reflections on metaphor and identification fundamentally deviate from both common and established critical interpretations. Through Morrison, I illustrate how lynching as the "metaphor of itself" exposes the irony of identification—an investment in racial symbols that only reveals the impossibility for blackness to be signified or contained. Such psychic capture, thus, reveals a profound irony: one is compelled to seek liberation through the very symbolic categories that ensure their entrapment. This enduring failure of representation returns us to the subjection of blackness in language, which structures a disavowal as a necessary but destructive psychic act. The process of disavowal finds its etymological shadow in the figure of the slave, where the notion *to serve* is deeply imbricated with the notion *to save*. Derived from the Latin *servus* or *sclavus*, "slave" carries a deep-seated etymological tension that binds the act of "to serve" to the possibility of "to save"—a critical ambiguity that structures the logic of disavowal. Placing these concerns together, I maintain that the substitutive image of lynching rests on a lynching of the image wherein blackness must be suspended to project a self. The focus now shifts to the question of the distinction—or the conversion—between image and symbol, and the identification produced by their difference.

In her introduction to *Race-ing Justice, En-gendering Power*, a dossier of essays reflecting on Anita Hill's testimony at the Senate hearings on the confirmation of Clarence Thomas to the U.S. Supreme Court, Morrison observes that "[l]ynching is also the metaphor of itself."[2] In this instance, the metaphor *of itself* refers to Thomas's remarks which directly cast Hill's hearing as a lynching of him. Hill, who was testifying about her experience of years-long sexual harassment by Thomas, had previously withheld these reports out of a well-founded fear of retaliation and the profound mental stress that followed. By invoking the specter of the lynch mob to shield himself from Hill's testimony, Thomas was not only deploying a trope, but was also enacting the "metaphor of itself" that Morrison identifies.

Over three days of testimony, Hill addressed questions from the Senate Judiciary Committee, a panel of fourteen white men, including Joe Biden, who was chairman of the committee. The C-SPAN media coverage begins with a pan shot of the hearing before zooming in to capture the individual senators poised for their respective interrogations of Hill (Figure 11). Caught mid-zoom, the camera frames the row of men with notable ease before a long, imposing wooden dais. The side angle emphasizes both the scale and the homogeneous gender composition of the panel facing Hill. Through-

Figure 11. Video still from the Senate Judiciary Committee hearings on the nomination of Clarence Thomas, October 11, 1991. The camera pans across the committee members before focusing on the interrogating senators. Source: C-SPAN Archives.

out the testimony, the gaze of the media image remains fixed on Hill as she methodically responds to the series of probing questions and accusations (Figure 12). One after the other, these inquiries would attempt to undermine her credibility as a professor of law and civil rights, probe the nature and scale of injury caused by Thomas's alleged sexual harassment, and pose leading questions about her psychological stability or any underlying political motives that might have led to her testimony.

For example, Senator Arlen Specter (R-Pennsylvania) attempts to neutralize Hill's testimony by reframing the harassment as commonplace. Informing her that discussing women's bodies at her previous workplace at the Equal Employment Opportunity Commission was reasonably normal and inoffensive, Specter remarks, "You testified this morning that the most embarrassing question involved—this is not too bad—women's large breasts. That is a word we use all the time. That was the most embarrassing aspect of what Judge Thomas has said to you."[3]

Figure 12. Composite of video stills showing Anita Hill's testimony during the Senate Judiciary Committee hearings, October 11, 1991. The sequence illustrates her steady composure during extended questioning. Source: C-SPAN Archives.

In another instance, the camera captures the institutional weight of the committee as Senator Howell Heflin (R-Alabama)—an older white man appearing in a tight medium close-up isolating him to the center of the image—leans toward his microphone to begin a series of leading questions. Heflin's inquiries seek to surface a latent pathology or underlying political "motivation" behind Hill's testimony. He asks, "Now, in trying to determine whether you are telling falsehoods or not, I have got to determine what your motivation might be. Are you a scorned woman?" to which Hill answers, "No." Immediately thereafter, Heflin asks a number of additional accusatory questions: "Are you a zealot civil rights believer that progress will be turned back, if Clarence Thomas goes on the court?" "Do you have a militant attitude relative to the area of civil rights?" "Do you have a martyr complex?" After each question, Hill calmly answers no. In response to the last question (as to whether Hill has a martyr complex or not), the camera captures a shift in Hill's composure: she offers a wry, slight smile followed by a moment of subdued amusement as she looks down toward her notes. The audience, visible in a soft-focus background, chuckles behind her, marking a brief moment of shared incredulity with Hill—a moment that disrupts the formal institutional logic of the hearing. They, too, seem to perceive the studied ignorance of Heflin's pathologizing inquiries.[4]

Time and time again, Hill has been both commended and condemned for her poise and cogency during a strenuous trial where rhetoric and figures of race, gender, and sexuality were gratuitously charged. Many scholars have pointed out that to consider her testimony a "high-tech lynching" of Thomas, as he put it, would require a disavowal of the racial *and* gendered sexual history of lynching violence that black people faced. Jacqueline Goldsby has observed:

> To allow Anita Hill's testimony to be heard, Thomas argued, was to sacrifice him for a crime he did not commit. To allow Anita Hill's testimony to be heard, Thomas insisted, was to mock the protocols of judicial procedure. To allow Anita Hill's testimony to be heard, Thomas accused, was to "destroy" him. To "caricature" him. To "lynch" him. . . . To rebut Anita Hill's testimony Thomas convened as his witness *the* image that compresses the horrific brutality of America's racial history with regard to African-Americans into a singular act: lynching.[5]

Perhaps even higher stakes are raised by the way in which the image of "high-tech lynching" can become a mode of concealment. Instrumentalized by Thomas, the image eclipses how the representation of racial, gendered, and sexual violence distorts blackness as anterior to these images. Anterior to the image of "high-tech lynching," the concealment of blackness becomes that which facilitates the image. As Rizvana Bradley has critically pointed out:

> Morrison reveals how Thomas' obsequious performance of masculinity, and his amenability to the public and to the legal conformation process, was not only enabled by the sexual displacement of race (specifically blackness) onto the image of Hill. This displacement of race onto the black woman constitutes the black woman as such. In other words, black femininity becomes the bearer of the burden of the racial mark, and of blackness.[6]

Goldsby's reading offers insight as to how "*the* image" of lynching is usurped by Thomas. Thomas endeavors to stage the hearing as a testimony to the racialized and gendered violence launched against him by hailing lynching's history of racial terror against black men to position himself as a victim, and the U.S. Supreme Court as the mob. Beyond what happens at the level of representation—that is, the discursive production of a racialized and gendered image—Bradley's reflections further elaborate the metapsychological function of a sexual displacement that shapes Thomas's image of Hill: race is displaced onto an image to conceal a fundamental absence. Such a displacement necessitates a critique of metaphor, not just at the level of representation, but as a site of identification and disavowal. Indeed, the structural nothingness of blackness and the sexual displacement onto the image of Hill are not mutually exclusive; rather, they are interdependent mechanisms: the structural nothingness provides the unrepresentable void that the sexual displacement is compelled to fill and conceal, thus enabling the metapsychological function—a psychic maneuver that preserves the subject's coherence by projecting its internal lack onto an external object. Critically, Bradley's reading exposes not only the gap between the metaphorical image of lynching and the negative positioning of blackness in the social construction of race and gender. She also shows how this difference is marked by the impossibility of black sexuality—the sexual displacement of blackness—that serves as the condition of possibility. The inscription of black sexuality is structurally impossible because the nothingness of blackness (the *n'est pas*) has no constituted symbolic position from which to assert a relational self or desire. This structural foreclosure makes the sexual displacement—the trafficking of blackness onto a pathologized image such as Hill's—a necessary symptom of racial representation that attempts to manage and contain the structural void at its core. The impossibility of black sexuality, Bradley tells us, is an originary difference that shapes a direct relationship between a hermeneutics of metaphor and the form that it takes on as an image. I argue that ultimately the act of compressing the violence of lynching into a singular, displacing image—which is enabled both by sexual displacement and concealing the nothingness of blackness—demands a psychic act of disavowal that allows the metaphor to function. This, I submit, is what Morrison perceives when she describes lynching as the metaphor of itself.

Indeed, Thomas's perverse use of metaphor distorts the repetition of racial history and positions the image of lynching in a peculiar place. Yet it also tells us that there is something in the metaphor of lynching itself that has been perverted. As the metaphor of itself, lynching magnifies the violence of the substitution—the trade of one image for another—while exposing the brutality of the compressed, captive image. By holding blackness captive with such compression, Thomas enables a substitution that captures the subject even as the metaphor claims to represent that subject's captivity. This suggests, in turn, an overdetermined meaning that precedes yet nevertheless comes with the substituted captivating image of the lynching of blackness as a self. The violence here is doubled, for it captures whilst it is also captivity.

Metaphor, in this moment, operates according to a structural law of representation—the law of a compulsory exchange: substitution acts as the mechanism that compels the rhetorical transfer of blackness into a manageable racial figure, a trope. Following Walter Benjamin, I understand this figure as an image because this linguistic exchange immediately takes on a spectral, material presence. As discussed previously, such materialization provides the legible, transferable currency required by the law to conceal the nothingness of blackness. In the context of antiblackness, the metaphor (the structural operation) and the image (its spectral, signifying effect) become functionally indistinguishable; the violence of metaphor relies on this compulsory imaging in order to enact its substitution and mask the abyss that blackness constitutes. Thus, the violence of "self-lynching" is part of the foundational psychic violence underpinning racial representation, while the violence of lynching *qua* the metaphor of itself is the symbolic violence that attempts to manage that terror through the successive production of displacing images.

Frank Wilderson discusses something similar when he explains the relation between the (non-)ontology of blackness and metaphor. He observes, "And it is well known that a metaphor comes into being through a violence that kills, rather than merely exploits, the object so that the concept may live."[7] "So that the concept may live"—or that it *can* only live—under the conditions of "a violence that kills" indicates something more insidious than simple repression or the mere substitution of images. What is exposed in this tension between life and murderous violence, between concept and metaphor, is the internal limit that facilitates the staging of such oppositions. It reveals the paradox of a force that attempts to overcome the limit, yet nonetheless maintains the opposition.

Let me pause briefly to clarify my use of the term "repression" and the notion of metapsychology. Doing so will allow us to understand how they relate to lynching as the metaphor of itself, as posed by Morrison. With Sigmund Freud, we can understand "the state of 'repression' ['*Verdrängung*']"[8] as contingent upon the change that the instinctual impulse might undergo: "One of the vicissitudes an instinctual impulse may undergo is to meet with resistances which seek to make it inoperative."[9] At the same time, resistance takes place due to a sense of rejection. Freud describes this "rejection based on judgement (*condemnation*)," and in this way "repression is a preliminary stage of condemnation, something between flight and condemnation."[10] Contrary to how repression is understood in a colloquial sense, Freud notes that here "repression is not a defensive mechanism."[11] Rather, repression, that is *primal repression*, functions with the representation of an idea of the instinct at the level of the imaginary; in other words, primal repression is not representative of the instinct, but an ideation of it—or what Freud characterizes as a psychical (ideational) representative of the instinct.[12] Jacques Lacan will later posit the signifier as a psychical representative (*die Vorstellungsrepräsentanz*), which he reminds his readers "means not, as it has been mistranslated, the representative representative (*le representant représen-*

tatif), but that which takes the place of the representation (*le tenant-lie de la representation*)."[13] Lacan's point implies that the psychical representative is in relation to the signifier. This will be relevant momentarily to another discussion in this chapter. For now, these preliminary conceptualizations of repression offered by Freud help us to acknowledge the meaning of a metapsychology. Freud's concerns about the psychical agencies and dynamics of repression were, perhaps unsurprisingly, in part what led him to define his use of the term metapsychology "in describing a psychical process in its dynamic, topographical and economic aspects."[14] With this definition in mind, I understand that the amalgamation of forces, dynamics, and psychical registers through which antiblackness takes place is not only unconscious but fundamental to the structuring of the unconscious. Wilderson's provocation that "metaphor comes into being through a violence that kills" stages the metaphor of lynching of itself as a metapsychological crisis, because it calls into question the mechanism of repression and substitution that characterizes metaphor. If primal repression is understood as that preliminary encounter with judgment, then the metaphor of lynching of itself points to a more radical severance. There is a lynching of blackness immanent in this preliminary encounter of condemnation and yet nonetheless enables the possibility of psychical representatives of (anti)blackness and the recognition of forms to appear.

Part of my attempt in what follows will be to consider how antiblackness works at a metapsychological level—that is, to consider how antiblackness is fundamental to the structuring of a sense of self, signs, objects, etc. In this instance, I mean antiblackness as the force that rests on and stems from the structural absence of blackness that is also foundational to the unconscious. My intent is to illustrate that these twin aspects, force and absence, shape the desire for judgment and representation, thought and concepts, as inscriptions of the unconscious. Blackness, in this vein, is not simply a marker of racial difference that drives the racial construction of gender and sexual identities. The exposure of the absence of blackness animates these differences, putting their appearances and representations to work. Furthermore, lynching as the metaphor of itself complicates the purported irrepresentability and untranslatability of blackness by allowing the metaphor of lynching to become unanchored. And while this book has argued thus far against the reformist and reparative illusions of juridico-legal representation, Thomas's assertion of a "high-tech lynching" prompts the question of what it means to rhetorically figure lynching in a law-preserving space like the U.S. Supreme Court.

To begin, let us consider the moments where Thomas points to an imagined lynching of himself. After the first full day of hearings, Thomas dismisses the proceedings as "a circus" and "a national disgrace," categorizing the FBI investigation into Thomas's case, Anita Hill's testimony, the intensity of media coverage, and the media's portrayal as a "high-tech lynching." Prior to this explicit naming in his response to the Senate Judiciary Committee, Thomas invokes the image of lynching at the conclusion of his opening statements. The camera captures him in a tight, unyielding close-up—his face illuminated by the hard overhead lights of the hearing room. The visual "pressure" supports his claim of being a victim, even as the televisual framing allows him to weaponize his own physical presence, utilizing the "institutional image" to reclaim a sense of sovereign authority. Here, the camera-work is indispensable to the labor of projecting Thomas as an ontological exception—a figure who adopts the very "violence of presence"[15] that violates and erases blackness to instead compel a national witness to his screened innocence. As he looks directly toward the committee to deliver his ultimatum of resistance, he refuses "to provide the rope for [his] own lynching."[16]

> Instead of understanding and appreciating the great honor bestowed upon me, I find myself defending my name, my integrity, because somehow select portions of confidential documents dealing with this matter were leaked to the public. Mr. Chairman, I am a victim of this process. My name has been harmed. My integrity has been harmed. My character has been harmed. My family has been harmed. My friends have been harmed. There is nothing this committee, this body, or this country can do to give my good name back. Nothing. *I will not provide the rope for my own lynching or for further humiliation.* I am NOT going to engage in discussions, nor will I submit to roving questions of what goes on in the most intimate parts of my private life or the sanctity of my bedroom. These are the most intimate parts of my privacy and they will remain just that: private.[17]

In this broadcast moment, the visual fixity of Thomas's close-up mirrors the rhetorical fixity of his refusal; his face, steeled against the committee, becomes the site where the "high-tech" apparatus of the media meets the historical specter of the noose. Lynching as the metaphor of itself is quite arresting in these two evocations. On one hand, Thomas frames Hill's accusation against him as a form of racial gendered stereotyping that casts black masculinity as sexually predatory, submitting that the injury to his own honor—the investigation targeting his character to undermine his nomination—is itself a form of lynching. He characterizes the probing into the "sanctity of [his] bedroom" as the essential mechanism of this assault. Yet, in the picture that Thomas paints, he is the one holding the rope. He positions himself as the arbiter of who can hand the rope over—as if victims of lynching ever possessed such choice. By asserting this capacity for resistance, Thomas uses the metaphor to eclipse his own discreditation and alleged sexual harassment of Hill. Despite Thomas's vocal distress at the fact that the media has caricatured him, he unabashedly puts his victimhood center stage through a rhetorical maneuver that only works because lynching is, as Morrison rightly observes, the metaphor of itself. This requires a repression of a primal repression: the suspension of blackness as nothingness. Thomas instrumentalizes his blackness as a racial gendered trope in service of animating the image of lynching while also foreclosing the dissemination of racialized, gendered, and sexualized images that denigrate Hill. Rather than analyzing what this might suggest for the construction of identity, I want to focus on how the double suspension (the repression of a primal repression) indicates the work of identification that coincides with it, and how the violence of the metaphor of itself necessitates and capitulates to a representational system of whiteness.

Thomas clearly seeks to convince his peers and the audience of a missed identification in respect to his race, gender, and lower-class background. But what does it mean to stage an interpellation of oneself while simultaneously naming the missed recognition that precedes the assumed need for an interpellation as a "high-tech lynching"? Thomas's use of the term not only characterizes and caricatures the media frenzy; by appending "high-tech," he also asserts a false distinction from what would be considered a "low-tech" lynching. As Goldsby notes:

> In a "high-tech" lynching such as his the terms and forms of violence metamorphose. Photographic flash guns make the torches and bonfires of a "low-tech" lynching obsolete; character malignment doubles for

> bodily mutilation; interrogation substitutes for castration, and rejection of his nomination symbolizes literal death. Attentive to these nuances, Thomas appears to be a perceptive witness of his own suffering.[18]

Goldsby importantly explains that "to cast lynching as the act and discourse defining his nomination hearing, Clarence Thomas placed himself beyond reproach."[19] While Goldsby's point regarding the transformation of terms and forms is vital, my concern here is less "the terms and forms of violence [that] metamorphose," and more the force facilitating that metamorphosis. There is a clear homology between the media relations in the coverage of the hearing and the relations that figure lynching as a racial trope. But in framing lynching as the metamorphosis of form, lynching becomes unanchored from any referents and violently displaces blackness only to recursively instrumentalize blackness as a medium. As Bradley describes it, "the brutal immediacy to which the black is subjected provides a constitutive mediation."[20] In this way, blackness raises a question of facilitation—what enables it and what it traces. Similarly, it calls into question not just what might facilitate the substitutive image of the racial trope in this context of metaphor, but what supports its production, its metaphorization.[21]

Morrison's observation moves away from most definitions of metaphor: in addition to the substitution of one image for another, she identifies a more volatile dynamic at work. She draws attention to a conjunctive adverb, the "also," thus indicating that the metaphor is forced to occupy a different (non-)direction, since lynching does not *become* the metaphor, but *is* the metaphor "of itself." The metaphor moves in a more excessive and forcible way that extends beyond the typical substitution. I submit that Morrison delimits an understanding of metaphor in her examination of Thomas's use of lynching as a way to contemplate what belies the use of figurative language. Morrison's deconstruction of figurative language parallels her gesture of bringing into sharp focus the collapse of the psychic life of antiblackness, its fantasies and hallucinations, into material reality. As discussed in *Beyond Abolition*, the image of blackness and its successive formations, including its displacements, house the necessary concealment of black death as *ante legem*. But here especially we must ask what the elision of black death might expose in its concealment so that metaphor works in a way "of itself" that is at the same time *against* itself? Or at least, this is what I believe Morrison to be suggesting: metaphor ceases to function when it attempts to establish itself as a stable, substitutive image. In the face of this failure, we encounter a magnification of the impossibility of being and becoming for blackness.

The image of "high-tech lynching," as Morrison and others have astutely observed, rests on a series of reversals and disavowals. For one, Thomas's imagined lynching can only take place at the expense, denigration, and foreclosure of Hill, her testimony, her subject position, and the repeated violence inflicted upon her.[22] Departing from common interpretations of metaphor as a trope of similitude, Lacan explains metaphor as "not a comparison but an identification."[23] In observing the privileging of the signifier over meaning in the semblance of metaphor, Lacan also points to how the signifier, in this particular case the metaphor, "occupies more and more place in the libidinal relation and invests all the moments, all the desires of the subject."[24] A crucial takeaway from Lacan's point is that when the privileging of the signifier takes place to the extent that the signified becomes emptied—"since the signifier is the instrument by which the missing signified expresses itself"[25]—we get a glimpse of the signifier's paradoxical centrality: it becomes the focal point of the entire representational field precisely because it is devoid of meaning. The point in all this is not to diagnose Thomas with a pseudo-psychological condition—though such a reading would not be a far reach. Rather, understanding metaphor as an identification allows us to see how the prototypical image of lynching—drawn from the fantasies of culture—structures relations of a self yet to be made.

Morrison pushes this point even further by troubling some of these aspects of identification when she notes a misrecognition of blackness that is nonetheless inseparable from racial doubt and the libidinal investment underlining it.

> With a black candidate, already stained by the figurations of blackness as sexual aggressiveness or rapaciousness or impotence, the stain need only be proved reasonably doubted, which is to say, if he is black, how can you tell if that really is a stain? Which is also to say, blackness is itself a stain, and therefore unstainable . . . Allegations of sexual misconduct re-raced him, which, in this administration, meant, re-stained him, dirtied him . . . In this case the search for the racial stain turned on Anita Hill. Her character. Her motives. Not his.[26]

Here, the metaphor of the stain is a mode of identification. Yet, unlike Lacan's privileging of the signifier over meaning, Morrison demonstrates how blackness complicates the centrality of the signifier, since blackness precedes what becomes signified by the metaphor of the stain, just as any signifiers of blackness can paradoxically take place without being signified (blackness as stain is positioned as unstainable). "The figurations of blackness," as they are libidinally placed, not only leave the subject with desire from these substitutive sexualized images, but the identification, in turn, also fixes blackness in an antagonistic corner: unstainable, blackness enters signification without being signified, and as stain, the privilege of privileging the signifier loses any capacity for those relations since it is without meaning. The privilege of the signifier collapses into the "nothingness" of the stain. This deconstruction, I argue, allows Morrison to ask how one can possibly relate to oneself as a black self in this perverse dynamic of identification.

By understanding lynching as the metaphor of itself, we might infer how a perverse dynamic of identification maintains the desires of fantasy—the pathological fantasies of the lynching of blackness—*for* culture. One perverse effect of this metaphoric collapse is the fixed staging of identity markers—race, gender, sexuality—without recourse to the latent forces in the production of meaning. The objective here is neither the retrieval nor recovery of an emptied meaning, but a speculation on the way the substitutive image of lynching functions as a fantasy-structure that stabilizes the categories of identity. Thinking through the limits of this image is a way to consider how the lynching of blackness—as a self within fantasy—stabilizes the performative grounds on which race, gender, and sexuality rest. At stake is a deadly judgment that is not juridical, but nonetheless arresting of blackness in language where now "the word 'language' is no longer secure against metaphor."[27] Peter Fenves notes: "Metaphor, as a correlate of judgment, begins its dominance over language, and this movement of metaphor, this metamovement in which something is carried from one spot to another . . . displaces the word 'language,' if not language as such."[28] In this sense, lynching as the metaphor of itself is the displacement of the violence of lynching and its racial terror, as it deracializes lynching and transforms it into a transferable trope. But if metaphor, according to Fenves, is also a correlate of judgment, what of the deadly judgment that is structurally prior to the image? What of the judgment that accompanies the structural execution before the image of language even appears? This priority compels us to ruminate further on the nature of this movement.

Certainly, this movement immediately raises the stakes of antiblackness as a constitutive violence. In conceptualizing this movement, I acknowledge that this theoretical turn runs the risk of collapsing the structural act into the realm of representation and predication—as forwarded by the work of Immanuel Kant and G.W.F. Hegel.[29] Moreover, to call this a judgment also hazards confusing it with the Freudian preliminary stage of condemnation. However, I argue that the deadly act that precedes the image of language—and even the preliminary encounter of condemnation described by Freud—is the constitutive foreclosure that renders blackness as an ontological void. The foreclosure here is not an act of predication based on rejection of an impulse, but a structural positing of non-being—the brute, non-representational assertion of the nothingness of blackness and the structural decision that blackness must be lynched in order for representation to cohere. The Freudian judgment is therefore not the origin of this terror, but rather a secondary, necessary symptom of it. When symbolic law encounters blackness, its response is not simply repression (*Verdrängung*) of an idea, but a severance or elimination that attempts to manage the terror resulting from that foundational foreclosure. The metaphor of lynching of itself is thus the mechanism that attempts to substitute this constitutive foreclosure with a manageable racial trope. As such, the violence—simultaneously veiled and structurally anterior to the systems of racial representation—only enters language and sustains the image through the disavowal of such violent displacements.

Morrison's observation of Thomas's evocation of lynching as a metaphor of itself is, therefore, critical to understanding how the adjournment of language paradoxically functions as a means of confinement through racial, gender, and sexual tropes. Insofar as language and meaning have been drained from the image—and language too possesses a carceral function[30]—the image conforms to a symbolic excess that forbids being outside the image. Such a functional exhaustion of meaning confirms that the metaphor of lynching, the metaphor of itself, never required a stable referent in the first instance. As Morrison explains:

> Those two major fictions, either/or, were blasted and tilted by a factual thing masquerading as a true thing: lynching. Being a fact of both white

history and black life, lynching is also the metaphor of itself. While the mythologies about black personae debauched the confirmation process for all time, the history of black life was appropriated to elevate it.[31]

As fact collapses as truth, the fantasy of one reality prevailing over another becomes all the more powerful and totalizing. Indeed, as Patricia Williams asks in her own response to Hill's hearing: "What account, in the name of law, are we to make of all this?"[32] At the very least, any deference to an account of positive law, and ergo the language of rights, leads into a dead end, since any interpretation of law must corroborate with the language of rights and recognition, from which Hill has been characteristically and ontologically excluded. It can be said then that possibilities of racial, gender, and sexual identities rely too uncritically on the law, thereby masking the ontological disinheritance of the self, a violence that precedes the trial. Such antecedent violence ultimately leaves Hill exposed, at the mercy of a language that cannot "hear" her. In effect, the instrumentalization of such markers of difference appears to work toward a juridical outcome of guilt or acquittal, but one that can only be determined by the whiteness of the court. David Marriott has described this authority in another context as a "sovereign power" experienced "by administering and safeguarding whiteness as a right via a law that announces itself as already transgressed, or perverted by blackness."[33]

The issue then is that lynching becomes a racial trope to maintain whiteness as the status quo; yet this raises the question of why such a substitution is so seamlessly fortified by the sovereign power of whiteness. Rodolphe Gasché recalls Paul de Man's reflections on metaphorical structure, in which the resemblances established by analogical links are "endowed with attributes of naturalness."[34] But at stake is neither simply "a foreclosure of this ineluctable difference" that comes via substitution nor the "subjugation of difference as such."[35] On the contrary, substitution, in its seemingly natural appearance, also presents the racial trope as real and having the capacity to represent. The question of the authority that presumably comes with metaphor emerges elsewhere in de Man's work. In "The Epistemology of Metaphor," de Man notes:

> The considerations about the possible danger of uncontrolled metaphors, focused on the cognate figures of support, ground, and so forth,

> reawaken the hidden uncertainty about the rigor of a distinction that does not hold if the language in which it is stated reintroduces the elements of indetermination it sets out to eliminate. For it is not obvious that the iconic representation that can be used to illustrate a rational concept is indeed a figure.[36]

De Man critically discloses the possibility that the metaphorical form not only might fail to correspond to a rational concept, but might also fail to be a figure at all. Thus, beyond the violence of and by the metaphorical image—the displacements and successive formations of metaphor—there also exists a violence fundamental to the metapsychological structure—the cognate figures of support and ground—that provides the conditions for the metaphor to function. But the capacity of the metaphor, or lack thereof, nonetheless masks the indeterminacy that gives rise to figurative language and its possible representations. In other words, "the language of mastery" enables "things [to become] 'truly real.'"[37] Wilderson might envision something similar when he explains that "analogy, then, is more than a rhetorical device . . . it often evinces generative agency where such transgressions [of violence] are concerned . . . and cradles that relation in the swaddling of conflictual harmony and shields the relation from the cold incoherence of [antiblack] antagonism."[38]

And perhaps this is where Thomas turns metaphor on its head, from substitution to something more akin to irony. Even within the metaphor's seeming naturalness, there is no doubt that this substitution is read, seen, and heard as inexact, imaginary, or even perverse. Certainly, Thomas is well aware of the trope that he instrumentalizes and the racial effects that such a trope produces. This suggests that Thomas exploits the notion of lynching not only to discredit Hill; by calling upon the racial guilt of whiteness in the service of his own self-victimhood, he also reifies the violent structures that pathologize blackness. Lynching as the "metaphor of itself" must be addressed as irony insofar as it is reduced to a reflexive structure.[39] As the "metaphor of itself," the irony is that lynching is without a referent. Here, the figure of irony lays bare how antiblackness is intricately interwoven with a psychic reality that is simultaneously posited as truth. To follow Marriott once more:

> The desire to *be* white can only confirm a failure of attainment; that it is indeed impossible to conform to it, impossible not to conform without

> conforming to it, to the point where being black is, inescapably, to be by right and by fact indebted to what one is *not*, for it is impossible, consequently, to be black without being enjoined to renounce being black in favor of the onto-stereotypical truths of anti-blackness.[40]

On this account, "guilt [that] constitutes moral incertitude"[41] is inseparable from the ontological uncertainty that blackness faces when positioned as a "flaw" (with Marriott) or a "stain" (via Morrison).

The ontological implications—"inescapably, to be by right and by fact indebted to what one is *not*"—tell us a great deal about the desire for the (blackened) figure in language and the movement of that desire. The way in which the figuration of blackness comes to be recognized as flaw or stain in language reveals a fantasy, one that Jared Sexton has described as "strung between the insecurity of whiteness and the fact of blackness."[42] Sexton's remark follows a comprehensive elaboration of Lacan's conceptualization of sexuation and his famous adage that "there is no such thing as a sexual rapport,"[43] or what he described elsewhere as "the impossibility of the sexual relationship"[44]—a point that we will return to shortly. More immediately for us here, Sexton's attention to the function of the fantasy of racial sexual relations is key. While the intertwining of "race" and "sexuality" is represented as "a union of race"[45] in the context of multiracial politics, Sexton makes the more significant argument that the fantasy of interracial sexual relations is asserted "to remedy" the racial antagonism of blackness. This ontological disposition, insofar as it elicits a distorted way of looking inward and reflecting on interracial sexual relations, suggests that desire (as it is translated into the symbolic) is only part of what we see. Blackness apropos of sexuation intensifies the psychic energies at the level of the drives, spinning the function of fantasy in the formation of interracial intimacy, not unlike Thomas's capitulation to whiteness. Such tension drives home the ontological negative positioning of blackness that makes possible what Morrison has described: blackness is both unstainable and a stain, the negative prediscursive determination of being a subject mediated by the social fantasies that drive the culture of racialization in politics. Perhaps counterintuitively, the irony of Thomas's "metaphor" interrupts the use of figurative language *as* figurative since it collapses the disjuncture between what is irreal versus what is real, demonstrating how antiblack social fantasies are perceived as real. The mediation of such fantasies posited as truth also exposes how antiblackness serves unconscious knowledge to an exceptional depth, even as its appearance in the knowledge (*savoir*) of the subject remains remarkably unexceptional.

The observations I have outlined above complicate Zakiyyah Iman Jackson's argument that "ontologizing racial characterization not only stratifies gender but also calls in question the very meaning of sexual difference." Jackson contends that "antiblackness itself is sexuating, whereby so-called biological sex is modulated by 'culture.' In other words, at the registers of both sign and matter, antiblackness produces differential biocultural effects of both gender and sex."[46] At first blush, Jackson's remarks might be congruent with our meditations on the necessary concealment of (anti)blackness and its conceit in both the politics of racial representation and the appearance of racist fantasies construed as real. However, because sexuation is not simply about the affirmation of gender or (non)gender expression, but also presents an internal limit, the formulation between antiblackness and sexuation—or the claim that "antiblackness itself is sexuating"—becomes reductive. Jackson rightly questions the biological construction of gender. Yet, by literalizing antiblackness as a discursive effect modulated "at the registers of both sign and matter," she risks treating antiblackness as an epistemological tool rather than an ontological limit. There is also another crucial distinction. Although Jackson discusses how antiblackness is positioned as an episteme, in the discursive formations of gender and sexual difference, and although Jackson discusses how blackness poses an ontological problem in the structuration of gender and sexual difference, it remains unclear how the two—ontology and epistemology—are differentiated in her arrangement. I submit that her use of antiblackness in relation to gender and sex is meant to explain an epistemology rather than raise an ontological question, even though Jackson observes the "ontologizing racial characterization" in the stratification of gender and sexual meaning. In this manner, ontologizing racial characterizations already suggests a re-ontologizing of sorts, a contingent effect of an ontological disposition. There are a few issues with narrowing antiblackness down to an epistemological problem. In this instance, "ontologizing racial characterization" reifies the dangers that this process is meant to caution against: racial characterizations propagate a racial ontology that brings forth the figures and tropes which must be unpacked in order for antiblackness to be (supposedly) revealed. In other words, racial ontology becomes an instrument of racial representation, as opposed to a more immanent structure latent to the discursive formations of representation and knowledge production in regard to gender and sex. The point, however, is less about revealing the ways in which antiblackness remain ostensibly occluded than it is about the fact that antiblackness is perpetually in conflict with the racial politics of representation. In this way, the notion that retrieving or questioning "the very meaning of sexual difference" via race is misguided, since an ontology cannot recuperate any missed meaning of sexual difference. Put slightly differently, such an approach implies the recuperation of sexual meaning via blackness whilst eliding the ways in which the incapacity of blackness is maintained.

Jackson's framing of "antiblackness," one that defines itself and is tied to gendered differences (sexuation), assumes that gendered signification can restore some missing meaning or original distinction to antiblackness. Though I do not take for granted her point that antiblackness is a continuous formation (which is perhaps why she utilizes the present progressive tense), there is an obscurity in her reliance, and in the seemingly clear point regarding the "itself": Does antiblackness sexuate itself—and what might this even mean, if not to reify the (un)ethical dilemma of turning blackness into a problem *of* gender and not *for* (non-)gender and ungendering? There is a strange irony in the grammar that Jackson uses—an irony that again assumes a self-reflexive structure. In this framing, antiblackness is in a position not only to signify sexual difference as the problem of sex, but also comes to occupy a position of itself in this signification. What are we to make of the double deracination of blackness in sexuation, where antiblackness is (or becomes) the subject of legislation and erasure? The question here is whether (a) antiblackness can ever truly be the subject who possesses such capacity to legislate sexual meaning, and (b) whether blackness, under any circumstance, can ever be free from the contaminations of sexual difference and meaning. That is, what does the ontologizing of racial characterization add to the construction of sexual meaning, if only to further obscure it?

The meaning of sexual difference is always, in part, a product of the "failure" of sex, insofar as the absence of sex gives rise to the signifiers of sexual difference. But in this way, the ontologizing racial characterization reifies this failure; it reinforces the assumption that the "failure" of sex and the "failure" of blackness share a common structure of self-difference. What is perhaps more problematic is that sexuation stands in here as a substitution for antiblackness—leading us back to the problem of metaphor as a trope of representation: antiblackness is made to bear a resemblance to itself via sexuation. As a consequence, we are left with the appearance of antiblackness, a spectacle that relies on the misrecognition of blackness, one which begets such appearances and possibilities of signification. Yet, unlike the "failure of sex," the failure of blackness permits no symbolic recuperation. The imagined restoration of blackness as a stable figure—the very "high-tech" spectacle of the lynching metaphor—serves to solidify the problem of racial representation by necessarily foreclosing the ontological absence, dispossession, and disfiguration that the image purports to represent.

We now arrive back at the unethical dilemma part and parcel of the problem of the lynching metaphor, the metaphor of itself. In order for the metaphor of antiblackness to function, blackness must become the locus of several displacements: rhetorical, sexual, historical, racial. This locus of displacements paradoxically becomes the site of accrual and excess; blackness gives the illusion of representation and of language's capacity to mean. Hence the problem of the metaphor of lynching of itself: if lynching no longer possesses a referent, what sort of questions does this pose *for* gender, and how might this absence restructure the figural possibility of gender? As the indictment of Thomas's sexual harassment leads him to discredit Hill through "a high-tech lynching," the metaphor performs a scotomization: it renders black men as the sole victims and occupants of the lynching trope, thus reinforcing the ontological displacement of black women. Such condemnation enervates insofar as it animates lynching as a trope of antiblackness only to dismiss and fortify the unrepresentable entanglements of black gender and sexuality. In attempting to explain that "antiblackness itself is sexuating," Jackson accurately highlights that signifiers of sexual difference may follow an antiblack racist representational logic. However, as Morrison brings to our attention, it is not simply that racial tropes themselves are racist; the signs of race and racism stem from a structural internalization that precedes their production. These signs of race are part of the psychic life of antiblackness, establishing the myth of the trope as real and necessary. Antiblackness is, in this vein, gratuitous. While it may establish gendered differences as a biocultural effect through the signs and (un)mattering of race, as Jackson suggests, she misses the point that antiblackness establishes a structure of fantasy where signifiers of difference both bear and mask the void, construed only to give a simulated value to the meaning of one's being.

Morrison portrays this as learning to internalize the master's tongue following the dispossession of the mother tongue—one among many modes of disinheritance in the figurations of blackness. What Morrison outlines for us here regarding structural internalization, in which one's racial subjection becomes masked via the language of difference, is fundamentally a problematic of the unconscious. She signals a structure in which the laws of unconscious knowledge are indistinguishable from those of racial power—a law that governs a sense of being and thinking in service toward the master. Rather than "the sole deciphering of the coherent meaning behind the distortions of the unconscious"[47]—which seeks "to make the symptoms disappear" by its symptomatic representations—the point is to grasp the structural forces that compelled the symptomatic problem of representation to materialize in this particular, decisive form. Though signifiers of racial and sexual difference provide insight into the racial ideologies, epistemologies, and laws that govern a perceived "reality," they indicate a greater problematic: how those signifiers and their racial meanings transform into the very surface or "mask" for the antiblack fantasies and hallucinations that are ultimately construed as all too real.

Perhaps this is why Morrison turns to the character of Friday from Daniel Defoe's *Robinson Crusoe*. Without piety or moral judgment, she makes a critical point: Friday, as a nonsovereign subject whose "loss of the mother tongue seems not to disturb [him], even though he never completely learns the master's" language, does not merely face the problem of being represented by a language or grammar that is his own. Morrison explains that "Friday's real problem . . . was not to learn the language of repetition . . . but to learn to internalize it,"[48] to the extent that "eventually, he learns more: he moves from speaking *with* to thinking *as* Crusoe."[49]

> The problem of internalizing the master's tongue is the problem of the rescued. Unlike the problems of survivors who may be lucky, fated, etc., the rescued have the problem of debt. If the rescuer gives you back your

> life, he shares in that life. But, as in Friday's case, if the rescuer saves your life by taking you away from the dangers, the complications, the confusion of home, he may very well expect the debt to be paid in full.[50]

Such debt is thought to be reconciled by the properties of speech; as Morrison tells us, "the *uses* of Crusoe's language, if not its grammar, become [Friday's] own. The internalization is complete."[51] And yet for Morrison, and for us here as well, there remains an essential question that cannot be answered only by examining symptomatic speech in the performance of some racial construction of gender: "In the absence of his master's desire to speak his tongue, did Friday forget completely the language he dreamed in?"[52] In Morrison's question regarding Friday's dream life, we glean a few additional concerns: What is the latent content, the dream-work, in respect to the dream of language? And how might blackness function at, or beyond, the navel of that dream, the point where the dream becomes unreadable? What unconscious wish is distorted in the manifest content, where dreaming in the master's language is experienced as a sovereign enjoyment? The pleasure is perhaps what allows Friday and Thomas to sleep at night. The issue of an unconscious wish—concealed, repressed, or distorted into another manifestation of language—coalesces in the problem of the metaphor of itself. For if the unconscious, in Lacan's famous maxim, is structured like a language, then what does the difference of language (and not just the language of difference) bear in the unconscious life of antiblackness? What does the metaphor of itself attempt to conceal about antiblackness that cannot remain hidden and, in its concealment, remains as violent as the force it attempts to repress?

In Thomas's use of the metaphor, there is, as Morrison has shown us with Friday, a sense of indebtedness that is imagined to be recuperated through the vehicle of language. But this indebtedness of being rescued indicates more than a desire to overcome the status of the Other; it demonstrates how the impossibility of inhabiting one's own language, and thus occupying the difference of otherness, structures one's internal and psychic reality. In this respect, Morrison pushes us to think beyond the violence of representation and the representation of violence, both of which attend the metaphor of lynching of itself. She highlights how such racial tropes of representation, though initially appearing as a desirable mode of recuperation, inflict irredeemable effects on the psyche. In this process, the hope of being "rescued" necessitates the dissolution of the self. As previous chapters have argued, such a dynamic functions as a psychical and carceral mechanism for the lynching of a self that signals a psychic injury initiated in the imaginary, leaves its scar in the *real*, and eventually finds its materialization in the symbolic. By "carceral mechanism" then, I am referring to the way that modes of representation—specifically racial tropes—act as a system of confinement and control over the psyche. In short, "carceral" highlights that the *psychical* damage is not arbitrary, but a structured, systematic process of the psycho-affective incarceration of blackness. The consequence of this carceral dynamic manifests as a paradoxical compulsion: that is, the subject seeks rescue through the very symbolic categories that guarantee one's capture. This inevitable capture stages an encounter with the irony of the metaphor of itself in one of its most rigorous articulations: a permanent disruption where the subject's attempt to claim sovereignty through the master's language only serves to verify one's total dispossession and dissolution. Such a rescue, of course, does not liberate; instead, it formalizes the subject's incarceration within a grammar that can only speak of them as an absence.

On this view, Morrison's observations on the conflation between a wish to be rescued and a debt implicitly track the etymology of slavery. As Mary Nyquist has explained in the context of premodern military conflicts that regulate war slavery, "slavery is first defined, with the slaveholder assigned the power of life and death, before the military victor's power is explicated etymologically: the word *servi* (slaves), substantive form of *servire* (to serve) comes from *servare* (to save)."[53] In a rhetorical sense, the "authoritative, seemingly timeless, etymological figure" elucidates the suspension of violence that drives the wish for slavery: "The already positive connotations of *servare*, to save, are enhanced by its unstated alternative, to kill or destroy, thereby adding luster to the priority of *servare* has over its supposed derivative *servire*."[54] As Nyquist points out further, "Indebtedness . . . appears to link *servare* to *servi*, constituting another, major sign of the etymological figure's ideological function. Rhetorically, the balanced complementarity suggested by *servare* and *servire* connotes a certain reciprocity: the victor willingly saves, the vanquished willingly serves."[55]

Morrison makes clear to us that the two, Thomas and Friday, represent the same difference: the metaphor of lynching itself cannot perform as and against the trope of racial representation without the disavowal of antiblackness that underpins lynching; for any deference to the master's language also requires an obliteration of blackness—even in the face of oneself.

> Minus one's own idiom it is possible to cry and decry victimization, loathing it when it appears in the discourses of one's own people, but summoning it up for one's expediently deracialized self. It becomes easy to confuse the metaphors embedded in the blood language of one's own culture with the objects they stand for and to call patronizing, coddling, undemanding, rescuing, complicitous white racists a lynch mob. Under such circumstances it is not just easy to speak the master's language, it is necessary. One is obliged to cooperate in the misuse of figurative language, in the reinforcement of cliché, the erasure of difference, the jargon of justice, the denial of history.[56]

Morrison's reading of Thomas's metaphor of lynching spells out the explicit deracination reminiscent of the etymological figure of the slave: the fragile split between being killed and being "saved"; the obligation to use the master's language (indebtedness) over the remains of one's blood language. Stripped of one's own idiom, it becomes possible to decry victimization in the discourse of one's "own people" while "summoning up" figurative language for an expediently essentialized self. In this uncertainty, it is easy to confuse the metaphors embedded in the "blood language" of one's culture with the objects they stand for. Even in its misuse, the endeavor to summon up figurative language indicates that another sort of judgment has already taken place: one that is not about a juridical decision regarding the meaning of words or how they enter a certain set of meanings, but a psychic negotiation with the terms of one's own capture and erasure. If metaphor, according to thinkers such as Fenves, "is distinguished from the analogical without ground and guarantee—and it also awakens an awareness of an indebtedness to textuality as such," Morrison shows us the stakes of its reversal. The psychic indebtedness to the master's use of language (its imagined quality and value) merges judgment into a kind of willing ignorance.[57] While ignorance might suggest another way of seeing that redeems one from the structure of indebtedness, it is filtered through and against the fantasies spun from the irredeemable place of black social death.

In this chapter, I examined Thomas's figurative uses of the word "lynching" in the context of Anita Hill's testimony at the Senate Judiciary hearings, turning to Morrison's meditations on Thomas's use of lynching as the metaphor of itself. By exploring the wider implications of the metaphor of itself and how it lends itself to the turns of irony, we have also seen how the relations between identification, the image of lynching blackness, and the signifier deviate from most standard conceptual operations of these terms. Likewise, we observed that while antiblackness often requires and utilizes the mechanism of primal repression, we must consider a more insidious violence that is antecedent to the repressive substitution inherent in the work of metaphor. The chapter concluded by suggesting the need to think more critically about the notion of willing ignorance, since we have demonstrated that the representation of violence and the violence of representation do not, in themselves, constitute the exhaustive horizon of the problem; for they are, in fact, secondary symptoms of the constitutive lynching of blackness that takes place anterior to language. Judgment of the visible and the apparent is fundamentally distorted by an anterior, metapsychological violence: the structural decision to lynch blackness by positing it as a non-being. To examine this question of seeing, a seeing without seeing the violence before one's eyes (or a seeing without eyes) and "not night darkness that show things once the eye get used to it,"[58] we will turn to the notions of the uncanny and of abstraction in the next chapters.

Five

Beyond Abolition

Unhomeliness, Perversion, and the Arrest of Jasmine Richards Abdullah

In the previous chapter, we were left with the fallacy of having a vision without seeing the violence before one's eyes. There, we discussed the violent turn of irony in which the "self-lynching" of blackness is without a referent yet nonetheless figures the explicit image of disavowal. In this chapter, we ask what it means to see without eyes. That is, we reflect, as psychoanalysis also does, on the principle that perception is never passive, but is always conditioned by unconscious wishes, wants, and desires. To ask what it means to see without eyes is also to ask what animates a sense of reality in which one not only sees blackness lynching itself or self-defense translated as a riot of blackness; it is also to interrogate the implications of seeing such a fantasy as if the event is real and seen for the first time. The irony here is that the "self-lynching" of blackness, evident in the interdependent relationship between the imaginary and symbolic, conceals the violent exposure of blackness to the *real*. Such a question becomes acute as we turn back to Jasmine Richards Abdullah's arrest. The book, thus far, has outlined an archaeology of the recent arrests in chronological order. In this chapter, we will home in on how the mechanism of disavowal underlies the "lynching" arrests and facilitates a reading of the arrests that reveals a peculiar sense of time and untimeliness. In troubling the appearance of these arrests and their "uncanniness," I consider the complex of law's perversion—a structure, I argue, that is crucial to the arrests and state's logic. To see without eyes, as I submit, exceeds the notion of vision and truth as mere redemption; it is, instead, concerned with the structural function that the "self-lynching" of blackness serves in driving the perverse dynamic that undergirds the "lynching" arrests.

The chapter is structured in three parts. First, it considers the racial politics of representation that shape the appearance of race and resistance in the context of the Occupy Wall Street movement in which the "lynching" arrests occurred. Drawing on Werner Hamacher's concept of the "afformative strike," I interrogate the limits of abolition when framed solely as a corrective to state power, arguing that the "lynching" arrests demand a reckoning with a violence that is foundational to the legal order itself—one that exceeds the traditional critiques of racial capitalism by insisting on a position that deposes the law as opposed to reforming it. Second, the chapter investigates the relationship between the unhomeliness of blackness and the uncanniness of the "lynching" arrests. In doing so, it explores the violence that renders the psychical image of blackness as the foundational threat underscoring Richards Abdullah's arrest. The chapter concludes by offering a close reading of the perversion that structures the justification of the "lynching" arrest by law enforcement. In doing so, we will also see how a perverse dynamic is reproduced through a reading and representation of black resistance.

My aim in this chapter is to extend my previous engagement with notions of *afterlife* and translation in order to complicate my earlier discussion of these concerns.[1] Throughout *Beyond Abolition*, I have demonstrated that the image and historical memories surrounding the California penal code and lynching, in its various forms, rest on a type of "self-lynching" in which the custody of blackness is not only carceral but also obfuscates the psychical phenomena that suspend a self, thus revealing the (non)sovereignty of blackness. We will further contemplate the stakes of this suspension, considering how blackness is not just unconsciously imagined to perform, but is explicitly solicited to do so. The wish to witness or to enlist blackness in the performance of resistance, I will argue, illustrates how the anxieties surrounding the unthought of blackness compel both the representation of and the desire to figure black resistance. Such a wish mirrors the perversion driving the responses of the police and the citizenry in their collective desire to strengthen state security and the enforcement of law.

Indeed, Richards Abdullah's arrest begs a number of questions that we have broached already in the book, but nonetheless stage once more in this chapter: If, by the definition of the penal code, "felony lynching" refers to the "taking by means of riot of another person from the lawful custody of a peace officer," and if, as we now know, the legal definition and legislative intent of the code displace and erase lynching's regime of racial terror, then what in this instance qualifies as a "riot" in its sociohistorical association with lynching? How is the conduct of "attempting to unlawfully remove a suspect from police officers," the charge Richards Abdullah faced, considered a felony, when interfering with the police is a misdemeanor in the State of California?[2] No less important, at what point did the perceived "riot" turn into "lynching" (or rather, when did these two acts ever become distinct from one another)? It is precisely this perceptual translation of "riot" into "lynching" that leads us to interrogate the racial politics governing the arrest and puncture the fantasies through which its representation has been read.

Arrested Developments

As noted in the introduction to this book, Richards Abdullah was not the first individual to face these charges. However, other protesters who were arrested under the charges of "felony lynching" had those charges dropped or reduced.[3] While the initial charges against Richards Abdullah were also dropped, she was later charged with "felony lynching" by Judge Elaine Lu, ultimately receiving a punitive sentence of "90 days in jail, with 18 days served, three years on probation, and one year of anger management. After posting bail for a separate misdemeanor protesting charge, Richards [Abdullah] is now free."[4] Critically, as her lawyer Nana Gyamfi notes, Richards Abdullah was the first African American to be tried on the charge—a distinction that discloses the underlying antiblackness animating the statute's application in this case.[5]

To be sure, the charge of "felony lynching" has been used across racial lines. In 2011, two non-white activists—Tiffany Tran, an Asian American woman, and Alex Brown, an African American man—were arrested on the charges of "felony lynching" at protests with the Occupy Wall Street Movement (OWS) in Oakland, California. In the case of Tran, she "was charged with *lynching herself* by yelling 'help' as the police arrested her"[6]—a legal interpretation that echoed the history of anti-Asian lynchings in the United

States, such as the Los Angeles Chinese Massacre of 1871 and the 1930 Watsonville Massacre. Yet, the peculiar fact that racialized subjects were arrested for the act of lynching themselves was largely eclipsed by the movement's broader focus on socioeconomic inequality part and parcel of late capitalism. Within this anti-capitalist critique and framework, racist police tactics were interpreted as symptoms of a political economy defined by structural and systematic inequality and inequity, rather than as a specific psychical or racialized logic.

Centering the "lynching" arrests of Tran and Brown within the logic of late capitalism—and the racial disparities it purports to explain—encounters a dual impasse. First, it assumes that capitalism might be the cause of racial targeting in law enforcement's use of "lynching" charges. Second, to read "lynching" as a multiracial phenomenon runs the risk of what Jared Sexton has described as a "*people-of-color blindness*, a form of colorblindness inherent to the concept of 'people of color' to the precise extent that it misunderstands the specificity of antiblackness and presumes or insists upon the monolithic character of victimization under white supremacy."[7] Together, these two issues—the explanatory limits of anti-capitalist analysis and the disavowal inherent in the category of "people-of-color"—expose an internal violence and dialectical reversal that enable their political representation. To better situate this critique, I briefly turn to Hamacher to illuminate the foundational violence that must already be in place before the language of capitalism and race can even begin to signify. We are thus compelled to shift our focus: to abandon the analysis of symptoms at the level of surface manifestation and, instead, confront the ontological conditions that determine the possibility of the social, political, and identitarian terms themselves.

Following Walter Benjamin's "Critique of Violence" ("Zur Kritik der Gewalt"), Hamacher's essay "Afformative, Strike" emphasizes the internal violence inherent in the preservation of law. Hamacher both deconstructs Benjamin's "Critique of Violence" and anticipates a liberal reading (and representation) of critique as a restorative gesture—one that masks the foundational violence Benjamin identifies as central to the positing of a law. Benjamin is clear that "in a critique of violence, the standard by which positive law classifies forms of violence cannot undergo its application but rather only its evaluation."[8] This demand for evaluation implies that any standard applied to violence must be questioned as to "what the meaning of this distinction is"[9] between law-positing and law-preserving violence. Hamacher's reading of Benjamin's critique of violence is distinctly pessimistic: there is no outside to the positing of violence because the "representation" (*Vorstellung*) of law's preservation remains trapped within a self-referential logic. As Hamacher explains, representation "is always a form of positing," thereby reinforcing the imposition that representation appears, on the surface, to mitigate or weaken.[10] Hamacher anticipates a resistance to the notion of resistance, arguing that critique itself can reify a dialectical law—an internal reversal (*Umschlag*)—that paradoxically necessitates and sustains the normative representation of law and its violence.

To illustrate the difference between a liberal critique of violence and a radical undoing of law's violence, Hamacher reemphasizes Benjamin's distinction between the political strike and the proletarian general strike. In short, the former works laterally with the institutions under critique—it "is only concerned with inverting the relation of domination, and is still based on the preservation and the strengthening of state violence"[11]—while the latter "aims at nothing less than the abolition of the state apparatus and the legal order maintained by it."[12] The stakes of such an abolition are critical and will be further elaborated in the following sections. For now, Hamacher's insistence that violence remains despite shifting political interests and legislation precisely resonates with our interrogation of the "lynching" arrests, which must be seen as more than a symptom of capitalism. By this measure, the "lynching" arrests are not simply political abuses requiring reform, but rather the structural manifestations that demand a foundational reckoning with the violence that precedes and constitutes the legal order itself. The ontological imperative here necessitates a theoretical break from reformist logic akin to the political strike, aligning instead with the general strike's non-recuperable abolition of the law.

Like the political strike, OWS's critique of capitalism maintains a relationality to both the institutions and the subjects of the state. In the context of the "lynching" arrests during the OWS protest, racialized subjects are positioned under the broad umbrella of late capitalism. Yet by omitting the internal violence of antiblackness that enables the arrests for "lynching" the self, the anti-capitalist critique becomes an unwitting vehicle for violence despite its opposition to state violence. As Hamacher explains, "The presence of violence—which is at least latent in every judicial institution—

complies with a dialectic that forces the disintegrations not of the principle of violence itself and of the power it institutes, but only of its respective forms."[13] Such a dialectic extends beyond judicial institutions to encompass liberal protests and the political strike alike. Consequently, the OWS protest, in its broad failure to acknowledge antiblackness as foundational to the general economies of late capitalism, does not dismantle either the violence of capitalism or the violence that the OWS movement itself might reproduce. Instead, the critique reinstitutes violence in a liberal, "anti-capitalist" form.

Though the "lynching" arrests seemed "out of sync" with the racial liberalism of the early twenty-first century, they were neither a result of late capitalism repressing the racial horrors of lynching nor simply a consequence of the now commonly used formulation of *racial* capitalism, a term that we will unpack more extensively in the following chapter. While "race" *appears* to be an effect of capitalism—as does the use of racist police practices—such an appearance raises the question as to what must necessarily be effaced in order for such effects to be seen. Here is an instance of seeing without eyes—a mode of perception that rests on the "self-lynching" of blackness to allow the positive identity of race to appear. And though these arrests occur across racial lines, they are symptomatic of an antiblack world that is, as Jared Sexton has explained, "inextricable from but irreducible to the history of capitalism."[14] The distinction—"inextricable from" versus "irreducible to" the history of capitalism—is vital: "inextricable from" registers the persistent collusion between antiblackness and capitalist formations, whereas "irreducible to" insists upon the antiblackness's anteriority—an independent structural logic that precedes and secures the racial system. The implication of this distinction is that conventional critique, which only addresses the effects of race and capitalism, remains epistemologically deferred, masking the foundational violence that makes its own language possible.

Frank B. Wilderson describes such violence as an "ensemble of direct relations of force . . . [marking] the emergence of capitalism *itself*."[15] Wilderson's argument points toward a political ontology of antiblackness that animates the relationality between civil society and politics, capitalism and a libidinal economy of antiblackness, the prison and the slave. The gravity of Wilderson's argument orients us away from indicting capitalism as the main culprit of racial discipline, exploitation, and expropriation, and instead allows us to ask how antiblackness sustains the relations between capitalism and violence as its undergirding force. Wilderson theorizes not only blackness's absence from the discourse of capitalism, but also the "conceptual anxiety"[16] symptomatic of phrases such as the "desire to democratise work."[17] Certainly, at this moment in time, there is no shortage of terms that attempt to convey the reach and effects of capitalism. "Racial capitalism" appears as nearly interchangeable with "carceral capitalism," or as the bedfellow of "finance capitalism," and so forth. But what if we consider, following Wilderson, the array of terms not as an opportunity to act on a common political impulse to further name "*the contingency of violence resulting in a 'crisis of authority*'" under the conditions of capitalism, and instead see the oversaturation of terms as symptomatic of a "conceptual anxiety" stemming from a thinking in which blackness remains unthought?[18] For instance, the notion of "carceral capitalism" leads Jackie Wang "to think about the carceral continuum alongside and in conjunction with the dynamics of late capitalism."[19] Carcerality is coterminous with capitalism, both of which include racialized techniques and procedures of racial disciplining, exploitation, and extraction. But the assumption that the violence and racist practices of policing are consequences of "the carceral" and "capitalism" leaves minimal space to examine the conditions enabling their entwinement—or the way they can stand in as analogy for one another. Take, for example, Wang's analysis of "racialized" techniques as part of the machinery of capitalism (i.e., extraction, exploitation, etc.), which she often exemplifies through the subjection of African Americans in cases such as predatory fines and fees imposed by the Ferguson Police Department and the deployment of prison and surveillance technology such as predictive policing. Her argument is often supported by personal anecdotes detailing her own encounter with the systemic violence of the student debt crisis, which she characterizes as a form of racialized violence and carceral control. The charge here is not one of misrepresentation; rather, I am placing pressure on how the exploitation of black labor is reified when blackness is positioned to provide the labor that makes terms such as "carceral capitalism" and "racial capitalism" work. The danger of this positioning is that Wang's own debt becomes an analogical bridge, simultaneously leveraging and diluting black unfreedom to a general condition, rather than acknowledging its structural and singular force as antiblackness. Here, the attempt to conceptualize "the carceral" and "capitalism" as intertwined presumes a structural symmetry; yet, the very possibility of this analogy also reveals a foundational antagonism that must be obscured to convey this shared difference and maintain that coherence. Wang's analysis rests on the explanatory power of capitalism and carcerality—a power that is only secured insofar as blackness is forced to perform the labor of meaning. As a consequence, the occlusion of (anti)blackness enables the normativity of capitalism and carcerality to integrate into a popular political vernacular and imagination. The coherency of these terms is, in short, a structured response to a conceptual anxiety in which blackness remains the unthought foundation.

The unthought of blackness seemingly stands in contradiction to Wang's close attention to the "racialized techniques" of labor launched by capitalism. But what if this is yet another instance of seeing without eyes—or rather, seeing blackness only when it is conscripted to produce the surplus images and terms required by an anti-capitalist vernacular to make "racial capitalism" appear. One cannot see or think the surplus without blackness, not as a figure or value at the levels of the imaginary and the symbolic, but as the blackness of the *real.*

Wang might express some investment (as it were) in the psychic life of antiblackness when she writes: "Though analyses of racial capitalism are much more nuanced than the caricatures of Marxism articulated by Afro-Pessimist thinkers, analyses that focus on how racism is incentivized by capitalism and instrumentalized for monetary gain can sidestep the intractable psychological dimension of racism."[20] Yet ultimately, following thinkers such as Rodolfo Torres and Christopher Kyriakides, Wang dismisses "pessimistic race doctrines, such as doctrines that psychologize racism and naturalize hatred, are politically untenable."[21] To some extent, Afro-Pessimism might agree that to psychologize racism and the effects of capitalism would be to essentialize the degree and kinds of antiblackness that operate within the political economy of capital. But this is also why a critique of political economy is inseparable from the question of the libidinal economy of antiblackness, which is fundamentally distinct from the psychology of individual and collective racism, consumerism, and capitalism. What becomes evident in Wang's misreading of Afro-Pessimism is her undertheorization of blackness that necessitates her own critique: it indicates an underdetermination of blackness that enables her to privilege racial capitalism as her primary analytic category.

Such a reliance on racial capitalism forces the effects of racialization to emerge from the material and conceptual operations of that model of capital. Under this rubric, "Black racialization, then, is the mark that renders subjects as suitable for—on the one hand—hyper-exploitation and expropriation, and, on the other hand, annihilation."[22] However, this formulation—by attempting to unify blackness and labor—collapses the distinction between the ontological condition of (anti)blackness and the social form of the worker. Such a view overlooks the violence and dialectical law that permit categories, including the social form itself, to be conceived. As Sara-Maria Sorentino, following W. E. B. DuBois, observes, "the additive character of racialized work is only one element of Du Bois's dialectic of slavery that *exceeds* 'work' in narrow and even expansive sense."[23] The double-bind, as Sorentino sees it, is in part what "continues to tether whiteness to work and renders the black worker-qua-worker *impossible*."[24]

In this light, Wang's mobilization of an anti-capitalist critique of carceral capitalism risks reproducing the oversights of OWS. As Emahunn Raheem Ali Campbell has observed, "For white activists involved in the Occupy Movement, appealing to a working-class consciousness located somewhere in the psyche of police offers will ultimately lead to police officers being on the side of working-class justice, which may lead to the immediate dissolution of racism."[25] Yet as Campbell clarifies, "This position, needless to say, is quite deterministic,"[26] illuminating how such a relational analysis offers only a momentary reprieve while establishing a deterministic reading of and response to racism. Such relational models leave these critiques epistemologically constrained and unable to apprehend the ontological necessity of antiblackness. Anchored in the continuous, structural act of blackness's "self-lynching," such violence necessitates an abolition of the *real* that exceeds the logic of (and desire for) political remediation. Anything less than this ontological demand merely reproduces the very epistemological limits and constrained political horizons that uphold antiblackness.

Just as the appeal to a (white) working class seeks a psychic reconciliation with the police ("somewhere in the psyche of police officers"), Wang's conceptualization of carceral capitalism presumes the possibility of abolition through material reform. But blackness—here black liberation and black working-class struggle—is once again usurped like ethnographic evidence to animate a fantasy of overcoming class exploitation. The presumption here relies on a notion of class where, as Sorentino explains, "class is thought to be liberated for the imagination, freed from its relegated role as 'structural *location*' unto its vitalization as 'social *relation*.'"[27] Situating this in the broader context of the "lynching" arrests, it is evident that the terms essential to an analysis and critique of capitalism and policing are insufficient for examining the "conceptual anxiety," symptomatic of antiblackness, that Wilderson describes. In respect to the possibility of political strategy, Wilderson distances himself from a Gramscian Marxist and conventional historical materialist method which might lend itself to what Antonio Gramsci described as a "war of position" as opposed to a "war of maneuver."[28] In contrast to Gramsci's notion of a sustained and gradual effort against hegemony (a "war of position"), Wilderson forwards "the value of reintroducing the unthought category of the slave, by way of noting the absence of the black subject"—a value that "expands the intensity of the antagonism" by extending the demand against state and capital beyond the limits of historical materialism.[29]

Wilderson's proposition, to say the least, is neither recuperative nor reconciliatory. For him, the unthought position of blackness is latent to the intensity of political antagonisms while remaining paradoxically anterior to symbolic law. Such a position renders the unthought of blackness beyond recuperation at the level of the imaginary, let alone at the register of dreams. This structural irreducibility stands in stark contrast to Wang's final provocation in her critique of carceral capitalism:

> Imagining and working toward a world without prisons—which is the project of prison abolition—would not only require us to fundamentally rethink the role of the state in society, but it would also require us to work toward the total transformation of all social relations. A project as lofty and ambitious as this is easy to dismiss as unrealistic, utopian, impractical, naïve—*an unrealizable dream*. But what if—instead of reacting to these charges with counter-arguments that persuasively demonstrate that the abolitionist position is the only sensible position—we instead use these charges themselves as a point of departure to show the prison itself is a problem for thought that can only be unthought using *a mode of thinking that does not capitulate to the realism of the Present*?[30]

The peculiar anti-intellectual tone nestled within the dismissal of "persuasive counter-arguments" aside, Wang's exhortation to reconceptualize abolition fosters "*a mode of thinking*" that secures itself through a lynching of blackness, its displacement and erasure. In her gestures to "unthink" the prison, blackness is subjected to a secondary displacement and erasure—sacrificed to maintain the coherence of a utopian project that remains tethered to the "social relations" it claims to transform.

Wang's approach productively shortchanges her commitment to a DuBois lineage by prioritizing the idiomatic conceptualization of the prison as the primary problem for thought. Such a move overlooks the depth of Nahum Chandler, whose extensive engagement with DuBois identifies "the problem of the negro as the problem for thought."[31] The appropriation, ironically, enacts Chandler's own concerns that portend the (un)thought of blackness as the catalyst for "the displacement of a question, indeed, a certain double displacement." In bypassing the singularity of blackness to reach the carceral, Wang evades the essential DuBoisian "question *of being*": "How does it feel to be a problem?"[32] As such, the "unthought," or the desire to unthink, the prison functions as a foreclosure of blackness to remedy the "conceptual anxiety" of the state by completing the exact erasure the state initially set out to perform.

The "self-lynching" of blackness, I argue, operates by suspending the ontological question of black non-being. Foreclosing the possibility of being, the suspension yields it to the utopian horizon of "the total transformation of all social relations" and to conjured dreams of abolition. Insofar as this "*mode of thinking*" might encourage us to imagine the reconfiguration of preexisting relationalities that make up the prison-industrial complex, it maintains the conceptual framework and representation of both the prison *and* abolition at the behest of—and for the sake of—(anti)blackness. In brief, the stakes of (anti)blackness are themselves lynched. As blackness remains unthought, it inhabits an unreachable and intolerable realm beyond the navel of the dream: the impossible point of reach for interpretation and meaning that nevertheless animates the conditions of possibility for thoughts and dreams of abolition. To this effect, we might ask, as Patrice Douglass has, "what happens to the centrality of Blackness in the visions of abolition?"[33]

Against the overreaching critique of capitalism that conjures "race" and "racism" as a relational effect, black criticism has often pointed out that the political banner of "Occupy," alongside the even broader agenda of the fight against capitalism, conveys a reactionary afterthought in respect to (anti) blackness. Stacy Patton's observations of OWS ground this critique, noting that "perhaps white Americans are now paying the psychic price for not answering the basic questions that blacks have long raised about income inequality."[34] The psychic toll Patton paints for us here reflects a more profound crisis of white self-coherence, where the erosion of economic security threatens to dissolve the categorical distinctions that stabilize whiteness. Therefore, in contrast to the view that racist police tactics collude with regimes of capitalism, why not consider, as Brian Jordan Jefferson suggests, that "nonwhite death induces a collective effervescence for a class that dimly senses itself in a state of ontological flux."[35] Indisputably, "drawing out relations between racialized police killings and lynching is quite apt"; lest we forget "that spikes in festival lynchings during the 1890s were linked to small farmers faced with a depression that threatened their property and sense of autonomy. When the institutions of civil society fail the white precariat, the state of nature will suffice."[36] As opposed to a breakdown of order, the failure of civil society indexes the exact threshold where the ontological repair of whiteness through antiblack violence becomes a structural imperative.

On this point, there is yet another facet of why capitalism, or even "racial capitalism," proves a misnomer in characterizing the lynching arrests during the OWS protests. While Tran's arrest might suggest an ostensibly "multiracial" targeting—upholding a deceptive "people-of-color blindness"—subsuming these arrests under the broad umbrella of "racism" only further obscures the *afterlife* of slavery. In the context of the anti-capitalist agenda, "racism" and "racial capitalism" often function as two sides of the same coin. "Racism," as kihana miraya ross has explained, "isn't a meaningless term. But it's a catch-all that can encapsulate anything from black people being denied fair access to mortgage loans, to Asian students being burdened with a 'model minority' label. It's not specific."[37] Calvin Warren reinforces this distinction when he notes that antiblackness cannot be reducible to a psychoanalytic account of the racial Other and thereby cannot be made synonymous with racism. He avers, "This understanding of racism . . . does not quite work for *anti-blackness* and, in particular, police brutality against black bodies. To put a finer point on it, racism and anti-blackness are not identical, interchangeable, or analogous."[38] Both ross and Warren respectively speak to the incommensurability of antiblackness that can neither be refined nor captured in a more precise term, nor compromised through a seemingly better moral standing driven by racial guilt. To conceive the "lynching" arrests as a problem that arises from racial capitalism or a broad notion of racism occludes the incommensurability of antiblackness that enables the perceptibility of a racial logic part and parcel of policing and the possibility of its political elaboration.

The perceptibility of this racial logic relies upon a specific distribution of bodies that often invites a reading of Tran's arrest—the only Asian American woman involved—as an instance of "exceptionality." Yet, to frame the arrest in this way is to participate in a perverse structural displacement. While such assertions of exceptionalism often invite counter-critiques, such as that of the "model minority" cliché or "the demand to go 'beyond black and white,'"[39] I am primarily concerned with how both positions—claiming exceptionality or demanding a "neither-nor"[40]—mirror one another by simultaneously displacing and incorporating blackness to substantiate their respective claims. While racialization and racial formation successfully address the discursive production of race and its social identities, they ultimately obscure the ontological conditions of antiblackness that render blackness as nothingness. This suggests that the disavowal of antiblackness must necessarily be elided for this "racial" logic to function: for this logic to work, blackness must be lynched. As we have discussed throughout this book, the "self-lynching" of blackness—the suspension of blackness from being and becoming, and its prohibition from formations of the self—maintains the "racial" logic of policing in respect to the racialization of Asians and Asian Americans.[41]

The recognition and imagined stability of racial identity categories rely on the misrecognition of blackness. In other words, the articulation of racial differentiations is inseparable from a necessary misrecognition—what psychoanalytic thought might describe as a "recognition . . . overlaid with misrecognition"[42]—which takes for granted the certainty derivative of being "*above all not Black*."[43] Such a rhetorical suspension of blackness parallels the displacement that conjures the arrests of "self-lynching." Asian Americanness is with certainty not black; yet blackness, in its definitive and violent exclusion, remains absolutely fundamental to that identity's framing and meaning.

In view of this structural framing, the reinforcement of a "black-and-white" framework, to whichever degree it strives to establish racialized identities, emerges as yet another iteration of multiracial politics. As Sexton notes in his rigorous critique of the politics of multiracialism and its coterminous movements of coalition:

> Multiracialism serves more as a rationalizing discourse for the continued and increasing social, political, and economic *isolation* of blacks. In this sense, I suggest that multiracialism arbitrates neoconservative racial politics as an indispensable libidinal accompaniment to an advancing neoliberalism that is itself oscillating between official (liberal) multiculturalism and the (conservative) posture of colorblindness.[44]

Sexton's analysis puts into sharp relief not only, nor simply, the internal contradictions that are at work in the politics of multiracialism, but importantly evinces how the varying displays of "race" prove to be a mechanism of containment. Containment, as well, makes false appearances. For if containment is counterintuitively a mode of inclusive formation "as a purely *formal* negation of racial blackness,"[45] then the liberal gesticulation of racial consciousness in mirroring its conservative counterpart would only maintain the displacement and dissimulation of blackness both within and beyond the scope of the lynching arrests. The failure then of any analysis that critiques liberalism or neoliberalism as the sole drivers of these "lynching" arrests is its tendency to reduce any political and philosophical meaning of blackness to the conciliatory registers of reform. Such a reduction evades the broader structure of racial anxiety that might, nonetheless, propel an itinerary of a politics of abolition.[46]

In following the chapter's provocation of having a vision without seeing the violence before one's eyes, the previous section concluded by challenging the racially liberal representation of the "lynching" arrests. Such a rendering, I argued, necessitates a reading that coincides with and corroborates a critique of late capitalism. By turning to Hamacher, we see that both liberal representations and readings of violence avoid addressing and therefore reproduce an internal violence—that of antiblackness—and reinforce a dialectical law that prohibits the possibility of going beyond a (neo)liberal protest of resistance, critique of violence, and by implication the symbolic calls for abolition. Our methodology, therefore, must not attempt to posit an alternative truth that risks becoming a new dogma; it is necessary, rather, that our critique remain committed to the ceaseless de-posing (*Entsetzung*) of the legal-violent structure to which antiblackness is foundational, lest the critique of antiblack violence reproduces the dialectical trap it seeks to expose. The un-setting of the legal-violent structure thus compels the exposure of analytic terms, such as "race" or "racism," that risk reifying the very violence they are meant to analyze. Such a diagnostic maneuver is essential because the liberal impulse to frame the "lynching" arrests as "multiracial" reinforces the internal violence of antiblackness that underlies both a "black-and-white" framework and "people-of-colorblindness." In the following section, we will consider the illusory sense of uncanniness that accompanies the fallacy of seeing the "lynching" arrests as if for the first time.

Afterlife: Uncanniness and Unhomeliness

In the introduction to this book, I argued that the language of law and race continues to codify antiblackness even in the gesture of removing racially charged rhetoric from legal texts. Thus far in this chapter, I have similarly examined how rhetorical banners of liberal politics, such as the anti-capitalist critique of Occupy Wall Street or the broader indictments of "carceral capitalism" or "racial capitalism," instrumentalize the figure of or proximity to blackness while ignoring its violent appropriation and seizure. These instances reveal the "self-lynching" of blackness, in which the castration or suspension of blackness is not only a necessity that makes such appearances possible, but also relies on and reproduces the refiguration and simultaneous disfiguration of blackness which enable the categories of "race" to appear. In what follows, I discuss how the lynching of blackness as a possible self or being is reflected in the way Richards Abdullah and the black witness, who repeatedly asks for her statement to be taken, are interpolated as non-subjects.

In Chapter 4, I argued that the forty-year gap between the enactment of the anti-lynching legislation and the court's first interpretation of the penal code does not imply that lynchings had ceased. On the contrary, the temporal gap exposes how antiblackness undergirds the violent strictures of the juridical archive, revealing the material constraints in recording a (black) witness's testimony of lynching. The *afterlife of slavery* has been commonly used to describe the periods following the institutional emancipation from slavery that still keep slavery's formal practices, policies, and *de jure* and *de facto* laws well and alive. More than this, however, we have seen that this *afterlife* also entails the lethal authority of racial perception—the deadly judgment imposed and projected upon blackness—and the aesthetic character that visually determines blackness as the structure of historical disappearance, a perpetual relic necessary for the appearance of the contemporary racial order. The survival of the image indicates the persistent labor of translating the untranslatability of blackness misleadingly as an epiphanic moment. Richards Abdullah's arrest is uncanny not merely because it takes place nearly seventy years after the enactment of anti-lynching legislation, nor because it highlights the classificatory failure of the law. Beyond linear time and shifting legal interpretations, the uncanniness of Richards Abdullah's "self-lynching" arrest distills how blackness brings *afterlife* into meaning and, likewise, how blackness, as non-meaning, brings meaning into the image, sustaining the very concept of *afterlife* itself.

To grasp the structural mechanism by which blackness, as non-meaning, invigorates the concept of *afterlife*, we can turn to Jacques Lacan's explanation of the *vel* of alienation. This *vel* of alienation is situated in a wider discussion on the properties of semantics where one side of language appears as meaning, as opposed to the other side that is characterized as disappearance.[47] He writes, "If we choose meaning, the meaning survives only deprived of that part of non-meaning that is, strictly speaking, that which constitutes in the realization of the subject, the unconscious."[48] Lacan thus highlights the capacity of survival that stems from non-meaning—the eclipsed side of the signifier. In doing so, he also illustrates the homology between non-meaning and the unconscious as the negative condition that constitutes language and the subject respectively.

Placing this feature of survival together with our earlier discussions of Benjamin's concept of *afterlife* as *Fortleben*, we observe how blackness enables the meaning of *afterlife*—the capacity of survival—of the contemporary racial order, but only insofar as blackness remains consigned to the side of non-meaning. Frantz Fanon succinctly captures this structural assignment when he writes, "And there you have it; I did not create a meaning for myself; the meaning was already there, waiting."[49] Such pre-assigned, structural meaning—predicated upon blackness as non-meaning—disrupts the viewing subject's sense of time and self when confronting the "lynching" arrest of Richards Abdullah. The resulting exposure of non-meaning simultaneously functions as a stimulus of upheaval and a foundation of systemic coherence—upheaval through the shock of the structural void, and coherence through the law's subsequent absorption of that void into its own antiblack criterion. The structural violence that lynches the black *imago* as non-meaning is thus what renders disparate elements of the arrests—the conversion from riot to lynching, the scene's (un)timeliness, and the ultimate "self-lynching"—perversely coherent.

In order to understand how Richards Abdullah's arrest belongs to the *afterlife* of lynching through the non-meaning of blackness, let us return to the ambiguous moment in which a nonviolent protest is perceived as a riot. This scene casts light on how the lynching of blackness in its non-meaning enables the possibility of meaning and capacity for *afterlife*. Recall the escalation leading to Richards Abdullah's arrest, which I described in the introduction. To legitimize the intervention, the police informed the business owner a citizen's arrest would be necessary, since the police did not witness the alleged incident in question. The officers further assured the business owner of their arresting powers, implying immunity from the potential litigation that a citizen's arrest often invites. Here, the private citizen and the state collude to purposefully interpret Richards Abdullah's resistance to her own detention as an attempt to initiate a riot by interfering with her own arrest, in an effort to lynch herself. Opposing this interpretation by the police and business owner is the witness recording the encounter. We hear her pleading with the police to accept her witness statement; a refusal to do so, as she rightly notes, is illegal. The gulf between the two—the business owner's deputized entitlement and the ontological rejection of the black witness—presents us with an image of antiblack police violence that is constituted by the simultaneous lynching and policing of blackness.

As mentioned previously, the definition of "lynching" has been maintained, even in the removal of the word "lynching," at the material symbolic level and for the purposes of a juridical interpretation that bolsters state security. Yet, we must critically move beyond viewing the police-sanctioned citizen's arrest as just another instance of law and order's failure or the carceral materialization of antiblackness. While the collusion between citizenry and the police is an explicit formation of mob rule designed to circumvent the boundaries of normative juridical rule, it is the image of a black riot turned into "self-lynching"—a fantasy weaponized by law enforcement and citizenry—that is taken as real. Taken as reality, this fantasmatic image of a black riot turning against itself reveals that antiblackness is irreducible to being the object of policing. While an image, of course, can be an object, the perceived image of a black riot as a lynching of blackness invites us to consider how desire filters not just *what* one sees in and as the image, but *how* and *why* one perceives that image as a real and persistent effect. Such perception, in turn, shapes the infinite here-and-now: the *afterlife* of the lynching of blackness.

By the same token, the exclusion of the black witness underwrites the collusion between police and citizen, rather than the converse being true. The former illustrates the necessary interdiction of blackness that conditions the transition of the fantasmatic image both into reality and to the *real*, permitting police and citizenry to enter the space of representation as sovereign subjects. The demand for the image also reveals the specific desire that animates it. Independent from the objects of antiblackness, desire revolves around a void, a void that can be understood as ontological, the non-being of blackness. It is precisely this prohibition of blackness within the image that makes the image of policing possible, and not the other way around.

In effect then, the staging of differences—authority and subjugation, the witness as the bearer of truth and the complete annulment of that possibility—points us to what falls outside the frame of the image: the frames of contract and contact between the police and citizen, the frames of the video, and so forth. When we ask what the conditions are that make these imagined representations of rioting as lynching appear real, the question here is not solely how or why one psychical content, but also why a specific psychical representative (*psychische Repräsentanz*)[50] takes precedence over the other. We, thus, find a process in which certain instinctual representatives (*Triebrepräsentanzen*)[51] hijack the representation of reality to exclusively occupy the *real*. These instinctual representatives revolve in some part around affect, the intensities felt through the libidinal charges of cathexis from an ideation, or an attachment to a set of ideas.[52] Lacan defines that which exposes a hole in representation as the *real*.[53] In a distinct account of the *real*, Fanon foregrounds the role of "real fantasy" that intrudes upon the symbolic, distorting the distinction between the *real* and reality. Or as Marriott explains, "The real fantasy of race is experienced only in the way the spectator is traversed by what she or he fails to see rather than what she or he sees, the gaze that judges and condemns, and/or solicits and seduces."[54] Such a gaze functions as a preemptive foreclosure of blackness, shaping the appearance of "race" before the arrest arrives—both at the level of the imaginary and symbolic. The traversal splits across the scene of the arrest and the subjects involved, serving to define their frames. Between the citizen's arrest and the denial of the witness's statement—at the edge of the shifting frames that mark the enclosure of representation—the real-fantasy of (anti)blackness and its hallucinatory effects beget an unbridled violence.[55]

The foreclosure of the black woman's right to provide a witness statement and the psychical dynamics that determine what is included in the frame bring us back to the beginning of this chapter, which asked what it means to see without eyes. In this vein, we are also invited back to the question of what it means to see the terror of the "lynching" arrests in an uncanny way. Sigmund Freud's definition of uncanniness (*das Unheimliche*) is to see something familiar *as if* unfamiliar—that experience of encountering something repeatedly yet also as if for the first time. If we understand this notion of uncanniness to be a sign of the return of the repressed, then we are presented not just with a concern of appearance and image, the repetitious image of black death, but also see how the tension between racial identification and unconscious knowledge, between what one sees and what one desires to see, manages to elicit meaning from where blackness is unhomely. Given our earlier discussions of *afterlife* as a mode of translation (in the footsteps of Benjamin), I argue that the *afterlife* of slavery materializes through blackness's unhomeliness in language. This prompts the question: Can blackness ever find a home or homeliness in language? It also raises the question why or how the (im)materiality of language would be different in any way, or free from the "the occult presence of racial slavery,"[56] in its pernicious translations and intensifications *as afterlife*.

To explicate further, let me clarify how I am using the notion of homeliness (*das Heimliche*), which stems largely from Freud's definition of the term "uncanny" (*das Unheimliche*). In his well-known essay, "The Uncanny," Freud reminds his readers

> that this word *heimlich* is not unambiguous, but belongs to two sets of ideas, which are not mutually contradictory, but very different from each other—the one relating to what is familiar and comfortable, the other to what is concealed and kept hidden. *Unheimlich* is the antonym of *heimlich* only in the latter's first sense, not in its second."[57]

Drawing on the work of F. W. J. Schelling, Freud clarifies that *unheimlich* complicates this supposedly neat opposition between the familiar and the unfamiliar, teasing out something "unexpected" from the meaning of *unheimlich* itself: "namely, that the term 'uncanny' (*unheimlich*) applies to everything that was intended to remain secret, hidden away, and has come into the open."[58] In this way, the uncanny is defined as a "species of the frightening that goes back to what was once well known and had long been familiar."[59] Freud goes on to explore "under what conditions the familiar can become uncanny and frightening"[60]—conditions that he explores through the use of other languages to illustrate how "we ourselves speak a foreign language."[61] The foreign language that Freud speaks of alludes to the most repressed dimensions of a self, which are, nonetheless, fundamental in the making of a self, the formation of the ego, in relationship to its surrounding objects. Importantly, Freud distinguishes the foreignness of language from how language appears to be foreign to oneself via modes of alienation concomitant with the process of repression. Freud's emphasis on language in respect to the appearance of the (un)familiar (that is, the return of the repressed) forwards concerns about the perceived threat of blackness and the implications of its recognition and misrecognition: the question of what it means to be out of sync with a shared sense of time despite the recurrence of the repressed, and what recourse, if any, to language might unsettle the familiar terror of antiblackness.

The uncanniness of the "lynching" arrest reveals then a double exposure: the familiar sense of estrangement screens out blackness without place, time, or term—which is to say that the sense of uncanniness is a distortion that masks the unhomeliness of blackness but is also constituted by this masking. This, to be sure, contrasts with Freud's explanation that the *Heimliche* activates the *Unheimliche*.[62] But it is not that far removed from his statement that "the double has become an object of terror."[63] These points are not mutually exclusive; rather, the invention of the double figure is something quite different from merely representing a mode of repression. It is significant that the content changes and continues to "acquire a new content." Perhaps more than this, "the meaning of the 'double' changes"[64] insofar as it shows that the object of terror is not just about the object itself. The double stands for something that manages in one way or another to cause such terror without any immediate explanation of how its representation comes to take place, and through what process of dissimulation, disfiguration, and distortion it can appear. The terror continues to be effective while the displacement of lynching's racial terror happens in real time and in plain sight.

Moreover, the displacement of lynching's racial terror is a force of terror in itself. In this respect, the uncanny terror of the "lynching" arrests has less to do with appearance and the image of the double (or what might be characterized as the repeated appearances of antiblack policing); but rather indicates how such appearances are inseparable from the pathological, since the latter's elicitation "[involves] a harking back to single phases in the evolution of the sense of self, a regression to times when the ego had not yet clearly set itself off against the world outside and from others."[65] Such a state of defenselessness, reminiscent of the infancy period during which one's exposure to the world is utterly vulnerable, also plays a crucial role in facilitating a sense of what is seen as if for the first time, yet overwhelmingly familiar. But while this intensity might induce a contingent sense of vertigo for some, it is positioned as, Wilderson notes, "objective vertigo" for blackness, "a life constituted by disorientation rather than a life interrupted by disorientation. This is structural as opposed to performative violence."[66]

Along these lines, Wilderson has emphasized the wanton scope of antiblackness, noting that "the world is not ready to think about policing the way that it affects black people. We are policed all the time and everywhere."[67] For Wilderson, the deceptively brief assertion that "there is no World without Blacks"[68] tarries with the unfathomable abyss between the solidity of the world and the unthinkability of policing blackness. In this schema, black death serves as the unthought that secures the coherence of the world. As Sexton indicates in reference to Wilderson's statement, "Not because police brutality as such is not a pervasive problem and a moral threat, but rather because the reigning political philosophy has been built on the fundamental concepts and categories inadequate for the analysis."[69] The production of knowledge corroborates with policing in the most unremarkable of ways: the unthought of blackness facilitates not only the ubiquitous surveillance in each corner of everyday life, but also the unrelenting psychic intrusions of judgment, scrutiny, aggression, and murderous desires.[70] Rizvana Bradley extends this logic when she explains, "Unworlding is the dehiscence which is immanent to black existence as nonbeing . . . Unworlding marks the condition of (im)possibility for every worlding's imperial promise."[71] Wilderson's, Sexton's, and Bradley's interventions elucidate for us a displaced ethical dilemma: antiblackness animates the world only to ensure that blackness remains policed, wounded, and unthought—violently exposed to the *real*. Under such a fatal structure, "the future belongs to the bullet."[72] This structural finality raises the rhetorical question of when and where policing begins, and whether it ever ends for blackness. If being in the world means being nothing—a nothingness met by the state's lead—then this void of meaning confirms blackness's perpetual nonsovereignty. Blackness thus occupies no positionality except through the violence of unhomeliness. As such, the unhomeliness of blackness provides the very meaning of the world's homeliness; it is the structural guarantee upon which the world's self-conception of its own homely existence is founded.

Wilderson's emphasis on the world's subsumption of blackness as a mode of defense reconfigures Freud's notion of the uncanny. In contrast to the subject who has established a defense mechanism in respect to the perception of an unhomeliness in their sense of self against "the world," Wilderson suggests that it is "the world" itself that must maintain a resistance to and against blackness. Such modes of resistance, in terms of a psychical dynamic, coalesce with the internal projections and external policing of blackness. Psychically speaking, policing blackness is never far from the lynching of blackness—the necessary castration and murderous suspension that authorizes the maintenance of law and order by force at the level of the imaginary; "the tension of force"[73] that, as we discussed in Chapter 2, is inseparable from the seduction of forms. To this extent, the psychical complex of policing and lynching blackness is an inextricable part of establishing the coherence of the world, including the sense of self which is established in and for it. As a sort of effigy, blackness must stand in as "a 'double' in the way death itself is the double of the living."[74]

In the introduction and in this chapter, we have explored the application and instrumentalization of force to police and lynch blackness—a force that precedes the actual "lynching" arrests, and the ways in which blackness is imagined to riot against itself. It follows that this unrelenting force, which provides the capacity for law and order to articulate what qualifies as reason, duty, self, rests on the incapacitation of blackness. Thus, antiblackness cannot *solely* be reduced to the policing of black social positionalities. Nor can an analysis of this force be limited to the discursive production of racial formation concomitant with dominant modes of power, since the force of antiblackness is a structurally ontological problematic rather than an epistemological or discursive one. Furthermore, extending the argument from Chapter 3, blackness cannot be reduced to a psychical *object* or the target of an antiblack drive, since the drive is indifferent to its objects and "desire is always directed at something other than—something more than—the object demanded."[75] To suggest that blackness is an object would falsely imply that it could be understood as a coherent identity at the level of the imaginary; such an assumption essentializes its existence precisely when it is construed as the drive's aim. These implications miss how blackness remains indelibly wretched, subtending the formation of a racial imaginary in respect to "the intolerable *real* of blackness."[76] As Fanon reminds us, "Such a [phobic] object does not come out of the void of nothingness . . . For the object, naturally, need not be there, it is enough that somewhere the object *exists*: is a possibility."[77] Fanon's observations paint a clear picture of how the phobic object is irreal in insidious ways which nonetheless function to compel and sustain the racial anxieties, fear, animus that circumscribe the exposure of blackness to the *real*. Such circumscription can be inferred through the ways in which the imaginary and the symbolic work together to dissemble (anti) blackness.

The impossibility of the black woman's testimony clarifies this point. The violence that renders her testimony disposable is symptomatic of the ways in which blackness—in its unhomeliness—resists the order and representation of language, not least in the language and procedures of the law. Yet, both in this resistance to language and the violence that constitutes the state's semblance of a symbolic order, blackness is registered as a threat—one that is immediately translated into a mandate for policing. The displacement of the black woman's possibility to witness parallels the transformation of Richards Abdullah's peaceful protest into an act of rioting and de-arresting herself, a hallucinatory shift that provides the opening for the implementation of juridical rule in the subjection and disciplining of blackness. In what follows, we will consider the wider implications of being seen as a threat from the structural vantage of a complex of perversion.

Perversions, Petrification, Policing

In an interview with Nana Gyamfi, Richards Abdullah's lawyer, and Melina Abdullah, at the time an organizer with BLM Pasadena, Abdullah makes a trenchant point: "Jasmine is a political prisoner and represents probably *the hugest threat* to the state, in that the folks at the bottom can recognize their own oppression and rise up against it."[78] Abdullah's observation of a perverse identification and modes of repression desired by the racial state—which views Richards Abdullah as an immovable threat—magnifies the Manichaean division and order that petrify the subject. Fanon uses these latter terms to describe a "world compartmentalized, Manichaean and petrified, a world of statues . . . A world cocksure of itself, crushing with its stoniness the backbones of those scarred by the whip."[79] Unequivocally, such racial division at its most ontological depth is an invention by the racial state—one that the law can neither exist nor function without, but one that also cannot be without the figure and figurations of the wretched. The invention of racial division is not only instrumentalized by the racial state system to enforce modes of policing and custody, but simultaneously reifies the racial judgment that casts blackness as wretched.

Custody is, thus, imposed by the racial state and executed by the police, but there is also the psychical custody that precedes the *event* of physical arrest—one in which blackness is held captive. Whereas in an earlier version of this chapter, I conceived Richards Abdullah to be positioned as an "eternal captive,"[80] we might better understand this sense of "timelessness" against the etymological evocation of the word "eternal," which implies an *existence* that lasts forever. However, rather than invoking *existence*, it would perhaps be more appropriate to limn Richards Abdullah's position within the wretchedness of an irredeemable void; she occupies an absence which Marriott describes as "the fear and hatred of an infinite unknown that has no bulwark with which one can surround it, and no plea that can deliver one from it. An ineffable blackness that has no witnesses: a timeless, *infinite* unknown."[81] Though this is nothing short of a life not lived, it reveals a (non-) being under the freight of foisted damnation—a figure that the law cannot function without, but which the law must invent, and in which blackness is the contamination of law.

The immediate necessity to position blackness as the contamination of the law—to hold blackness in custody and maintain the circuits of policing—offers a glimpse into a perverse dynamic where the subject (here, the law) asserts its necessary right to enjoyment and fulfillment. The complex of perversion exemplified in the lynching and policing of blackness clarifies why the language of rights remains essential to the law's operation. Such language is less about the law's duty or command and more about its modus operandi in the incapacitation of blackness. The discourse of rights—a language shared by law and psychoanalysis—is fundamentally teleological. In the determination of rights as telos, we find a basic privilege that blackness is without, since the determination of the subject—let alone the subject of rights—is untenable against the lynching and arrest of blackness as a self. To this end, the shared grammar of rights also betrays a metapsychological fracture: it presumes a subject whose sovereignty is sutured by the foreclosure of blackness—the unthought and psychical violence of antiblackness.

Take for example Abdullah's observation of Richards Abdullah's arrest as a state symbol of singular power used to punish those who try to circumvent normalized juridical rule. Abdullah incisively notes the irony of a conviction for "felony lynching":

> [I]t's ironic that she's charged and convicted with felony lynching, when the real lynching that's carried out is done in the same way it was carried out in the late 19th, early 20th century, where it's supposed to punish those who dare to rise up against the system. But also, you leave the body hanging from a tree to send a signal to the rest of those black folks who might want to get out of line, and remind them that the state has more power than they do.[82]

On the one hand, much of what Abdullah describes as the state's desire to assert itself as the sole authority of the law follows a basic psychoanalytic definition of perversion in which "a manifest perversion may express not defiance of the law of the father, but rather obedience to [the law of the father] . . . which confines perversion to its marginal status, or obedience to the same law."[83] On the other hand, more perverse than this demand for conformity is when the law's conviction as the sole proprietor of representations—of freedom and unfreedom, life and death—is taken as an absolute necessity. The collapse between the state and white citizenry is rendered as a requirement of order, and so too is their joint mutilation, murder, and hanging of blackness. In this perverse logic, lynching is no longer construed as racial terror but is recast as a symbol of requisite power, authority, and order. The charge of "felony lynching" is itself a lynching of blackness; both irreal and real, perverse yet normalized, the lynching of blackness brings into view the machination of laws but also the violence within the laws of representation.

Such perverse structural logic requires us to reflect on the foundational positioning of the enslaved who ostensibly "consents" to submitting to the law. In her landmark essay, "Mama's Baby, Papa's Maybe," Hortense Spillers explains at length the double-bind of the slave in the law's application and intent. Spillers chronicles the continuum of violence emerging from the logic of property and the Middle Passage that inaugurates what she incisively conceives as "perversions of juridical power," the operations of law that were necessarily enacted as *high crimes* against the flesh of the racial slave.[84] Following the study of slavery's juridical codes by abolitionist and reformer William Goodell, Spillers observes how "the rhetorical and moral passions of the abolitionist project . . . also lend insight into the corpus of law that underwrites enslavement."[85] For Spillers, this window reflects how the juridico-legal codes of slavery "crystallize in the precise moment when agitation against the arrangement [of slavery] becomes articulate."[86] Critically elaborating on Goodell, she writes:

> The "slave" is movable by nature, but "immovable by the operation of law" (24). As I read this, law itself is compelled to a point of saturation, or a reverse zero degree, beyond which it cannot move in the behalf of the enslaved *or* the free. We recall too, that the "master," under these perversions of juridical power, is impelled to *treat* the enslaved as property, and not as personality. These laws stand for the kind of social formulation that armed forces will help excise from a living context in the campaigns of civil war.[87]

Spillers outlines the excess of violence in the law that also grants its power by incapacitating the slave. Gesturing to the essential construction of the "slave," Spillers insinuates how blackness—as the "enslaved *or* the free"—is rendered necessarily static under the logic of property and as operationalized by law. Crucially, the perversion of juridical power, Spillers explains, is not isolated to the logic of property as it underlies armed strategies of bodily and psychic removal of blackness, that is, a militaristic operation moving across key historical moments that remain decisive in the deliberation of freedom and abolition at the level of rights and constitutional discourse. In this sense, perversion can be seen in the use of disavowal by the subject of law. The enslaved is called into existence only to be enjoyed, manipulated, and violated by the law. Law and the rule of juridical power are enabled by the same dynamic of racial sexual violence enacted by the master. Typically, within the complex of perversion, the subject makes itself available as the enjoyment, the object, for the Other's *jouissance*.[88] Here, however, the enslaved is kept from any possibility of enjoyment. The perverse dynamic, as Marriott has critically pointed out, exceeds the scope of "sexual intimacy between masters and slaves."[89] The condemnation of black desire extends beyond master and slave, because the taboo of black desire is essential for maintaining a racial state system that is "also the effect of the perceived *unconstraints* of black being and desire."[90]

Reorienting the analysis moves our view of perversion from a relational dynamic to a structural function. Spillers's framework of the "perversion of juridical power" helps us interrogate further the incredible scale of antiblack policing as a mode of lynching that has as one of its aims the incapacitation of blackness. Primarily, this framework amplifies how prior to identifying blackness as flesh in regard to the captive's "body," blackness is seen as available for the "zero degree of social conceptualization that does not escape the concealment under the brush of discourse."[91] By incapacitating blackness in this way, "perversions of juridical power" exploit not just the slave's body but any imagined figures and figurations of blackness as the surface upon which the law inscribes its operations and justifies its application. As Sexton elaborates in regard to Spillers's ruminations:

> Spillers finds useful the conceptual discrimination between the domain of the *operation* of the law (in which it is historically determinate of social, political, and economic existence) and the domain of the *application* of the law (in which it solicits the consent of the governed or, in another parlance, the identification of the dominant position). A law may be inapplicable, enabling an array of subversion and resistance at the level

> of infrapolitics, or better, providing preconditions for effective opposition, but that does not thereby make it inoperative—maybe not even a little bit.[92]

Sexton outlines the operative intent that enables both "the effective opposition" and the drive of its entire operation. The conceptual discrimination between *operation* and *application*, which is often overlooked or conflated, fades completely in the slave's apparent "consent" to the submission of law. The resulting perversion of juridical power here happens on multiple levels. On one hand, there is the unfettered abuse that renders blackness into flesh at the expense of the law's application and operation. On the other hand, the conceptual discrimination that Sexton delineates based on Spillers also elucidates the obfuscation of the law's means and ends, disclosing the instrumental purposes of the representation of laws, but also the laws of that representation. With regard to the "felony lynching" arrest of Richards Abdullah, perversion plays out insidiously as a carceral course of action that relies on the racial determination of self-restraint. As Marriott limns the underlying logic and what it dictates: "The very notion of self-restraint is racially determined: the act of reining in, or better still, the act of self-repression, encodes a social hygiene whose sources are racial and therefore, not natural."[93]

Perversion operates before and beyond the visible executions of law enforcement and (non-black) citizenry, since it actively suppresses expressions of black desire that strive for liberation from an imposed slavishness and criminalization. Such a libidinal economy explains why any gesture of black life that transgresses the desires of the state, namely in the movement for black life, is charged with excess beyond what can be juridically or legally represented. Black life, in the context of the arrest, is imagined and represented as carrying out the utmost perverse acts against itself—imagined as "*the hugest threat* to the state" and represented as rioting against and lynching itself, as if self-defense were unimaginable. Any expression in the movement for black lives thus appears in the eye of civil society as a depth of depravity to which only blackness can descend.

The perversion of juridical power exceeds the discrete historical events concerning constitutional rights and freedom or the formal domains of law. Perversion also ensnares the deferral to law and rights as a telos—a lived conviction (or, more precisely, a conviction that becomes *alive*) that becomes internalized as the absolute limit to reason and being, meaning and interpretation. When narrowed to the domain of juridical power through its own linguistic representations, perversion functions by rendering black desire as inherently deviant and, consequently, criminal. In the case of Richards Abdullah's arrest, such a perversion manifests in the state's capacity to imagine nonviolent protest as both rioting and an act of self-lynching.

Throughout *Beyond Abolition*, we have discussed how the repudiation of blackness, underscored by the force and violence of antiblackness, subtends the appearance of what is deemed lawful custody, arrest, and the police and court's interpretation and translation of the anti-lynching statute. In examining the dissimulation of blackness and its untranslatability, unthinkability, irrepresentability, it becomes clear that to inquire about blackness solely at the level of representation (image and forms) or in the register of (the language of) law not only perpetuates carceral effects, but also maintains a psychical dynamic in which the lynching and policing of blackness as a self take place. Blackness then is forced to appear in ways it is not nor can ever be—haunting the law with what Marriott evokes as the *n'est pas* of blackness. As established in Chapter 3, what blackness resists in respect to representation and language are antithetical to translation and form. Yet, this resistance, that which escapes representation and language, cannot be construed or defined as resistance proper or conceived as a mode of flight without capitulating to the laws of representation it eludes. The arrest of Richards Abdullah brings this impasse in sharp focus: the scene of her arrest and its preceding events can only be represented through what Sexton characterizes as "the material and symbolic terms of blackness whose spacetime presents itself in a paradoxical display."[94]

Bearing in mind this "paradoxical display," the language of performance proves insufficient to construe the criminalization of blackness or the state's transition from imagined rioting to a "self-lynching." Such a framework fails to account for the psychical structures of antiblackness—the logic of fantasy, perversion, and aggression that subjects blackness to terms in which blackness is never deemed worthy of being. The language of performance or non-performance of blackness, frequently utilized in recent scholarship to locate opacity and freedom before the law, hazards reducing ontology to a problematic of representation.[95] The question remains whether blackness, specifically when nefariously projected as criminality or resistance, can ever escape reduction to a "performance." In this context, the relationship between the body and the signifier must be interrogated through the lens of incapacity.[96] Moreover, reading (and rewriting) blackness through the lens of performance only mirrors the law's subjection of blackness into the scene of a crime. Under such a regime, blackness is animated to be seen as acting criminally—as crime itself—and, thereby, corroborating the wishful thinking and fantasmatic structures of a law that furnish what Hartman has described as "the capacities of the performative in doing (as in making) and undoing the subject and . . . the status of the enslaved as a curious hybrid of person and property."[97] It is "this dramatic seizure of the will [that] figuratively expropriates the power of the (would-be) master that animates and annexes the captive body."[98] As the following analysis elaborates, this annexation becomes problematically reproduced even within the language and representation of tenable freedom.

In contemporary black critical thought, perhaps no one has utilized the notion of performance and fugitivity more than Fred Moten, who throughout his oeuvre has conceptualized fugitivity as the "stolen life" of blackness—a movement that operates as an escape from the strictures of logic, language, and materiality. For Moten, blackness as a *case* of an "anoriginal impurity" signals "the flaw that accompanies impossible origins and deviant translations."[99] His use of the term "deviant translations" corresponds to questions he poses as he frames fugitivity as inextricable from reimagining the conditions of possibility for black life. In this sense, the notion of "deviant translations" reclaims a lawlessness raised by these questions—questions that themselves waver between inquiry and assertion. He writes:

> Is the designation of this or that thing as lawless, and the assertion that such lawlessness is a function of an already extant flaw something more than that trying, even neurotic, oscillation between the exposure and replication of a regulatory maneuver whose force is held precisely in the assumption that it comes before what it would contain? What's the relation between explanation and resistance? Who bears the responsibility of discovering an ontology of, or of discovering *for* ontology, the ensemble of political, aesthetic, and philosophy derangements that comprise the being that is neither for itself nor for others? What form of life makes

> such discovery possible as well as necessary? Would we know it by its flaws, its impurities?[100]

Let us dwell on the relation between performance, race, and the signifier, and the specific problematic of translation and disturbance. For here, deviant translations pose a double act: Moten's text illustrates a particular deviancy—oscillating between the questioning and asserting a *case of* blackness—while simultaneously evading the distinctions that such oscillation creates. As Marriott has already rigorously outlined, an originary disturbance functions, for Moten, as both cause and case for fugitivity.[101]

On this view, the text performs what Moten conceptualizes as a fugitivity against zones of attainability and governance, positioning fugitivity as the zone of unattainability. Yet, the notion of "deviant translations" transgresses the discussion of untranslatability established in Chapter 3, forcing a confrontation with the prior conditions of the translation apparatus itself: Mustn't translation adhere to some degree of law at the level of grammar? And doesn't translation rely, to some effect, on an overdetermination of what is deemed untranslatable? As Benjamin notes, "Translations . . . prove to be untranslatable not because of any inherent difficulty, but because of the looseness with which meaning attaches to them."[102] Considering the fleeting nature of translation, a deviant translation appears as a productive oxymoron—a rhetorical method that allows "fugitivity" and "deviant translation" to *appear* irreducible specifically by establishing a perverse relation to ontology, one that internalizes its own politics and aesthetics. Moten continues:

> What's at stake is fugitive movement in and out of the frame, bar, or whatever externally imposed social logic—a movement of escape, the stealth of the stolen that can be said, since it inheres in every closed circle, to break every enclosure. This fugitive moment is stolen life, and its relation to law is reducible neither to simple interdiction nor bare transgression. Part of what can be attained in this zone of unattainability, to which the eminently attainable ones have been relegated, which they occupy but cannot (and refuse to) own, is some sense of the fugitive law of movement that makes black social life ungovernable, that demands a paraontological disruption of the supposed connection between explanation and resistance.[103]

Here, Moten assume a relation between explanation and resistance to be intelligible. But why does he think that there is a missed interpretation or, more fundamentally, a misplaced one—hence it being a "supposed connection"?[104] As established in Chapter 3, how one reads an originary disturbance in language dictates the successional formations of translation, including the shaping of explanatory power. Such a maneuver assumes that the relation itself is intelligible, even if misguided; it critiques a misplaced intelligibility instead of questioning the foundational possibility of the connection. As Hamacher elucidates, "The elements of language explicate one another. They speak for that which still remains to be said within that which is said."[105] The issue, then, is not the falsity of the relation, but Moten's failure to account for the structural condition that undergirds and enables the very link between resistance and explanation.

Since resistance remains necessarily obscure(d), clarification and explication arise squarely from that obscurity—a connection that rests on the resistance of blackness in the first instance. This connection between explanation and resistance is assumed here as a structural necessity, derived from the Fanonian critique where the *Weltanschauung* (worldview), in its antiblack structure, outlaws ontological explanation and denies blackness the possibility of ontological resistance.[106] Yet, how or why the para-ontological disruption of blackness assumes this connection between explanation and resistance—even *if* supposed—also remains unclear. As Axelle Karera explains, the uncertainty accompanying such a disruption should radically question this connection—whether supposed, imagined, or real—rather than reinforce its relation.[107] Ironically then, blackness as fugitivity demands an assumption fixed within an assumption: it requires the unthinkable be treated as synonymous with the unintelligible, which is why Moten must place fugitivity in proximity to law or *écriture*, even as he embraces fugitivity as a mode of lawlessness.[108]

As Moten returns fugitivity to a site of unattainability and indistinction—as an unthinkable act—fugitivity still remains within a system that is thinkable; ergo, it is effective for Moten to think about blackness as a fugitive case *under* law. But when blackness *as* fugitive—or resistance, for that matter—becomes legible or thought through such a system, even when imagined as unthinkable, it only affirms the structure in which its negativity generates its signification.[109] Moten's fugitivity as a case of blackness is tethered to and must perform within the law's juridical strictures; as such, resistance and explanation remain bound to the juridical register. Because blackness indicates an irrepresentability within the language of the law, forcing blackness into the legibility and politics of the human is all the more problematic.[110] Thus, Moten's fugitivity not only affirms the structure in which blackness attempts to escape, but also involves a perverse notion of resistance: one in which resistance can only take place through a fidelity to a particular level of power. This represents a resistance to the question itself—a recognition that resistance can only ever be deemed "radical" insofar as it remains perverse to the powers that be.

Hence, when Moten explains that blackness "is stolen life, and its relation to law is reducible neither to simple interdiction nor bare transgression" yet "breaks every enclosure" of law, he installs a contradiction in which fugitivity's resistance serves as law's prohibition. Moten reproduces the respective connections among blackness, explanation, and resistance. Yet, fugitivity emerges not as an escape from the laws of governance, *logos*, or the social, but as a mechanism of repression, an unwillingness to open blackness to and from itself. This is not a problematic at the level of "explanation and resistance," but that of an impossible desire to translate oneself into a *sense* of self as a form of non-knowledge. This also explains why Moten quickly succumbs to the illusion that escape will relinquish blackness's "stolen light, stolen life,"[111] when he turns to Michel Foucault in his essay "Knowledge and Freedom" to contextualize "the regulative and disciplinary powers," a "disposed and dispossessive fugitivity" that ostensibly precedes power. The deference to Foucault is peculiar. It is not that (black) life escapes the administrative and governing techniques that enable varying degrees and kinds of power. In Chapter 3, I referenced Joan Copjec who makes clear that differences are not what threatens or feeds the gaze of power.[112] For the gaze is not a surveillance of differences to be managed, but a confrontation with an internal limit of sight—a lack that no "fugitive" movement can fill. Thus there is no position that can define blackness, nor can blackness be defined through a position that does not establish an antagonistic interplay among power, identity, and recognition—one that remains irreconcilable via "escape." The questions with which we are left are: What exactly is being imagined as an *outside*—and what, and where, would escape even be a possibility?

By conceptualizing an escape, an "out" perceived with an already extant flaw, Moten marshals a representation of fugitivity as if it were somehow liberated from the violence that he endeavors to guard against. However, as Barbara Johnson explains, this "doesn't mean that the thing repressed can't be resistant to naming in another sense."[113] Thus, the affirmation that Moten offers through fugitivity problematically facilitates translations from negation to positive representation—in law or otherwise—that only reinforce the violence trafficking blackness as something *other*. Notwithstanding Moten's later endeavor to elaborate his meditations on performance by turning to what he describes as "the non-performance of blackness," the latter term, in its restorative goals, yields to the carceral enterprise of antiblack representation. Worse still, it employs the same language of the master's tool to fortify and reproduce the master's house under the veneer of fugitivity.[114] In either instance—performance or non-performance—fugitivity itself becomes a *form*, if not figure, for a being, or a self, to be judged and to be had: captured and in captivity, stolen yet again. In this vein, the subjection of blackness to perform (even if conceived *as* a performance of freedom, fugitivity, transgression, etcetera) reifies a stage that mirrors the arrest of Richards Abdullah. Here, the performance forces the signifier of "race" into a perverse signification of difference while upholding the terms of the law. Yet, to position the non-knowledge of blackness as a performance of fugitivity is to (un)consciously place blackness within a "philosophy [that] would be *legitimated* juridically."[115]

Further, given that blackness is structurally available in the flesh for endless impersonation (*pace* Spillers and Marriott respectively)[116]—a condition that provides the pre-authorization for others to claim blackness—the stakes must be relocated to the libidinal attachments that procure the terms of blackness as fugitivity. Without an explicit account of desire, drive, or sexuality, Moten's argument overlooks how the conceptualization of blackness as performance inadvertently sanitizes the libidinal economy of antiblackness—the very structure that makes an ontological masking so effective. In her own critique of Moten's "anoriginal twist," Sorentino asks:

> Can the invitation to dance paraontologically ever not be what Ann duCille has identified as the desire to "have that 'signifying black difference' without the difference of significant blackness"? Do not the seductions of the prior operate in tandem with the master's mode of seduction, which is to say, antiblackness' mode of reproduction?[117]

For as she notes further, "there is no way of knowing whether the authorization of everyone to claim blackness means reinvigorating antiblack violence in the form of ontological minstrelsy."[118]

To come to the point: whenever and wherever blackness is asked to perform, it is never without force or perversity. This much is clear from the ways we have seen blackness animated in order to be criminalized—even imagined as rioting and "self-lynching." Still, if the lynching and policing of blackness ad infinitum also evince ontology's racial terror—its accompanying images, representations, and forms—then we can also infer that the stakes are irreducible to the bereavement of a self or being that was never possessed. Within the blinding enclosure of ontology's field stands a hall of mirrors: structures that maintain the reflections of blackness as distortions, disfigurations, and disorientations. No doubt, these mirrors can only stand as they do unless shattered. But even with such destruction, those fallen shards form some semblance of possibility—an image indicating how even the most abstract fragments can reflect insomuch as they deflect and conceal.

Our discussion of uncanniness and perversion in the context of Richards Abdullah's arrest has demonstrated an incommensurability between blackness and place as well as between blackness and representation. These two domains in their incommensurability expose the laws of judgment as image and event, in which the assertion of blackness is positioned against a common set or sense of rules. On this account, blackness troubles the terms of representation; its appearance—simultaneously familiar or unfamiliar—suggests a non-ontology that can only be considered an abyss. To read blackness in alternative or new materialist ways perversely reproduces a structure of disavowal that not only makes such aesthetics possible but also fosters the illusion that such a structure of disavowal could be free from or less than a perverse violence itself. Between the racial politics of aesthetics and this vertiginous plummet, blackness puts into crisis the diremption between the familiar and unfamiliar, the material and immaterial. We have also laid out that any attempt to eradicate law's antiblackness by way of restaging blackness through an alternative schemata of representation, such as performance, cannot do so without repeating the perversion of and by the law. This is because any unconscious or conscious wish for representations and images of blackness, even among those that are intended to be the arbiters of anti-racism or anti-capitalism, reifies blackness as a trope of representation and disavows antiblackness as an internal violence and dialectical law in the structure of representation itself.

The supposed *uncanny* appearance of Richards Abdullah's "lynching" arrest registers as unfamiliar and unreal, despite the familiarity of antiblack violence and the violence of (blackness of) the *real*. The "lynching" arrests distill the petrification of blackness in its most perverse depths: to know what one sees while simultaneously disavowing it—as if to see without eyes. The "uncanniness" of the "felony lynching" arrests tells us, in the end, that they are neither unusual nor do they take place for the last time. Never far estranged from the familiarity of slavery, the lynching of blackness demonstrates a world that cannot—or will not—see the proof of its own antiblack making and conditions, a violence that always remains, and already is, present before naked eyes.

Six

Black Abstraction?

Real Abstraction, the Artworks of Melvin Edwards and Torkwase Dyson, and the Abolition of the Real

Objects are not things.
Among the poplars
the lynched body does not resemble
an image.
–David Marriott, "Lorem Ipsum"[1]

"Objects are not things." Against the density of an image ("among the poplars"), as David Marriott's verse suggests, the lynched body outstrips the logic of the figure and the status of vestigial racial representation. If the preceding analysis has traced the aesthetic and psychic (non-)sovereignty of blackness—the image of sovereignty and the sovereignty of the image linked to the condemnation of blackness—this final chapter confronts the point where the law's desire for a judgment in the symbolic collapses into abstraction that reverberates from the *real*. We have seen that abstraction can be operative at multiple registers—juridical, aesthetic, representational, economic, and psychical—driven by the unrestrained force of antiblackness. As discussed in Chapter 1, this force is inextricable from what Derrida pinpoints as the laws of law: "what remains invisible and hidden in each law."[2]

The fifth chapter concluded with the fallacy of a type of seeing without eyes. The 2015 "felony lynching" arrests of Jasmine Richards Abdullah and Maile Hampton are not solely localized anomalies; they are the terminal manifestation of a sovereign desire to translate the irreducible nothingness of blackness—the unmanageable *real* of blackness—into the finite capture of the carceral sign. The failure of such a vision is, therefore, neither a simple identificatory disappearance nor an equivocation of sight. For the lynching of blackness is antecedent to, and saturates, any representation and appearance of the self. This excess culminates and is exposed in specific legal phenomena, yet it also signals the threshold where the general economy of representation—the effort to provide a mask to the unthought—falters against the very nothingness that sustains the impossibility of the being of blackness.

In this chapter, I further explore the compulsion, an unconscious desire, to reconcile the failure of such vision and the unthought of blackness through the explanatory power of race and abstraction. I argue that the wish to fill these lacunae through the categories of race and abstraction reproduces blackness as fundamentally constitutive of the problem of, and for, representation. The objects that drive law, historical memory, sovereignty, and aesthetics in the lynching of blackness at the level of the imaginary shape the materialized images—the symbolic representation—of blackness in custody and arrest. Together, the symbolic and the imaginary conceal and distort the violent exposure of blackness to the *real*.

Psychical concerns of blackness and antiblackness, often framed as abstractions, present an aesthetic dilemma that permeates through critical interventions in the field.[3] For Rizvana Bradley, the disfiguration and disembodiment of blackness not only precede aesthetic forms but also are ontologically positioned as antithetical to form. In this way, discourses of art, theory, and aesthetics mirror this elision. Yet, even as "the cataclysm of trans-atlantic slavery marks the conditions for the emergence and consolidation of capitalist modernity, the human, subject, and the relays of material-discursive exchange that sustain the accumulation of capital and the fabrication of civil society,"[4] she brings into sharp relief why an approach to value and form in relation to blackness must be delimited from an analysis that solely concentrates on a capitalist mode of production. She writes, "My invocation of the law of value suggests that the predatory abstractions of capital may be regarded as simply one moment within the more general operation of the 'calculative thinking' that [Martin] Heidegger critiqued, even as his refusal to think the antiblackness of metaphysics ultimately reinscribes it."[5] Bradley's approach is vital as it raises a concern that is similar to what I hope to explore in this final chapter—that is, the need to excavate what might underlie the latent infrastructure of aesthetics "even when," in Bradley's words, "considering artworks held under the rubric of abstraction."[6]

In view of this, I explore the implications of the compulsion to turn *to* abstraction as a primary analytic of (anti)blackness. Another way of articulating this concern is to ask what the analysis and critique of a "racial logic of capital" and abstractions might conceal just as they might expose "race itself as an abstraction."[7] Might the rhetoric of race and abstraction (or even the notion of real abstraction)—in its allusion to the materialization of antiblackness—nonetheless reify a violence not unlike that of racial representation? Do conceptions of abstraction, in other words, neglect a violence of disavowal that precedes abstraction? And if race is an abstraction, then how should we contend with the lynching of blackness that precipitates the materialization of "race" and "value" in their abstract forms? While abstraction suggests an imperceptible presence for which some other form of representation, ethics, or politics must stand in, the materialized "picture-thought" of abstraction functions as a veil over an underlying structure of antiblackness. To move beyond the common invocation of the term—which often serves only to gesture toward the "abstract" nature of racial violence—and to instead inhabit what Gillian Rose, following G. W. F. Hegel, describes as the "pure abstraction" of the concept, might hazard reproducing a structure of disavowal.[8] We must, therefore, contend with the fact that the "abstraction of race" often functions as no more than a *Vorstellung*—a representational picture that fills the void of the unthought. To *begin* with race as a static and reified "concept" of the truth is to bypass the antagonistic *Darstellung* of the lynching itself: the systematic unfolding of a labor of the negative—a violence that forces into being the categories of "race," "value," and "abstraction" before they can even be thought.

One challenge of discerning abstraction in relation to blackness and antiblackness is that the term "abstraction" has accumulated many competing valences—from Marxism to phenomenology to aesthetics and art. Indeed, there seems to be something quite seductive, almost reparative, about the notion of abstraction when speaking about (anti)blackness; the pairing of "race" plus "abstraction" has, to some degree, achieved unchecked explanatory power and critical purchase in the contemporary field. Yet, because of this, abstraction presents a quandary where libidinal attachments to blackness—and the violence they carry—necessarily recede from view.

Choosing an unorthodox way to approach some of the questions outlined above, I turn to two artists, Melvin Edwards and Torkwase Dyson, whose uses of "abstraction" not only interrogate the neat opposition between abstraction and figuration, but also offer a reflexive critique of the conditions that cast valences of antiblackness *as* abstract or concrete. I turn to Edwards's and Dyson's works because they notably consider the limits of representing and articulating policing and lynching as reductive abstractions of carceral structures and systems, including capitalism. Their works respectively call into question the ontology of racial abstraction by initiating supplemental yet critical readings; they discern the dissimulation of blackness as constitutive of the conditions of the image and representation through which "race" appears. Furthermore, these artists' engagement with abstraction forces us to move beyond the prevailing argument that focuses on the representation of race and racialization. Instead, their works compel us to recognize antiblackness's foundational role in both representation and abstraction, exposing how the latter is often encoded within the image while simultaneously being conceived as outside of representation itself. That is, these works put into question the abstraction of racial codification, regardless of whether such codes are made referential through the signs or authority of race. At issue is why abstraction—when conceived as a form or figure of violence in the discursive productions of race—elides yet reinforces its own presuppositions of a duality between the concrete and abstract, the immaterial and material. More critically, commentary on the abstraction of blackness and antiblackness turns their irrepresentability and escape from representation *into* something, as if the nothingness of blackness could be restored or recuperated by the sovereign decision of self-representation[9]—a sense of sovereignty, as this book has discussed, that is withheld in the lynching of blackness as a self.

"The Direction of Poetry"

Let us begin by exploring examples from Melvin Edwards's series of sculptures titled *Lynch Fragments*. Edwards, a black American sculptor born in 1937, is a pioneer of the Black Arts Movement whose work is defined by the use of welded steel to create sculptures that are simultaneously abstract and figurative. He began the *Lynch Fragments* series in 1963 during the height of the Civil Rights Movement and has continued to produce pieces for it across six decades. The longevity of his practice and series marks a defining and continuous thread in his oeuvre—a persistent return to the industrial and social materials of antiblack violence in America.[10]

The series consists of about eighty-five pieces that are not always displayed as a whole series. The titles of the sculptures—each alluding to black figures, events, or places—appear more arbitrary, akin to contingencies as opposed to references or signs through which each sculpture should be identified and interpreted. In this way, Edwards's sculptures, individually or as an ensemble, throw referentiality into crisis, and so too unsettle any question regarding how to read fragments of lynching. This feeling of disorientation and interruption stands in sharp contradistinction with—yet perhaps also functions as a consequence of—the sculptures' mounting: the small reliefs are arranged in a disciplined row along the gallery wall. While the row of small sculptures creates a sense of order, it is a fragile, somewhat administrative symmetry that only amplifies the jagged, metallic discord of the fragments themselves. This order stands against a vast emptiness. The straight line cuts through the wall's bare whiteness like a serrated knife, leaving puncture marks when pressed upon the surface (Figure 13). The stark contrast is held in a precarious manner. But in that precarity, the space between negative and positive, literal and metaphor, abstract and figural, becomes highly acute. The gallery describes Edwards's works as follows:

> Composed as small welded reliefs mounted on the wall, the *Lynch Fragments* occupy a charged space between painting and sculpture. Their intimate scale and careful positioning suggest both the presence of a body and the psychological weight of lived experience—conveying identity as something at once personal, historical, and political.[11]

Edwards himself elaborates:

> The work has nothing that is literal. It tends to be more the direction of poetry. There are some elements like chains, people love to jump to slavery and oppression—that can be, but nobody remembers why chains were invented. Well, I'm a sculptor who works in steel. I'm a blacksmith. I know that that's the human invention of a stronger rope. Everything else is implication. You can use a chain to anchor a ship, you know, or bind somebody.[12]

The two descriptions of Edwards's work share a concern regarding what goes missing in the gaps of a "charged space," and the difference between what is representable and knowable—a difference manifesting in the tension between mediums (painting and sculpture), the literal and the poetic, and history and invention. Yet, they speak radically differently about the logic of that difference. The gallery text describes a mapping of difference in identity—locating it between the presence of the body and the psychic life of blackness, or between the personal and political. Edwards's reflection on his own work, however, indicates a difference that remains unthought: the desire for a *human* invention of chains as a stronger rope—a difference that cannot be reconciled by representation *or* abstraction. Accordingly, representation and abstraction function repressively against a structural antagonism that gives rise to the invention (chains), while censoring the underlying desire for a stronger rope.

In any gaps of representation—whether figural, formal, or abstract—there remains the trace of something withheld from knowledge and lan-

Figure 13. Installation view: *Melvin Edwards*, Alexander Gray Associates, New York, 2014. Source: Courtesy Alexander Gray Associates, New York.

guage—a trace that troubles the common understanding of whether language is an effect of knowledge, or knowledge an effect of language.[13] And yet, significantly, this trace is not an abstraction. To grasp this distinction, we must realize that to confuse the trace for abstraction would be to take abstraction literally. The trace does not denote a removal from a prior presence, but rather the structural impossibility of presence itself. Such structural impossibility is predicated upon blackness, which serves as the pre-original mark of difference that then manifests as the "trace" and makes the subsequent operations of abstraction and sovereign categorization possible. Abstraction, by contrast, is a calculative gesture of the law or capital designed to remove and negate blackness in order to produce a universal form (as in value, citizenship, or the human). Thus, the trace is not simply the remainder left behind by abstraction, but is the effect of the pre-original aperture of blackness that structurally resists the sovereign project of categorization and universalization.

The structural impasse, maintained by the impossibility of blackness, necessitates a critical methodology that avoids the literal and calculative imperative of abstraction and instead finds movement by critiquing and undoing established representational form. "Nothing literal" might assume that the literal is the opposite of metaphor. The problem with the literal mode is that it rejects the difference and deferral that defines the trace, insisting instead upon a final, fixed referent. Indeed, racial abstraction functions by taking the social construct of "race" literally, treating blackness and whiteness, for example, as static and essential qualities that require corresponding literal, fixed social treatment (slavery, segregation, etc.). Yet Edwards's his work is positioned closer, as he states, to the direction of poetry (Figure 14); ergo, or so I assume given this heed, the opposition between the literal and metaphor loses sight of poetry's direction, its movement; that is, the movement of writing, reading, thinking, undoing, and unknotting. Such movement is more radical than any uncovering or representation of abstraction, as it resists the capitulation to read the work through the referentiality of race. The direction of poetry here is, therefore, not just the creation of an artistic object (poeisis); rather, it is a direct collision with a knowledge that asserts itself by way of a violent desire to place blackness under the human invention of a stronger rope, of chains. Edwards troubles these oppositions without any guarantee or affirmation of knowledge; nevertheless, the work

Figure 14. Melvin Edwards, *Poetry*, 2012; welded steel, $10^1/_2 \times 7^5/_8 \times 9^3/_4$ in (26.7 × 19.7 × 24.8 cm). Source: Alexander Gray Associates. Courtesy Alexander Gray Associates, New York; Stephen Friedman Gallery, London; Galerie Buchholz, Berlin. © 2026 Melvin Edwards / Artists Rights Society (ARS), New York.

raises the question of a type of (unconscious) thinking, seeing, and reading that refuses all deference to the authorial signs of race.

In this sense, Edwards's series seems to ask viewers what it would mean to apprehend abstraction as neither a removal from the uninterpretable *real* nor a concrete object, but to consider blackness as the (non)relation constitutive of these distinctions. In other words, Edwards queries what establishes the abstract and concrete relations at the level of desire—the libidinal links that bind them.[14] By splintering the apparent differences within this constitutive nonrelation, Edwards invites his viewers to observe, think, and unthink through the direction of poetry—a movement that resembles Aimé Césaire's invocation of a turning point, a shift away from the triangulation between the image of the history of the world, black resistance, and a coming into consciousness that previously "had no relationship to each other."[15]

To view *Lynch Fragments* neither as abstractions nor as literal objects, one must recognize Edwards's "direction of poetry" as a rigorous dialectical process. This is not because poetry is necessarily dialectics or dialectical per se, but because blackness constitutes a fundamental resistance to the naming—the infinite array of references—that seeks to capture blackness through the authority of racial signs. The direction of poetry is dialectical then not because it traverses across a duality (abstraction/formalism, literal/metaphorical, concrete/abstract) as if abstraction were purely outside the mind—but because it uncovers the production of difference that remains irreducible to representation (or abstraction).[16] In this poetic register, blackness exposes the friction between truth and untruth, functioning as the fissure through which difference is written. This movement serves as a stark reminder of the misapprehension inherent in the desire to name blackness, which forever escapes both the strictures of representation and the abstractions that reside outside of thought. Thus, the direction of poetry does more than bring contradictions between blackness and its referents and signs into view; it also reveals that these contradictions are set in motion by the violence that comes from blackness of the *real*, the foundational impossibility of blackness that conjures the very conditions for abstraction to exist.

Edwards's dialectical reading de(con)structs not simply the set of references evoked by his sculptures, but also undoes a type of metaphorical reading of (black) abstract art that might otherwise reduce the work's form of abstraction to a representational index of blackness. Such a dialectical maneuver cautions against the common aesthetic descriptive of "a black aesthetics *of*" and the prescriptive reading that coincides with such unassuming denominations. Even when a "black aesthetics of" is deployed to signal a resistance to dominant modes of aesthetics, such a framing is, nevertheless, an idealism that reminds us of Marx's wariness toward certain conceptual abstractions becoming ideal forms. *Pace* Marx, the value-form—as an abstraction of labor—acquires a false autonomy that obscures its material origins. The resulting power of idealization formally parallels the aesthetic repression that Edwards challenges by questioning the reading of any signifiers that emerge from *Lynch Fragments* and the supposed coherence of their meaning. As such, any interpretation that reads the form of abstraction exclusively as a metaphor for race or racial violence yields to the exact terms that structure meaning for abstraction; it neglects the more radical structure (and structuring) in which blackness is without term.

Perhaps this is why, as a strategy to move beyond this reification in which the abstraction of lynching reduces blackness and antiblackness to a trope of representation, Edwards provides his viewers with a complex set of references that are attached to the pieces. The titles of the individual sculptures span from "Poetry" to "Takawira-J" (in reference to Zimbabwean sculptor John Takawira) (Figure 15), to "Strange Fruit," "Frantz Fanon," and others. On one hand, it could be argued that the individual titles, as a set of references to black art, culture, and thought, establish the very markers of blackness. On the other hand, contrary to the titles serving simply as markers—as if blackness were a stable referent—the point is precisely not to apply these markers where blackness does not appear or is not. Nor do these titles facilitate an identificatory disappearance. Instead, because knowledge and thought enter through this set of black references—or, at least, this is how the artwork is staged—what becomes evident is the fragility of the sign as an abstraction of blackness and the antiblack horrors of lynching. The sign is a fabrication, but also a screen that has been run paper-thin in its defensiveness and defenselessness against the *real*. Indeed, a paradox emerges between the tumbling wall, the surface of the sign, and the abstraction that it is meant to docket: abstraction within *Lynch Fragments* appears interlocked with the dissimulation of antiblackness. Said differently, abstraction becomes the mechanism that brings what blackness is *not* into appearance, while maintaining a structure of disavowal.

Edwards's work highlights this paradox of the image of abstraction and the abstraction of the image: the abstract image of the mask differs critically from the abstraction of an image that masks. By staging knowledge through a set of references that simultaneously identify and withhold, Edwards suggests a condition in which, as Werner Hamacher writes, "If knowledge can be a mask, it can no longer be known what is mask and what is not mask."[17] Within this indistinguishability, dialects do not resolve the image into a higher legibility, but function as an un-setting critique—one that refuses to stabilize the referent. To read these fragments dialectically is thus to

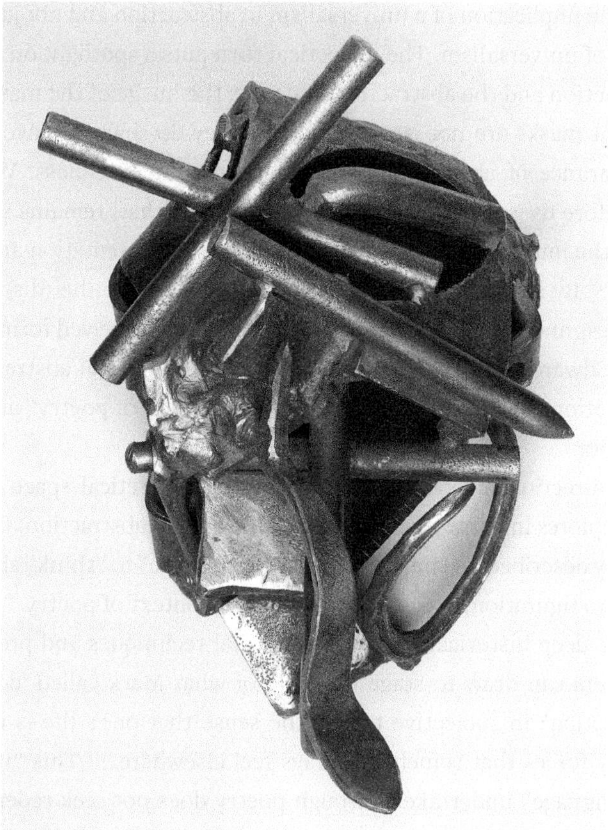

Figure 15. Melvin Edwards (American, 1937–2026), *Takawira - J*, 1989; welded steel, 14 × 10 × 9 in (35.56 × 25.4 × 22.86 cm). Brooklyn Museum, gift of Edward A. Bragaline, by exchange, 1990.104; © 2026 Melvin Edwards / Artists Rights Society (ARS), New York. Photo: Brooklyn Museum.

remain within the aporia of this indistinguishability, where the "knowledge" provided by the titles does not unveil the object but instead participates in the opacity of its masking. Edwards thus critiques a symptomatic reading which works as a screen that occludes the desire for the abstraction of blackness—or for blackness only in and as abstraction. My analysis of Edwards's commentary resembles Slavoj Žižek's proposal to supplement a "standard Marxist hermeneutics of unearthing the particular bias of abstract universality" with "its opposite: . . . the properly Hegelian procedure which uncovers the *universality* of what presents itself as a particular position."[18] At stake is the implication of a universalism in abstraction and not just the abstraction of universalism. The dialectical turn puts a spotlight on the desire for abstraction and the abstraction of desire; the image of the mask and the image that masks are not isomorphic, but they do share an investment in the appearance of abstraction that disavows (anti)blackness. What then stands before us is, in Marriott's words, a "vision [that] remains suspended between the image and its designation, between representation and its subtraction."[19] By attending to the relations that structure the (dis)figuration of blackness and lynching in their most commonly conceived forms and references, Edwards homes in on the limits of placing racial abstraction into representation—insisting, instead, on "the direction of poetry" as a refusal of metaphor.

The "direction of poetry" constitutes the theoretical space that Amy De'Ath explores in her work on language and formal abstraction. De'Ath has eloquently described an "impossible feat in language" to "think" abstract relations into figuration, specifically within the context of poetry.[20] She identifies "the deep historical reservoir of formal techniques and problems on which poets can draw to stage the *agon* of what Marx called 'domination by abstraction': in subjective terms, the sense that one's life is intimately shaped by forces that somehow always feel elsewhere."[21] This "impossible feat in language" undertaken through poetry does not seek redemption or restoration through the materiality of language or conventional modes of abstraction. Instead, the impossible endeavor of language to figure abstraction distills poetry's "dialectical unravelling"[22] of form and formlessness. Here, the direction of poetry offers a dialectical engagement that unearths a sublationary suppression (*Aufhebung*) which produces the differences and contradictions that set abstraction into motion.

The dialectical unravelling of form and formlessness that mobilizes abstraction in the direction of poetry establishes a crucial theoretical benchmark. Nevertheless, my contention here is that the dominant paradigm of "real abstraction" remains an insufficient critical instrument when positioned against (anti)blackness and the context of "racial capitalism." Despite the range of interpretations and readings of "real abstraction," the term typically attempts to pin down abstraction as both a totalizing mechanism of dispossession—alienation and violence—and as a site of potential aesthetic agency. The problem with this dual pinning is that it often fails to account for the foundational structural violence that constitutes the terms of abstraction itself.

Moreover, such a failure persists despite the fact that abstraction is commonly mobilized both as a critical lens of capitalism and the particularities of "race"—insofar as capitalism is what opens up abstraction—and as a potential route to resist capitalism's most oppressive forces and forms. However, the dual potential of abstraction lies in its capacity to serve as both a critical tool and a site of reification and violence. As we have explored in regard to Edwards's work, reading representations of abstraction as a lens through which race appears can just as easily be instrumentalized by crystallizing (anti)blackness *into* the references and signs of race, identity, and politics. Such a reading ignores that abstraction cannot be decoupled from the violence that underlies it—a violence that is distinct from the violence of abstraction itself. In other words, the triangulation between abstraction, capitalism, and race collapses when abstraction is misconstrued as the racist sign (or the sign of racism) that facilitates the dispossessive and exploitative mechanisms of capitalism. This misconception treats abstraction as a means to interpret the production of racial formations while losing track of how such mechanisms might conceal blackness as being constitutive of the conditions of violence. These conditions, as I have argued throughout *Beyond Abolition*, necessitate and are predicated upon the lynching of blackness.

Abstraction, an Underdetermination of Slavery?[23]

To further illustrate the limitations of reducing antiblackness to the dialectics of racial capitalism, I turn to the abstract paintings of Torkwase Dyson. Dyson's abstract paintings engage directly with the historical memory of lynching, yet they have also been discussed through the lens of political economy and racial capitalism—both by critics and the artist herself. Here I argue that her paintings offer a more extensive critique of antiblackness and its abstractions; it is a critique that cannot be isolated within, nor reduced to, the logic of capitalism and its attendant terms of value, labor, property, and expropriation. I submit that Dyson's interrogation of abstraction—both as an implied form and as the abstraction of lynching within historical memory—pushes the concept of abstraction to the edge of what it can represent. Her movement through painting, thus, brings us to abstraction's representational limit, compelling us to question how abstraction functions in representation and how it might serve as an impossible mode for making antiblack violence or white supremacy more thinkable.[24]

Upon first glance, Dyson's paintings from her *Strange Fruit (Series)* use methods of abstraction (Figure 16). The work, particularly her *Strange Fruit (Series)*, draws inspiration from "architecture plans, [using] repeating symbols of trees to blot out the canvases with the memory of thousands of known lynchings that took place from 1882 to 1968."[25] The metaphor of "strange fruit" conveys the bodies of lynching victims hanged from trees, a reference to "Strange Fruit," the title of both a poem by Abel Meeropol and a song by Billie Holiday. Such a formal strategy—which renders a horrific historical materiality through the visual language of abstraction—dialectically reflects on the very limits of that language, thereby providing a crucial site for critique. Dyson (b. 1973), widely recognized for her interrogation of black spatial politics and the relationship between architecture and systemic oppression, engages with the historical memory of lynching through a painterly vocabulary of abstraction.[26] The series emphasizes the compositional tensions between geometric hypershapes, layered, near-black pigments, and liquid washes. Through these formal techniques, the paintings treat the visual language of abstraction not as an escape from materiality but as a structured, spatial record of historical memory and systemic oppression. Forms elude figuration yet nonetheless follow a technical erudition of placement and composition. The visible, labored brushstrokes resist the monochrome blackness, asserting the presence and density of the canvas surface against any implied spatial void. Like the abstract artwork of Mark Bradford, Julie Mehretu, Quentin Morris, Rashid Johnson, or Jack Whitten, Dyson's paintings enact a rigorous "formal manipulation of tone and texture in the abstraction of black monochrome" that conveys what Jared Sexton has called "cultural resonances."[27] The tension found in Dyson's work, thus, echoes the arduous labor required to work against the illegibility of the violent history of lynching and antiblackness more broadly within an abstract idiom. Dyson's work indexes an experience that emerges not from an ostensibly black phenomenological experience, but rather an experience that blackness is structurally without. In this way, Dyson's use of abstraction is a formal study of her subject, the historical memory of lynching. Her practice also unsettles the commonly conceived relationship between abstract art

Figure 16. Torkwase Dyson, *Strange Fruit (Blue Note)* from the *Strange Fruit (Series)*, 2016. Photo: Allison Meier. Source: Courtesy GRAY, Chicago/New York and Hyperallergic. Photo: Allison Meier.

and theory, in which the painting refers to a *Vorstellung*—a secondary representation that defers to a concept or a text to justify what is supposed to be *seen*. Dyson is an abstract painter, but she is, just as importantly, a painter of abstraction.[28] Her work operates as a staging—a *Darstellung*—of an impossible logic underscored by the void of blackness; it does not simply illustrate a history of violence, but registers its material forces and its unmediated relations to the *real* as radically present.

In her *Strange Fruit (Series)*, a dual process of abstraction is at play. Abstraction reveals that the image of lynching only "works" through the realization that there is something deeply unknowable, unthinkable—beyond what can be perceived as abstract—while the lynching of blackness remains all too real, persisting against the abstraction of forms. The persistence of such violence, together with this irreducible tension in representation, establishes the imperative to put blackness "to work" in images of lynching against their assumed abstractions (and what abstraction assumes). Such a critical imperative, however, immediately raises a concern that touches upon two interconnected issues: the material and economic exploitation of blackness, and the psychic exploitation inherent in the conceptual usurpation of black figures and forms by an antiblack unconscious. Dyson's work demonstrates that, consequently, the dominant aesthetics of abstraction are rendered effective only through the unconscious co-option of blackness as the raw, consumable (im)material of form. Put differently, Dyson's *Strange Fruit* paintings argue that black labor and exploitation cannot be confined to purely discursive productions of racial formation and processes of racialization. By rejecting this confinement, the work insists on a reading of abstraction that acknowledges its structural density, resisting its reduction to a facile metaphor for these processes by pushing beyond a purely materialist critique. The formal tensions in her work urgently demand an extension beyond a purely materialist analysis; instead, they require a reexamination of the canvas surface itself as the paradoxical site, not of material substance or a simple object of exchange, but rather as the unanticipated rupture for de-posing critique in respect to the inscription and violence of antiblackness. This shift transforms the surface from a mimetic representation of struggle into a critical plane that reveals the nothingness composing the non-being of blackness and exposes the foundational (il)logic of antiblackness. Much of the "work" of blackness in the paintings stems from what is not or cannot be known about blackness. Dyson's paintings dialectically reflect the impossibility of blackness to be shown through representation. While blackness is composed through abstraction and surplus, blackness simultaneously renders these terms void because it can neither be fully shown nor known. Though this approach can be seen across her *Strange Fruit (Series)*, it is more prominent in *Strange Fruit (Blue Note)* (Figure 16) in which blackness both recedes from view and foregrounds the other components in the painting.

Critically, Dyson's *Strange Fruit* paintings revolve around a void—the structural impossibility for blackness to come into being.

What is consequentially (mis-)represented and (mis-)identified as the appearance of racial abstraction relies on the elision of blackness—an elision that shapes the production of aesthetic value and form. Such a displacement puts Dyson's critique at odds with views that reduce the dynamic of social exchange to an "articulation of race, property, and capitalist abstraction." This includes the framework advanced by Brenna Bhandar and Alberto Toscano who endeavor "to understand *abstractive powers* of property law—and their articulation with and use of racial difference in processes of propertization and profit."[29] In contrast, Dyson's paintings compel us to examine how slavery and lynching, as both conditions for and an excess to capitalist logic, do not entirely participate in these circuits, but instead directly unsettle and exceed them.

We turn, then, to Sara-Maria Sorentino's analysis, which argues that slavery fundamentally disrupts the circuit of abstraction, including the commodity form that conceals the social relations through which its appearances take place.[30] Unlike Bhandar and Toscano, Sorentino identifies the limits of the Marxist theory of value in the underdetermination of slavery within its conception of abstraction. More specifically, blackness, "a negative substance,"[31] becomes the condition of possibility for the appearance and cohesion of forms. This operation reveals the core paradox of blackness in respect to abstraction: slavery is, on one hand, foundational to capitalist relations, yet its excess is also incommensurable with capitalist abstractions. In this light, race is not simply an articulation of "capitalist abstraction," nor can it be reduced to the "*abstractive powers* of property law." On the contrary, as Sorentino argues, "The coherency of the wage relation—the very absence of substance it necessarily comes to circulate—is sustained by the ways slavery stands in for the excesses that money (and race) seeks to overcome."[32] The function of race and property law, then, is to systematically shroud the absolute non-subsumable negation of slavery that paradoxically stabilizes the wage relation.

Dyson's abstract paintings, I submit, are concerned with the exposure of this structural paradox: the foundational excess of slavery and lynching versus the concealment required for capitalist coherence. Such an exposure, however, is not an unveiling that promises a materialist resolution, but one that compels us to confront the terms of the image and political economy as suspended in an unresolvable abyss. Whereas the core of commodity fetishism illustrates that the commodity conceals the social relations of labor—where an "unveiling" leads to a potential materialist resolution—Dyson's paintings suggest that the excess of slavery and lynching—the non-subsumable negation—ruptures this logic profoundly. The viewer's encounter with the work does not facilitate a realization of "true" material relationships; rather, it forces a confrontation with the incommensurable non-being of blackness that haunts the very conceptual coherence of abstraction.

Dyson's *Strange Fruit* paintings display an altogether different and disruptive dialectic—one that refuses the promise of historical resolution and compels us to reconsider the joint problem of slavery's underdetermination (which enables the coherence of Marxism's critique of political economy) and slavery's excess (which gives rise to the cohesion of forms). This operation suggests a form of critique that, much like Walter Benjamin's concept of de-posing critique (*Entsetzung*), arrests the movement of contradiction to expose a structural truth rather than to achieve synthesis. In this regard, Dyson's paintings not only disturb the Marxist dialectic between the concrete and abstract; more significantly, they gesture toward the impossibility of the image of lynching to correspond with the (non-)being of blackness. The question, then, is how the image of abstraction in Dyson's paintings tarries with the violence emerging from this impossibility of correspondence. In no way can the image of lynching—be it formal, figurative, or abstract—the excess of slavery, and the negativity of blackness correspond in a fashion that satisfies the rationalizing logic, the ledger, of capital. Nor, as Sorentino demonstrates, can capitalist abstractions (including, ostensibly, the abstraction of race) reconcile the absence of blackness as substance. Dyson's paintings confront the viewer with an antagonism between racial abstraction—articulated through historical structures, social forces, and commodity forms—and the impossibility of blackness. Her paintings disclose that the articulation of property and race cannot be overcome through the material structures in which abstraction is enfolded (or what Marx sees as the positive transcendence of property). Here, the Marxist notion of a materialist resolution falls short, leaving the confrontation suspended in an abyss. This suspension is formally enacted by Dyson's composition: the visible, labored brushstrokes together with the wash assert the canvas's dense presence against the monochrome of blackness. The resulting materiality is an inversion that does not just imply a spatial void, but also a resistance to that void. To this effect, Dyson's paintings stage a critique through the impossibility of blackness—a stark sense of friction—which is perhaps why the viewer also is left with an intense feeling of suspense. The paintings function not as political prescription or critique demanding materialist resolution, but as a methodological demonstration of the limit of the materialist structure itself. By inverting the canvas's ground through the black paint and wash, Dyson provokes an intangible encounter with and an impossible knowledge of (anti)blackness—an encounter staged in the void.

The fact that Dyson chooses to work with abstraction tells us a great deal about the racial—and racist—knowledge of the imaginary (*connaissance*) that positions blackness as an irredeemable difference under subjection, judgment, captivity. What one thinks is knowledge, or what one believes they know within the imaginary, is not knowledge at all, but a profound misrecognition (*méconnaissance*). The purpose of Dyson's abstraction, then, is neither "to see" nor "to see better," with or from abstraction; it is not an attempt to discern what is simultaneously veiled and revealed. For as psychoanalysis suggests, seeing is never simply innocent, but is always already conditioned by this structural misrecognition.

Such a contaminated vision compels a different objective: to stretch beyond what seeing can offer, since even with the sharpest reality testing, as Fanon writes, "for the colonized subject, objectivity is always against him."[33] The violence of this objectivity is compounded by the fact that the signifiers manifesting in one's preconscious life are not necessarily abstractions at all. As Vicky Lebeau has noted in respect to Fanon's account of dream interpretation, "crudely, sometimes a rifle is a rifle on both sides of the dream-work. Or, sometimes what we dream is real; there is no work of transformation between culture and dream."[34] For this reason, within the lived experience of blackness, the symbolic realm offers no refuge from the material world—a reality that explains why for Fanon, "a Marxist analysis should always be slightly stretched."[35]

This necessity to stretch the analysis points directly to a critical divergence in the concept of transformation. While the Freudian and Marxian work of transformation entails masking truth and inscribing value, Fanon demonstrates that the content of the dream is not far from the traumatic realities of blackness in waking life. Just as "the economic infrastructure is also a superstructure,"[36] according to Fanon, the traumatic division of race establishes blackness as valueless, in a way that assumes the weight of objective fact.[37] To this effect, the work of transformation (including "the mechanisms of condensation, distortion, displacement"[38] and, to add, social forces) is less about a masking that is unveiled than a testament to "the fact that economic reality, inequality, and enormous disparities in life-styles never manage to mask the human reality."[39] The theoretical stakes are clear: abstraction does not become the place or mechanism of transformation through which knowledge is eventually acquired. The critical question, instead, is how abstraction might presume a knowledge—or non-knowledge—of blackness, thereby conscripting blackness in the service of abstraction's own epistemic effects.

Here, the question is what it would mean to separate something inseparable in Dyson's abstract paintings on lynching: the knotted image of non-being and blackness, of space and self, and the horrors of dreaming and living in an antiblack world. What are the conditions and preconditions that position one to see distortions for what they are, rather than what they stand in for? It follows then that the "auction blocks and lynching sites . . . [that] inspired the paintings and sculptures"[40] in the *Strange Fruit (Series)* present themselves as holes in the brushwork—at times fading into the negative of the painting's background and at others rising to the fore. These gaps, which disappear alongside others rendered more concretely through and in whiteness, complicate our reading. Upon closer inspection, it is unclear whether the dashes of black paint pull the background into the surface or vice versa; it remains uncertain whether they function as ground or figure. If what appears as abstraction of antiblack violence in the painting conveys that "the paintings . . . at their core are a form of data visualization,"[41] then the appearance of abstraction also makes evident what fails to appear: the violence coterminous with the irrepresentable. The irrepresentability of blackness—the condition of possibility for the appearance of abstraction itself—cannot be read at the level of forms, nor can it be interchangeable with what is positioned as "the abstract." Thus, what remains is not abstract form, but the irresolvable, constitutive tension between abstraction and antiblackness. That is to say, the resulting abstraction is not a depiction of absence, but the inscription of an impossible presence.

Though Dyson herself explains that "the abstraction [she refers] to is also the political abstraction used to enact hyper-capitalist and white conservative racist agendas upon black and brown geographies,"[42] I argue that the artistic strategy of turning to abstraction in painting—when read through the lens of racial capitalism—risks collapsing the distinction between symptom and diagnosis. Such a collapse confuses the appearance of an effect with the underlying structural problem. As I have discussed throughout *Beyond Abolition*, misinterpreting the appearance of blackness at the level of form and representation does more than reinforce the racial politics of antiblackness; it ignores the fact that such abstractions emerge fundamentally from the absence of blackness and the lynching that precedes it. Nonetheless, Dyson's paintings evoke a serious crisis in respect to the images and forms: blackness cannot be *read* simply as a gap or as negativity—features that recur through Dyson's work—nor can blackness afford to be literalized as abstraction. Insofar as blackness is severed from knowledge and experience only to underpin the relations of value, exchange, and labor, the incapacity reveals that blackness remains without telos, even when confronted with the presumed dialectical progression of abstraction.

The crux, then, is not how to overcome an impasse seemingly created by capitalist modalities of abstraction and abstractions of "race" and "racialization," but rather how the indeterminacy and incapacity of blackness make the abstraction of race possible in the first instance. This point runs counter to Jaleh Mansoor's reflection on Dyson's use of abstraction which, as she emphasizes, refuses the limits of "white representational terms." Mansoor locates this refusal as part of the "remaining recess of creative capacity under capital: abstraction."[43] For Mansoor, "Once we locate the vanishing point from which racialization and abstraction conjointly issue, we recognize that no representational intersection can begin to probe the limits of a problem so foundational as to be part of the social infrastructure"; that is, "the social-political relations that issue from the extraction of value are historical consequences."[44] However, utilizing abstraction as a refusal of racialization and abstraction is contingent on the exact limits of this foundational problem: a reduction of the problem to historical material causation. Such a refusal can only occur to the extent that the recognition Mansoor describes relies on a misrecognition of blackness—a misrecognition that is not only a historical necessity, but a necessity that itself must go unremarked. Rather than construing refusal as illustrative of a "creative capacity" that blackness is structurally and systematically denied, I ask what assumed logic must take place in order to imagine blackness as refusal in Dyson's paintings.

My question echoes Omnia El-Shakry, who insists in regard to her examination of clinical drawings:

> The silent gestures, corporeal hesitations, and movements of the subjects in question, may of course be viewed as individual acts of refusal. However, rather than a liberal feminist signal that would reclaim these gestures as the agentive acts of refusal of an undivided subject, I parse these gestures and hesitations alongside Winnicott's claim that the subject has the 'right not to communicate . . . a protest to the frightening fantasy of being infinitely exploited.[45]

While "the right not to communicate" might too be a privilege regarding the possibility of signification and who can be(come) a subject, what I value and take seriously about El-Shakry's point is how the desire to center refusal as agency overshadows "the frightening fantasy of being infinitely exploited." This fantasy, of course, is not separate from the wish to see refusal as agency through modes of abstraction, but in fact drives this wish toward a particular demand for recognition. Along these lines, I submit that Dyson's abstract paintings of lynching speak to my earlier point: any recognition of blackness is a necessity which must remain misrecognized.

The pressure Dyson places on the question of abstraction as form requires a dialectical reading of (anti)blackness—one that cannot be reconciled through materialist solutions, such as conceiving the process of abstraction in her paintings as a mode of retrieval or an attempt to reify abstraction against racialization and under capitalism. On this score, the impasse that Dyson's paintings illumine is not a failure of representation that must be overcome through more abstraction; rather, abstraction in painting uncovers how blackness of the *real*, in its very impossibility, generates the possible abstractions from thought and appearance. This stands in direct contrast to what Mansoor asserts: "Abstraction comes to saturate the field of the real and to be mistaken for it."[46] Instead, I contend that exposing blackness to the *real* lays bare the impossibility of blackness regardless of its many appearances, including abstraction.

In Mansoor's argument, the "vanishing point"—resting on the joint operation of racialization and abstraction—points to a limit in thought and critique of representation that is inextricable from what Marx might describe as social forms and exchange. Mansoor notes the "linkage of architecture and abstraction, and problems of racialization that [Dyson's] work also addresses." However, as I have argued, centering "abstraction" as the starting point to interrogate the violence of antiblackness and non-being through social forms risks reducing the violence of abstraction to the structures of capitalism. Such a reduction elides the ways that antiblackness underpins the material and immaterial structures of value and exchange (or of capitalism and abstraction), thus foreclosing an engagement with foundational questions of ontology—namely, the non-subsumable negation of blackness upon which the logic of capitalist abstraction is founded.

The tendency to collapse the infinite anxieties of ontological critique into the finite bounds of material structure remains a pervasive habit of thought—a refusal to tarry with the abyss I identified in Chapter 3 in Cheryl Harris's formulation of whiteness as property, which reappears with renewed literalism in Eunsong Kim's "aestheticization of abstraction." Kim, who subscribes wholesale to Harris's now well-known formulation, makes property the central term in her notion of "aesthetic abstraction,"[47] which along with "its assumed vacancy precedes propertization."[48] As a consequence, within the aesthetic and artistic context of property, she examines how "with the ontology of property rights, race is rendered invisible and denied and whiteness is vitalized."[49] For Kim, "property, then, must be understood as the combinatory forces of singular abstraction and exclusion."[50] Following thinkers such as Grace Kyungwon Kim and Jodi Byrd, in addition to her piety to Harris, Kim explains "the abstraction of space" (the term is hers) as:

> a purposeful, uneven political endeavor, one that works to actively negate spaces of difference, life, and injury. Dispossession is activated through the creation of abstraction, and abstract space continues to foreclose materialist, political inquiry. Rather than opposing the *real*, abstraction and the creation of abstract space can be witnessed as continuing to normalize structures of violence by forcibly creating notions of property and ownership, such as vacancy.[51]

Kim's remarks echo those of Mansoor, insofar as the naturalization of abstraction simultaneously constructs and reinforces the racialization of nonwhite subjects and the material realities of their marginalization. Hence, the claim that "race is rendered invisible" serves as a necessary premise for her argument: it allows her to position property as the central vehicle for dispossession. However, while Kim explicitly claims that abstraction works with "rather than oppos[es] the real," her analysis reinstates the conceptual separation she denies. To establish the distinct roles of abstraction and the "creation of abstract space" in "foreclosing the materialist, political inquiry," her reading must first disengage abstraction from the material real it purports to constitute. This conceptual slip—an unacknowledged, implicit separation between the material real and abstraction, relying on a gestural use of the word "the real"—becomes, in essence, the site where a Marxian materialism fails to register its own impossibility. By grounding its critique in an abstraction that must be "created" to render race invisible, rather than an abstraction that is ontologically fundamental, this framework ensures that the contradictions of antiblackness cannot be registered as constitutive limits, but only as temporary problems susceptible to material resolution.

"The creation of abstraction" assumes perhaps too impetuously a capacity for conversion (or collapse) between the legal form of property and the aestheticization of property as an aestheticization of abstraction. The creation of abstraction, at least in Marxist terms, is somewhat of a conceptual oxymoron, as it, in fact, "has nothing to do with the level of 'reality,' of the effective property, of an object."[52] As opposed to being "created," abstraction functions as a constitutive relation "always already" within the social space of the world. Or as De'Ath illuminates, abstractions are "shaped by forces that somehow always feel elsewhere."[53] Hence, abstraction is neither about the creation of its abstraction nor is it a matter of "witnessing" or discovering its forms for what they truly are or where they come from. Instead, the tasks of "witnessing" and thinking abstraction encounter a "supra-sensible" limit. It is at this boundary that the materialist project of unveiling, again, fails. Such a method—a "bad dialectics" which assumes that contradiction can be overcome through materialist resolution—halts at this absolute boundary. By insisting that abstraction is a creatable form, Kim's analysis both collapses back into the very materialist framework it seeks to critique and betrays the new materialist conceptualization to which she aspires. At the same time, as we have discussed throughout *Beyond Abolition*, blackness as a non-relation challenges the universality of this Marxist claim (i.e., the assumption that all contradictions are susceptible to dialectical resolution). The abstraction constituting the legible social world (e.g., commodity and labor) is not merely a social relation, but a non-relational necessity. What Frank Wilderson might deem a "grammar of suffering" is thus built on the principles and social relations of reciprocity and equivalence—a logic fundamentally at odds with the non-relation of blackness. Such necessity persists because the social world requires an unaccounted-for foundation for its own internal logic of equivalence (e.g., wage labor, value exchange); it also ensures that the non-being of blackness is structurally foreclosed from participation to condition the coherence of social relation itself. What is ultimately revealed is that the tools designed to penetrate the veil of commodity fetishism are futile before the irreducible opacity of antiblackness. For such opacity is not a veil to be lifted, but the irresolvable unknowability—the indispensable condition for the operation of all legible social forms.

The notion of "the creation of abstraction," particularly the creation of abstract space, thus dismisses Fanon's fundamental critique of a Marxist logic of abstraction—the realization that for blackness, abstractions are not always abstractions (the rifle, as it were, is a rifle). More profoundly, Kim's framework ignores Fanon's critical observation that spaces of reality and the imaginary, as they are conceived and structured through the terms of capitalism, are fundamentally insufficient to both apprehend and account for the psychic realities of antiblackness. Because the critical capacity of a materialist structure is vitiated by antiblackness, any critique relying on those terms is forced into a conceptual substitution—the inevitable outcome of a Marxist framework unable to process ontological limits. As a result, the endeavor to "unveil" or recuperate the invisibility of race collapses into the same logic of racial fetishism it intends to overcome. Such an inversion is stark: by assuming that abstraction is nothing but a screen that leaves race invisible, the critique treats race as a hidden object to be recovered, reinforcing the abstract mechanisms of masking and veiling that naturalize a language of racial difference.

The unwitting reification of racial fetishism in Kim's formulation of aesthetic abstraction makes clear the critical imperative of Fanon's reevaluation of a materialist logic. For Fanon, the base is, at once, the superstructure in the colony; conversely, the concrete of material conditions is always overwritten by violence, which is how (and why) race becomes enshrined in the notion of value. Or, to reiterate Fanon's warning: "Objectivity is always against the colonized." Dispossession, in other words, is never simply a matter of a "creation of abstraction." Racial divisions and the ontological violence that subtends them emerge from and are maintained by, as Fanon puts it, "a world with no space."[54]

In this vein, "the theorization of property" does not necessarily "shed light on the coemergence of private property and the racial,"[55] as Bhandar suggests. Nor does it explain the incapacity of blackness in the projection of the slave as property. The nonvalue of blackness precedes its "racial mark" (Chapter 1). And while property *and* slave law inscribed the fungibility of the slave—in both the psychical and the economic sense of the word—the perversion of such laws was not simply ratified in practice *de jure* or *de facto*. Antiblackness, *ante legem*, makes abstraction as a fact appear real: the impossible recognition of blackness necessitates the conditions of abstraction—conditions that are irreconcilable and irreparable in the face of the foundational constitution of antiblackness.

As I have also argued in Chapter 3, the uncritical adoption of "whiteness as property" ignores that racialized subjects can oppose white supremacy while nonetheless aspiring to whiteness—or, more specifically, desiring the erasure of blackness as presence. Such a desire is exercised through the privileges of ownership and the right to enjoy property, which are structurally denied to blackness.[56] By marshaling an implicit, assumed "we" of those who are non-white, Kim's "aestheticization of abstraction" ironically reproduces not only the abstraction of blackness as property; it reinforces and perpetuates an underdetermination of slavery for the sake of its own aesthetic utility. This conceptual framework, based on a ruse of recuperation, cannot be reconciled nor redeemed via "better" representation nor a mode of "seeing" which might foster a more critical understanding or critique. Thus, while Kim's critique attempts to be abolitionist and aspires to a kind of new materialism (or alternative Marxist methodology),[57] it ultimately devolves into miming the rhetoric of liberal reform.

All that said, what Dyson establishes in her paintings is not about rendering blackness (or antiblackness) more or less real *through* abstraction, nor does she try to position her paintings as more or less real *than* abstraction—

quite the opposite. If an ominous sense of disquiet emanates from her abstract paintings, it is not simply because her abstract representation of lynching—and the violent misidentifications inherent in the gratuity of those events—leaves us with the devastating realization that such horrors often remain abstract at the level of knowledge and the unconscious life of antiblackness. The structural impossibility of fully grasping this horror through conceptual capture makes any project reduced to the level of representation not only theoretically redundant, but one of disavowal. Precisely because the horror of the event exceeds the capacity to name it, Dyson's work abandons the ruse of "unveiling" altogether. Her methodology suggests that the only way to inhabit a world structured by the violence of abstraction is not to "create" more of it, but to find a way of "surviving abstraction through abstraction."[58]

The transition from a critique of abstraction to an ontological necessity marks the limits of the materialist project. What remains is an irredeemable ruination, confronted by the realization that abstraction may be the only possible articulation of the imperative that, as Frank Wilderson has posited, "we need a new language of abstraction to explain this horror."[59] The necessity of a "new language" might appear as a reformative gesture in and for language. However, Wilderson's urgency is not a call for a revision of language; his assertion arises from the paradox of antiblackness: fundamentally structural and pre-discursive, antiblackness is the condition that subsumes and exceeds the representational capacity of conventional materialist discourse. In other words, the intensity of abstraction is focalized around the impossible void created by the circumvention of blackness. The primacy of this void in Dyson's paintings reveals a relationship that is essentially chiasmic: the non-being of blackness is indexed by architectural space, while the violence of antiblackness constitutes the very space of that non-being. Such non-being occupies a state never afforded a place within the social world, yet it remains the foundational condition that enables the infinite range of segregative acts and violence impinged on this non-ontology (Figure 16).

In this regard, the supposed critical purchase of race and abstraction (whether too abstract or not abstract enough, or too abstract yet all too real) colludes with the dissimulation of blackness when expressed through the logic of racial capitalism. It may be that any interrogation of abstraction and race in relation to (anti)blackness is tautological so long as "real abstraction" is identified as "an abstraction other than that of thought."[60] However, my interrogation of abstraction as a mechanism of dissimulation stresses that while the capture of blackness—both the formalist capture of the aesthetic[61] and the materialist capture of political economy—is an unavoidable condition of the social world, blackness is never fully exhausted by these terms. Specifically, I contend (a) that blackness is not a problem to be solved through static concepts or compositional arrangements, and (b) that its ontological weight cannot be accounted for by the metrics of property or exchange. To center the void in Dyson's work is to acknowledge that blackness is the very thing that enables and remains after these systems of capture have reached their conceptual limits.

Despite attempts to retrieve some ground from whiteness, the materialist reading of property—however original its attention to race—ultimately reduces property to a violence of metaphysics. In Chapter 3, we discussed Harris's point that "property is thus said to be a right, not a thing, characterized as metaphysical, not physical."[62] By deferring to the notion of whiteness as property and appearance of race, Harris, Mansoor, and Kim necessarily overlook the structural function of (anti)blackness in the constitution of abstraction, form, and value in the aspiration to recuperate race. In orienting their analyses toward the transcendence of private property—Marx's observation that property moves from a physical object to an abstract legal relation—they retain a metaphysical bias that prioritizes the creation of abstract equivalences (the commensurable foundation for value and exchange in commodity circulation). The mode through which property is examined thus reproduces a metaphysical mode of retrieval, leaving blackness suspended from the interrogation of abstraction and forms. At the same time, blackness is instrumentalized as the unacknowledged condition for the analysis of property, facilitating a violent metaphysical (re)turn that rests upon antiblackness. Such an oversight echoes Calvin Warren's explanation that "metaphysics uses blacks to maintain a sense of security and to sustain the fantasy of triumph."[63] This "fantasy of triumph" resonates in the intonation of reform in Harris's, Mansoor's, and Kim's critiques of capitalism, abstraction, and race.

Expanding a critique of the metaphysical turn requires an engagement with Warren's analysis of legal form. In his scrutiny of contract law, Warren elaborates how "contract law conceals an ontological project" through which the contract of form "is predicated upon an ontological difference that it disavows (or more precisely forgets)."[64] Although contract law is distinct from property law, Warren's reading is indispensable here, as the two are inextricably bound through the legal logic and history of slavery—the site where the "thing" is converted into an "abstract right." By bringing into sharp relief that "the contract performs important ontological work," Warren demonstrates why it "has become central to legal metaphysics."[65] In this light, the contract is irreducible to a legal instrument; it is a primary mechanism of abstraction that renders blackness a void, both prior to and through the act of formalizing its capture under the criterion of property. In essence, Warren identifies that antiblackness is that which weaves together the interdependent relations between contract, metaphysical violence, and ontology. On this score, rather than offering a redemptive presence, Dyson's work draws from abstraction to index the sheer gratuity of this capture; her compositions do not "resolve" the void, but rather highlight its impossibility as a permanent, stable condition of the architectural and legal frame.

The compulsion to reduce blackness to the categories of race and abstraction—treating (anti)blackness solely as an effect of these larger structures—reifies blackness as a problem of representation. Such a reification provides the ground for historical materialists to charge Afro-Pessimism with "[denuding] the slave of meaningful qualities to the base abstraction of social death." This line of critique, however, ignores how Sorentino's expansion of "real abstraction" critically destabilizes the Marxist reliance on ostensibly meaningful social categories. For Sorentino, the materialist insistence on such qualities signals a symptom of a deficiency within Marxism itself:

> Instead of diagnosing the slave as the opposite of the laborer, with the former representing concrete domination and the latter its abstraction, we can address Marxism's underdetermination of slavery as a problem for Marx's critical reach. When slavery is considered (only) a matter of empirical-historical significance, it is impossible to grasp why its organization of "white-over-black" compulsively reappears in scenes of antiblack violence. When abstraction is realized primarily within the purview of capitalism, with Marx writing "individuals are now ruled by abstractions, whereas earlier they depended on one another" (*Grundrisse* 164), black thought and action become limited to pre-capitalist revolutionary potential. Irreducible to the critique of political economy, the critique

> of epistemology, or the critique of political theology, Afro-pessimism's critique of political ontology tarries with excesses encoded in historical representation and their unreflexive abstractions.[66]

The appearance of abstraction, race, and violence born out of capitalism is often met with the resistance and indeterminacy of blackness masked by the ideological fidelity to abstraction at the level of representation, but also as a misplaced essence and misconstrual of possible redemption. It follows then that the unthought or unthinkability of blackness is what puts the abstractions of race, as they become indexed by the slave, property, or the nonhuman, through various structural mechanisms and social forces. Yet whereas critical theorists of race such as Bhandar argue that "abstraction lies at the basis of an ontology of property and the racial, and that the each of these phenomena rely upon the other for their actual, material realization,"[67] for Sorentino the wager is more critical. She suggests that the symbolic and ideological materialization of race actually obscures blackness as the negative substance through which these forms appear: "The vanishing mediator . . . is blackness, a negative substance whose flexible uses and appearances are driven towards its own actualized disappearance in scenes of racial violence."[68]

Rather than viewing abstraction as merely a problem *for* ontology, we must consider how articulations of race and abstraction actively suspend—or lynch—blackness in order to render the violence of capitalism thinkable. It is only through the lynching of blackness that the terms of race and forms of abstraction appear. Sexton might explain this tendency as an attempt to critique how the "manifestations of racism, its forms of appearance—what we might call its restricted economies of meaning or its instrumental practices—are called forth by something else, something other that escapes definitions, its evasive 'real purpose.'"[69] In this vein, abstractions of "race" or the "racial" do not merely establish racial formations; they facilitate their manifestations through the occlusion of (anti)blackness.

So, does the language of (racial) abstraction reify the problems of representation for blackness, inadvertently halting thought without going beyond them? If so, does, or must, thinking race through abstraction inevitably capitulate to the very systems that uphold the dissimulation of (anti)blackness? To conceive an abolition of the economies, structures, and systems in the face of the abstraction of race requires a leap beyond the generic and ubiquitous call for abolition at the level of institutions, law, and policymaking. It demands nothing short of an abolition of the *real*—and not just a real abolition as an imagined, humanistic, and idealistic aspiration—to confront the void of blackness itself.

Such stakes reverberate through our interrogations of "self-lynching" and the psychical modes of lynching that take place in the imaginary, where the desire of a self is conceived and continuously made and unmade. As Lacan reminds his readers, "Le réel n'est pas le monde. Il n'y a aucun espoir d'atteindre le réel par la representation" [The real is not the world. There is no hope of reaching the real through representation].[70] This statement follows from his earlier work that the unbarred self-realization remains impossible. Lacan situates this impossibility in one's first encounter with the Other—the enigmatic desire of the mother. For Lacan, such a desire "cannot be satisfied because it is the end, the terminal point, the abolition of the whole world of demand, which is the one that at its deepest level structures man's unconscious."[71]

Lacan's point is not strictly about the abolition of the Other's desire, but rather the abolition of what he sees as an ineffable *x* that inaugurates "the whole world of demand." Yet, such an abolition is impossible, for it would also require overcoming and dismantling the split and the incompletion of the unconscious itself. In other words, abolition would require the impossible destruction of the double inscription characteristic of the unconscious—the radical estrangement from the world already within. Perhaps this is why Sexton says that "slavery is the threshold of the political world, abolition the interminable radicalization of every radical movement [. . .] but a radicalization through the perverse affirmation of deracination."[72] If, following Sexton, "slavery is the threshold of the political world" and the unconscious is the threshold through which the symbolic interacts with the self, a real abolition of lynching—as it is tethered to the bonds of slavery—might be nothing short of the end: "the terminal point, the whole world of demand." And while these bonds are material, legal, and even psychical, they remain structural coordinates of a world that an abolition of the *real* seeks to depose entirely. Such radicalization requires moving beyond the annihilation of bonds, the most fundamental relations, toward the abolition of the *real* that the bond, in its exactitude, aims to contain. Without this, any "real abolition" risks merely re-inscribing the void within new configurations of the bond.

Moreover, what if—as we have seen through Fanon's insights on the real-fantasies of antiblackness—the exposure of blackness to the *real* in all its violence already indicates an abolition of sorts, here and now? Does this mean that a descent into the terminal point has already arrived—a *fait accompli*, one that lacks any possible way to reference its beginning or end? The ethico-political implication is critical: under the strain of antiblackness, there is no way to reference that the end of the world has already happened. It is this unknowable encounter—the confrontation with an unfathomable *x*—that Marriott, following Fanon and in contradistinction to Lacan, describes as having a double valence: at once "understood by all, for while the other only sees a non-me, a non-assimilable counterpart, the black sees a figure—a metaphor—woven through and through by a prescription that separates as a kind of subtractive abolition, by which the entire universe is split in two and/or abolished."[73]

Coda

And so only by contending with the impossible encounter with (the blackness of) the real—the inexpressible void around which desire revolves—can one begin to fathom what would be entailed by not just a real abolition, but an abolition *of* the *real*. The idea of a real abolition might still rest on real abstractions that take place outside of the mind—the objective social forms of exchange and law—and henceforth neglect how the social bonds of antiblackness are libidinally sustained in the imaginary. Yet an abolition of the *real*, its very impossibility, asks what conditions of possibility even remain thinkable, imaginable, realizable with or without blackness.

Our examination demonstrates the structural necessity of "self-lynching" across the juridical, aesthetic, and psychical domains, revealing a paradox where blackness serves as both a target of accrual (policing, punishment, erasure) and a constitutive elision necessary for the image of sovereignty to cohere. In this final chapter, we evoked the urgency of an abolition of the *real* as a way to move beyond the limited imaginary of a "real abolition." The unimaginable possibility of such an encounter takes us back to Marriott's stark assertion from this chapter's epigraph: "objects are not things" and "the lynched body does not resemble an image." The "lynching" arrests of Richards Abdullah and Hampton—much like "the lynched body [that] does not resemble an image"—force a confrontation with the profound failure of the image to contain or represent antiblack violence that underwrites the distinction between object and thing. As such, this chapter turned to the limits of abstraction in art and theory to analyze how attempts to figure or represent violence disavow the very structural subjection they aim to disrupt. The imagined "self-lynching" of blackness—as prosecuted under the language of the law—runs through psychical economies of violence that endeavor to name, represent, and hold captive blackness in the most ineffable ways to perfect the unimaginability of captivity. That "the lynched body does not resemble an image" also leaves us with the unbearable intimation of a nothingness through which the image of sovereignty and the sovereignty of the image are born. The arrest of blackness under the conditions of a lynching of the self cannot possibly correspond to an image, but thereby constitutes the condition of untrammeled violence.

The unrequited demand placed upon blackness by law, knowledge, and aesthetics urges the need to "stretch" a Marxist analysis (as Fanon has informed us). This unthinkable and unrepresentable position of blackness—exposed to the unmediated violence of the *real*—renders impossible the dialectical resolution between the abstract and the concrete that underpins critical thought and racial capitalism itself. As we have seen in the works of Edwards and Dyson, the risk of reifying the very violence they seek to critique is ever-present, especially whenever a literal reading of abstraction is foregrounded; such a reading risks placing blackness within a form or figure that extends its perpetual judgment and capture. The lynching of blackness, as an act that is both concrete and hyper-abstract, confirms that the violence is not simply an implication of an underlying abstraction such as capital, but rather the originary and dialectical law that precedes and sustains the appearance of all such categories and forms. The sovereign fallacy lies in the wish to "know" the unknowability of blackness—and, therefore, the wish to contain that unknown—through abstraction. Such an attempt only proves the power of the unconscious desire to sustain the illusion of sight through a constitutive foreclosure. Since abstraction proves incapable of containing, or, for that matter, realizing, the unknown, we must instead turn to the structural mechanism that produces and maintains this unaccountable difference as a foundation of law. Having demonstrated the impossibility of escaping dialectical traps through representation, our methodological commitment has been the ceaseless de-posing (*Entsetzung*) of the legal-violent structure—a procedure which refuses to posit an alternative mythology, and instead attests that antiblackness remains the un-settable foundation upon which the modern world rests. This de-posing, however, must remain attuned to the Benjaminian danger of merely preserving the law of violence through its dialectical articulation.

The necessary consequence of this un-settable foundation is the production of a specific mechanism of internal capture that stabilizes the entire social, juridical, and aesthetic order. The difference of "self-lynching"—a complex of structural subtraction, psychical operation, and policing of correspondence—is the process that grants law (and not just positive law) its foundational, concealed legitimacy and its explicit, visible violence. Thus, the problem is not simply misrepresentation or a lack of rights, but a foundational uncertainty where blackness is held captive, elided, and displaced at the structural threshold of law's legitimacy. This internal and recursive lynching makes unthinkable what actually drives the thinkable and knowable social, juridical, and aesthetic orders—the blackness of the *real*. Thus, the critical language used to describe this mechanism must itself remain highly self-reflexive and maintain the constant dynamic of undoing without resolution, lest the dialectical effort to articulate the structure of violence risk re-inscribing the law it seeks to dismantle.

Beyond Abolition inexorably suggests that the stakes of antiblackness leave us with a project that cannot be finished through a "real abolition" at the level of the social, nor a critique of violence at the level of the symbolic alone. It demands, instead, an abolition of the *real*: a descent into the terminal point where the world of demand ends. The "self-lynching" of blackness, exposed to the *real*, compels an inquiry that contends with the constitutive fracture of the racial state, a fracture driven by antiblackness. The question remains whether the violence that is always present before naked eyes can ever be seen by a world that cannot see the proof of its own antiblack making—or whether the irrepresentable dynamic of "self-lynching" is the unending condition of the image of sovereignty and sovereignty of the image. The occlusion implies that the violence constituting the racial state must perpetually displace itself onto the image of blackness—and the (anti)blackness of the image—in order to sustain its own coherent appearance. For the image never ends, and the abolition (of the *real*) begins again.

Notes

Introduction

1. "Black Lives Matter Activist Convicted of 'Felony Lynching.'"

2. See Chabria's "Black Woman's 'Lynching' Charge" and Chimurenga's "In Strange Twist of History."

3. I employ the term "self-lynching" not as a psychological description of self-harm, but to designate the structural, psychic effect of antiblack violence, wherein the foreclosure of blackness enacts the symbolic violence that already defines the non-being of blackness. This term thus captures the dual pressure of the state's legal transformation of "felony lynching" into "self-lynching" and the internalized terror resulting from the constitutive foreclosure that grounds the symbolic order.

4. Park, "The Eternal Captive"; Gray, "Anti-Lynching Laws Were Never Meant to Defend Black Lives."

5. Siders, "Jerry Brown Signs 'Lynching' Law Bill"; Mason, "Gov. Brown Signs Measure Striking 'Lynching' Charge From California Law."

6. Cornell, *Beyond Accommodation*, 20.

7. Among the many other places in the manuscript where I have benefited from the incisive comments and interlocution of Jayden Johnson, I appreciate his reminder of how this passage from Lyotard has its immediate resonance with Sexton's article, "The Social Life of Social Death." Sexton, "The Social Life of Social Death," 31.

8. Cornell, *Beyond Accommodation*, 20.

9. Kaufman-Osborn, "Capital Punishment as Legal Lynching?," 31.

10. Kaufman-Osborn, "Capital Punishment as Legal Lynching?," 31.

11. Kaufman-Osborn citing Charles Mills, "Capital Punishment as Legal Lynching?," 24.

12. Mills, *The Racial Contract*, 13.

13. Sexton, *Amalgamation Schemes*, 93.

14. See Marriott, *Whither Fanon?*

15. The expression refers to the Pauline notion of a time before "the time of the laws" (*ante [aetatem] legum*). I thank Mario Telò for his insight on this.

16. See Nolan, "Defendant, Lynch Thyself."
17. Marriott, "The Crisis of Truth," 84.
18. Sexton, "People-of-Color-Blindness," 35.
19. Vismann, *Files*, 3.
20. Johnson, *The Feminist Difference*, 45.
21. Johnson, *The Feminist Difference*, 46.
22. Johnson, *The Feminist Difference*, 46.
23. Johnson, *The Feminist Difference*, 38.
24. Johnson, "Using People," 262.
25. Johnson, "Using People," 265.
26. Johnson, "Using People," 265.
27. Johnson, "Using People," 266.
28. Johnson, "Using People," 266.
29. Teo, "Non-Event," 73.
30. Teo, "Non-Event," 73.
31. Bradley, *Anteaesthetics*, 238.
32. Wilderson, *Red, White, and Black*, 91.
33. Butler, "Blackout."
34. I define my use of the term *metapsychology* more extensively in Chapter 4.
35. White, "History as Fulfillment," 41–43.
36. White, "History as Fulfillment," 40.
37. White, "History as Fulfillment," 40.
38. White, "History as Fulfillment," 40.
39. Hartman, *Scenes of Subjection*, 11.
40. Fanon, *Black Skin, White Mask*, 146. See also Lebeau, "Psycho-Politics," for an insightful reading of this passage and Fanon's notion of the real.
41. https://www.sup.org/books/series/inventions-black-philosophy-politics-aesthetics.
42. Sexton, "Afro-Pessimism: The Unclear Word."
43. Sexton, "Afro-Pessimism: The Unclear Word."
44. Lebeau, *Psychoanalysis and Cinema*, 8.
45. Lebeau, *Psychoanalysis and Cinema*, 8.
46. Han, *Letters of the Law*.
47. Mulvey, "Visual Pleasure and Narrative Cinema," 9.
48. Farley, "Perfect Slavery."
49. Benjamin, "Critique of Violence," in *Toward the Critique of Violence*, 60.
50. Weigel, *Walter Benjamin*, 68.
51. Benjamin, "Critique of Violence," in *Toward the Critique of Violence*, 60.
52. Benjamin, "Critique of Violence," in *Toward the Critique of Violence*, 57.
53. See Hamacher, "Afformative, Strike," 3.
54. Fanon, *Black Skin, White Masks*, 35.
55. Cited from Sorentino, "Abstraction."
56. Marx, "Economic and Philosophic Manuscripts of 1844," 84.
57. Marx, "Economic and Philosophic Manuscripts of 1844," 84
58. Marx, "Grundrisse," 237.

59. Marx, "Grundrisse," 237.

60. See Sohn-Rethel, "Intellectual and Manual Labor," 51.

61. Sohn-Rethel, "Intellectual and Manual Labor," 51.

62. Sohn-Rethel, "Intellectual and Manual Labor," 51.

63. Toscano, "The Open Secret of Real Abstraction," 19.

64. Toscano citing Roberto Finelli, "The Open Secret of Real Abstraction," 21.

65. Toscano, "The Open Secret of Real Abstraction," 18.

66. Žižek, *The Sublime Object of Ideology*, 17.

67. Žižek, *The Sublime Object of Ideology*, 19.

68. Žižek, *The Sublime Object of Ideology*, 19.

69. Lacan, *The Four Fundamental Concepts*, 22.

70. Lacan, *The Four Fundamental Concepts*, 22.

71. Lacan, *The Four Fundamental Concepts*, 60.

72. Fanon, *Black Skin, White Masks*, 145.

73. For example, in Chapter 2 of *Black Skin, White Masks* ("The Woman of Color and the White Man,"), Fanon highlights an encounter between the distortion of truth and reality at the level of fantasy in respect to blackness and sexuality. He describes the encounter as a "[confrontation] of a real black aesthetic" (*Black Skin, White Masks*, 40). See Park, "'A Real Black Aesthetic.'"

74. Lacan, *Four Fundamental Concepts*, 41.

75. Fanon, *Black Skin, White Masks*, 146.

76. Freud, "The Dream-Work," 507.

77. Freud writes: "But now that analysts at least have become reconciled to replacing the manifest dream by the meaning revealed by its interpretation, many of them have become guilty of falling into another confusion which they cling to with equal obstinacy. They seek to find the essence of dreams in their content and in so doing they overlook the distinction between the latent dream-thoughts and the dream work" (Freud, "The Dream-Work," 506).

78. Freud, "The Dream-Work," 506–507.

79. Lear, *Freud*, 90.

80. Lear, *Freud*, 90.

81. Didi-Huberman, *Confronting Images*, 141.

82. Didi-Huberman, *Confronting Images*, 141.

83. Freud, "Instincts and Their Vicissitudes," 122.

84. Freud, "Instincts and Their Vicissitudes," 123.

85. Bradley, *Anteaesthetics*.

86. Bradley, *Anteaesthetics*, 43.

87. Bradley, *Anteaesthetics*, 45.

88. See Hegel, *Phenomenology of Spirit*, *Philosophy of Mind*, and *The Science of Logic*.

89. See Lacan, "Mirror Stage."

90. Rose, *Broken Middle*, 81–84.

91. See in general Jackson, *Soledad Brother* and *Blood in My Eye*. Specifically, see Jackson, *Soledad Brother*, 215–217.

92. Marriot, *Haunted Life*, xxi.

93. Lacan, *Four Fundamental Concepts*, 167.

94. Gonzales-Day, *Lynching in the West 1850–1935*.

Chapter 1

1. Marriott, "The Perfect Beauty of Black Death."

2. Marriott, "The Perfect Beauty of Black Death."

3. On the "rotten" cycle, see Benjamin, "Critique of Violence," in *Walter Benjamin: Selected Writings*, 1:242.

4. For *Setzung* (Positing), see Benjamin, "Critique of Violence," in *Toward the Critique of Violence*, 45.

5. Benjamin, "Task of the Translator" (Zohn trans.), 70.

6. My emphasis. Here, I cite Waldrep, "Word and Deed," 232. Waldrep in turn cites from *The Galenian*, as quoted in *Nile's Register*, July 19, 1834.

7. White, *The Content of the Form*, 11.

8. White, *The Content of the Form*, 9.

9. Vismann, *Files*, 8.

10. Benjamin, "Task of the Translator" (Zohn trans.), 71.

11. See Žižek, *Incontinence of the Void*, 185.

12. Žižek, *Incontinence of the Void*, 186.

13. His emphasis. Cover, "Nomos and Narrative," 108.

14. Cover, "Nomos and Narrative," 109.

15. To this point, Cover, following the passage cited above, notes: "Such real integration occurs around particular constellations of creed and ritual . . . concurred in by a particular group of brothers and sisters. And to their common understanding of creed and ritual is added a common understanding of their relation to the primordial, imaginary, *true* unity that occurred in a vanished instant long ago" (108–109).

16. Fanon, *Black Skin, White Masks*, 204.

17. Johnson, "Vigilance and the Law," 559.

18. Forbes, "The Early African Heritage of California," 89.

19. Waldrep, *The Many Faces of Judge Lynch*, 50.

20. Waldrep, *The Many Faces of Judge Lynch*, 50.

21. Anderson, *The Second*, 70.

22. Anderson, *The Second*, 71.

23. For instance, Kiser brings up the example of Judge Kirby Benedict, an "official from Illinois [who] had established himself as the face of antislavery judicial activism in New Mexico by ruling in favor of a peon in an 1857 lawsuit." Kiser, *Borderlands of Slavery*, 58.

24. LeMenager, *Manifest and Other Destinies*, 164.

25. LeMenager, *Manifest and Other Destinies*, 164.

26. LeMenager, *Manifest and Other Destinies*, 164.

27. LeMenager, *Manifest and Other Destinies*, 165.

28. LeMenager, *Manifest and Other Destinies*, 143.

29. See again, LeMenager, namely her chapter, "The Nation's Mouth," 164.

30. LeMenager, *Manifest and Other Destinies*, 166.

31. Marriott, "Judging Fanon," n.p.

32. LeMenager, *Manifest and Other Destinies*, 165. LeMenager explains further, "Like legal slave traders, Murrell has to disguise his slaves to ensure their marketability; moreover, he recognizes that his profits from slaves will increase the farther he moves them from centers of supply . . . to less accessible regions of demand."

33. Cited in LeMenager, *Manifest and Other Destinies*, 165–166.

34. LeMenager, *Manifest and Other Destinies*, 166.

35. LeMenager, *Manifest and Other Destinies*, 166.

36. Haley, *No Mercy Here*, 94. See also Hartman, *Scenes of Subjection*.

37. See Lacan, *On Feminine Sexuality*, and Sexton, "The *Vel* of Slavery."

38. Sorentino, "Money, Slavery, Myth," 14.

39. Sorentino, "Money, Slavery, Myth," 14.

40. Sorentino, "Money, Slavery, Myth," 14.

41. Marriott, "On Decadence."

42. Marriott, "On Decadence."

43. Marriott, "On Decadence."

44. Tomšič, *The Capitalist Unconscious*, 194–195.

45. Tomšič, *The Capitalist Unconscious*, 195.

46. Tomšič, *The Capitalist Unconscious*, 194–195.

47. Žižek, *Incontinence of the Void*, 184.

48. Fischer, *Modernity Disavowed*, 19.

49. Weigel, *Grammatology of Images*, 69.

50. Waldrep, *The Many Faces of Judge Lynch*, 45, citing a lynch mob.

51. Žižek, *The Sublime Object of Ideology*, 33. See also Fischer's critical reading of Žižek's *The Sublime Object of Ideology* in her *Modernity Disavowed*, 142–144.

52. Kiser, *Borderlands of Slavery*, 32.

53. Le Menager, *Manifest and Other Destinies*, 154–155.

54. Kiser, *Borderlands of Slavery*, 33.

55. Kiser, *Borderlands of Slavery*, 19.

56. Kiser, *Borderlands of Slavery*, 19.

57. Kiser, *Borderlands of Slavery*, 47.

58. Kiser, *Borderlands of Slavery*, 47. Elsewhere, Kiser notes that after "the United States secured possession of California, Utah, and New Mexico," the "political disposition" for chattel slavery was not based on the possibility of plantation-style agriculture or the extension of involuntary servitude. The "arid climates" of those regions prevented the former, and "Indian captivity and debt peonage as alternative forms of involuntary servitude already satisfied regional demand for labor" (Kiser, *Coast-To-Coast Empire*, 10). Rather, in securing the Southwest, "Southerners sought to make New Mexico a slave territory or state not because they actually intended to transport large numbers of black slaves there, but rather to exercise ideological control over the area in advancement of their own sectional economy and political relevance" (Kiser, *Coast-To-Coast Empire*, 10–11).

59. Morrison, *Playing in the Dark*, 38.

60. Morrison, *Playing in the Dark*, 38.

61. Among other places, see Tomlins, *Freedom Bound*, 116–120 and 143 for a comprehensive understanding of *terra nullius*.

62. Johnson, *Critical Difference*, 142.

63. Rose, *States of Fantasy*, 23. I paraphrase the end of Rose's citation here. In the original, she writes, "where this particular dialogue between literature and politics will begin," situating her intervention within wider debates of politics in literary theory.

64. I am informed here by Jared Sexton's use of "bodies as images" as opposed to images *of* bodies, a distinction that he conceptualizes following the work of Kara Keeling in his *Amalgamation Schemes*, 29. For a separate but informative discussion on this, see Georges Didi-Huberman's *Images in Spite of All.*

65. Laplanche and Pontalis, *The Language of Psycho-Analysis*, 206.

66. Marriott, *Whither Fanon?*, 213.

67. Lapp, *Blacks in Gold Rush California*, 2–3.

68. Juliet Hooker has explained in detail the complexities of U.S. and Latin American racial formations. Relevant here is perhaps her observation of how "the term 'race' during this era [the second half of the nineteenth century] reflected the historical strand's restriction of its racially deterministic arguments about 'white superiority' to Nordic or Northern European populations" (7). To this end, she critically notes that "Latin Americans who accepted the premise of white supremacy but who believed that their populations could be 'whitened' via racial mixing with European immigrants tended to gloss over the distinction between Latins and Anglo-Saxons, as most Europeans immigrants to Latin America were from Southern Europe (i.e., Latins)" (7). Hooker further illustrates how Western ideas of race and scientific racism that were well established in the United States would influence Latin America: "Eugenics also played an important role in debates about the consolidation of national identity in Latin America, as hereditary science came to be seen as something that could assist in the biological homogenization of various national types" (9). Citing Nancy Stepan, she explains in the context of Mexico: "Thus the Mexicans praised racial hybridization as itself a form of eugenization that would help consolidate the nation around the mestizo" (9–10).

69. Terada, *Looking Away*, 15.

70. Sexton, *Amalgamation Schemes*, 31.

71. Lapp, *Blacks in Gold Rush California*, 3.

72. See for example Miles, *Dawn of Detroit*; Wheeler, *Black California*; Beasley, *The Negro Trail Blazers of California*; de Graaf, Mulroy, and Taylor, eds., *Seeking El Dorado*; Lapp, *Blacks in Gold Rush California*; Roberts, *Mining for Freedom*; and Nokes, *Breaking Chains.*

73. See Roberts, *Mining for Freedom.*

74. Lapp, *Blacks in Gold Rush California.*

75. Sexton, *Amalgamation Schemes*, 196.

76. Derrida, *Before the Law*, 36.

77. Fischer, *Modernity Disavowed*, 18.

78. See, for example, Cornell, "Citizens of Nowhere" and Pfeifer, ed., *Lynching Beyond Dixie.*

79. Roberts, *Mining for Freedom*, 11. It is important to note that similar modes of black exclusion took place in Oregon and other parts of the Pacific Northwest. See, for example, Coleman's *Dangerous Subjects* and Nokes's *Breaking Chains.*

80. Roberts, *Mining for Freedom*, 12. See also Smith, "Pacific Bound."

81. Roberts, *Mining for Freedom*, 13.

82. See "The Crime of Testimony Laws," https://www.aclunc.org/sites/goldchains/explore/george-gordon.html.

83. https://www.aclunc.org/docs/FINAL_California_Testimony_Exclusion_Laws.pdf.

84. Smith, "Pacific Bound."

85. Smith, "Pacific Bound."

86. Rose, *States of Fantasy*, 23.

87. Johnson, "Anthropomorphism in Lyric and Law," 202.

88. Johnson, "Anthropomorphism in Lyric and Law," 202–203.

89. Hartman, *Scenes of Subjection*, 88.

90. White, *Content of the Form*, 13.

91. Lapp, *Blacks in Gold Rush California*.

92. Wells-Barnett, "Lynch Law in America." See also in particular Goldsby's chapter, "Writing 'Dynamitically,'" in her *A Spectacular Secret*; Park, "Whence Disinheritance Holds."

93. To name only a few examples, see Dayan, "The Law Is a White Dog"; Davis, "Reflections on the Black Woman's Role in the Community of Slaves"; and Harris, "Whiteness as Property."

94. Derrida, *Before the Law*, 36.

95. Waldrep, *The Many Faces of Judge Lynch*, 45.

96. See Waldrep, *The Many Faces of Judge Lynch*.

97. Waldrep, *The Many Faces of Judge Lynch*, 45.

98. Winnicott, "Psycho-Analysis and the Sense of Guilt," 24.

99. Bahti, *Allegories of History*, 76.

100. Bahti, *Allegories of History*, 74.

101. Bahti, *Allegories of History*, 76.

102. Derrida, *Writing and Difference*, 4.

103. David-Ménard, "Kant, the Law, and Desire," 352.

104. Marriott, "On Decadence."

Chapter 2

1. I am relying on Emily Apter's use of the term, which she draws from Jacques Derrida. I expand on this notion of "indefinite sentence" in the next chapter. See Apter, "Armed Response."

2. Goldsby, *A Spectacular Secret*, 66.

3. See Collins, *Black Feminist Thought*.

4. See Gonzales-Day, *Lynching in the West*.

5. See Park, "Unhomeliness."

6. Here, I position this argument in the context of representation and question the construction of the image, but I follow the argument of Sara-Maria Sorentino who extended what Frank Wilderson has described as the "ruses of analogy." In her reflections on what she describes as the virtual slave that traverses philosophies from Aristotle to the present, she notes that "when the long-fabled Aristotelean Word finds fruition in the grammar of the flesh, it turns to the ruse of analogy to conceal the fact that it has nothing to hide. Blackness

is, insofar as it is semantically and gratuitously captured and substituted." Sorentino, "Natural Slavery, Real Abstraction," 646. This dimension of capture and substitution, I find, is key to what I try to conceptualize in the role and function of representation in the compulsive and insistent valences of antiblackness that underlie slavery's *afterlife*.

7. See Morrison, *Playing in the Dark*.

8. See Farrell, *Swift Justice*.

9. See Goldsby's chapter "Lynching Photography at the Turn of the Nineteenth Century" in *A Spectacular Secret* for a compelling analysis of the gaze, identification, and visual cues of the image that serve a critique of lynching.

10. Goldsby, *A Spectacular Secret*, 231–232.

11. Marriott, *On Black Men*, 6.

12. My emphasis. Wood, *Lynching and Spectacle*, 216.

13. Laplanche and Pontalis, *The Language of Psycho-Analysis*, 211.

14. Wood, *Lynching and Spectacle*, 214.

15. On an underground economy and cultural logic of the terror formations of lynching, see Apel, *Imagery of Lynching*; Goldsby, *A Spectacular Secret*; Wood, *Lynching and Spectacle*; and Woodward, *Delectable Negro*.

16. Wood, *Lynching and Spectacle*, 215.

17. Wood, *Lynching and Spectacle*, 214.

18. Freud, "Instincts and Their Vicissitudes," 129.

19. Freud, "Instincts and Their Vicissitudes," 130.

20. See also Goldsby's *A Spectacular Secret* on the contrast and distinction between white men and black men regarding the display of their bodies in lynching photography (231).

21. Apel, *Imagery of Lynching*, 135.

22. Apel, *Imagery of Lynching*, 136. See also Marriott's *On Black Men* and Woodward's *The Delectable Negro*.

23. Lacan, *The Object Relation*, 30.

24. Nolan, "Defendant, Lynch Thyself."

25. Nolan, "Defendant, Lynch Thyself."

26. See Nolan, "Defendant, Lynch Thyself."

27. National Association for the Advancement of Colored People (NAACP) anti-lynching papers, Newspapers and Microforms Library, Doe Library, University of California, Berkeley. Brackets indicate author's interpolations where the original manuscript is indiscernible. The identification of "race" and "Messrs. Knowland and Levy" is based on Beasley's contemporaneous reporting in *The Oakland Tribune*.

28. National Association for the Advancement of Colored People (NAACP) anti-lynching papers, Newspapers and Microforms Library, Doe Library, University of California, Berkeley. William Pickens is identified as the author of the January 29 response based on his role as NAACP Field Secretary (1920–1942) and the direct address to him in Beasley's preceding correspondence.

29. Nolan citing William F. Knowland in "Defendant, Lynch Thyself," 78. In particular, see also Nolan's footnote 119 where he elaborates on the fallacy of Knowland's memory. I quote it partially here: "It must be noted that Knowland's memory was not entirely accurate

about the circumstances surrounding the law's enactment. He told the interviewer that in fact the law was passed as a result of the San Jose tragedy . . . This of course is impossible, since the law was introduced several months before the lynching in San Jose. However, it is easy to understand how the two became linked in the Senator's mind, and how the details of the timelines may have become confused after 40 years," 78.

30. Nolan, "Defendant, Lynch Thyself," 78.

31. Nolan, "Defendant, Lynch Thyself," 77–78.

32. Johnson, "Moses and Intertextuality," 136.

33. Douglass and Wilderson, "Violence of Presence," 117–118.

34. Douglass and Wilderson, "Violence of Presence," 117.

35. https://kengonzalesday.com/projects/erased-lynchings/ (accessed November 11, 2022).

36. Gonzales-Day, *Lynching in the West*, 16.

37. Quoted in Rose, *Sexuality in the Field of Vision*, 97.

38. Rose, *Sexuality in the Field of Vision*, 97.

39. Bradley, "On Black Aesthesis," 21.

40. Lacan, *Écrits*, 225.

41. Higginbotham, "African-American Women's History and the Metalanguage of Race," 253–254.

42. Sexton, "The Rage."

43. Hartman, *Scenes of Subjection*, 57. The notion of phobogenic objects in relation to antiblackness can be traced to Fanon. Fanon writes: "The choice of the phobic object is thus *overdetermined*. Such an object does not come out of the void of nothingness; in some situations it has previously evoked an affect in the patient. The phobia is the latent presence of this affect on the core of his world; there is an organization that has been given a form. For the object, naturally, need not be there, it is enough that somewhere the object *exists*: is a possibility." (Fanon, *Black Skin, White Masks*, 133).

44. Hartman, *Scenes of Subjection*, 58.

45. Gray, "Necrophagy at the Lynching Block," 13–14.

46. See Barthes, *Image-Music-Text*.

47. "Counting the Dead" refers to the title of the first chapter of *Lynching in the West*. The chapter outlines his methodological approach to the archive, census data, and other source materials where he quantifies the number of summary executions across racial lines.

48. Gonzales-Day, *Lynching in the West*, 12.

49. Da Silva, "No-Bodies," 119–120.

50. Da Silva, "No-Bodies," 120.

51. Benjamin, *Race After Technology*, 99.

52. See Goldsby, *A Spectacular Secret*.

53. Goldsby, "In the Mind's Eye," 303.

54. Gonzales-Day, *Erased Lynchings*.

55. Marriott, "On Revolutionary Suicide." For an extensive critique and meditation on the relationship between black gender and sexuality, technology (namely the camera and photography), and lynching, see also his *On Black Men*.

56. Marriott, "On Revolutionary Suicide."

57. Johnson, "Ego Sum Game," 286.

58. Weigel, *Grammatology of Images*, 108.

59. Weigel, *Grammatology of Images*, 108

60. Weigel, *Grammatology of Images*, 106.

61. Weigel, *Grammatology of Images*, 91.

62. Wood, *Lynching and Spectacle*, 49.

63. Wood, *Lynching and Spectacle*, 48.

64. Goldsby, *A Spectacular Secret*, 7.

65. Haley, *No Mercy Here*, 9.

Chapter 3

1. See Nolan, "Defendant, Lynch Thyself."

2. *People v. Anthony J.*, 85 Cal. 2d 783 (App. 4th 1999).

3. Gray, "Anti-Lynching Laws Were Never Meant to Defend Black Lives."

4. I thank the anonymous reader who reviewed an earlier version of this chapter published in the journal *Diacritics* (2021). They encouraged me to specify this point regarding the language of the state that contradicts its own intent to protect racialized citizens from lynching violence only to inflict violence on those same subjects as means to secure the power of the state.

5. Nolan, "Defendant, Lynch Thyself."

6. Martinot and Sexton, "The Avante-Garde of White Supremacy," 176.

7. See Goldsby, *A Spectacular Secret*.

8. I am grateful for the archival and research assistance provided by Saphronia Carson regarding the limitations and strictures of the archive that I outline in this chapter. Her assistance confirmed that the information regarding *Jones* has been restricted as the result of a move in the jurisdiction of the case from the Fourth Appellate District to the Third. Further, while attempting to find additional information on the case, it was noted that the courthouse destroyed records for any criminal cases after twenty years. There are similar barriers regarding the case of *Anthony J.* Because *Anthony J.* was processed as a juvenile case, the request to access the case records was denied.

9. *People v. Jones*, 19 Cal. App. 3d 437 (Cal. App. 4th 1971).

10. Hazel Carby, Jacqueline Goldsby, Sarah Haley, and Leigh Raighford, to name only a few, have explained the impossibility of recording extrajudicial antiblack violence and the insidious pathology of black criminality's construction. Specifically in the context of lynching, Goldsby explains the pervasive nature of a dynamic in which such violence was not recorded, yet naturalized as a quotidian state of affairs by both the state and (white) citizens (see Goldsby, *A Spectacular Secret*).

11. See Hartman, "Seduction and the Ruses of Power."

12. Wilderson, "The Vengeance of Vertigo," 20.

13. Wilderson, *Red, White, and Black*.

14. Here, I lean on Sigrid Weigel's interpretation of Freud's notion of *translation* against the context of repression, which she draws from his letters to Wilhelm Fliess (see Weigel, *Walter Benjamin*).

15. See Derrida, *Of Grammatology* and *Writing and Difference*. See also Lacan, *Seminar III: The Psychoses*.

16. Apter, "Armed Response."

17. *People v. Anthony J.*, 85 Cal. 2d 783 (App. 4th 1999).

18. Reiter, "The Pelican Bay Hunger Strike," 581.

19. Hartman, *Scenes of Subjection*, 52.

20. Johnson, "Anthropomorphism in Lyric and Law."

21. Benjamin, "Zur Kritik der Gewalt," 48.

22. Vásquez, "Illegalist Foucault, Criminal Foucault," 939.

23. Weigel, *Walter Benjamin*, 60.

24. Weigel, *Walter Benjamin*, 60.

25. Here, Weigel's citation refers to Michael Jennings's edition of *Walter Benjamin: Selected Writings*.

26. Ng, "Benjamin on Law," 4:04–5:01.

27. Benjamin, "Critique of Violence," in *Reflections*, 283.

28. Benjamin, "Task of the Translator," in *Illuminations*, 70.

29. To name only two of his works that engage with this thesis, see Marriott's *Whither Fanon?* and *Of Effacement*.

30. Marriott, *Of Effacement*, viii. There, Marriott notes his use of the term, "I borrow the word *invisable*—meaning unable to be intended or aimed at—from Jean-Luc Marion's *The Visible and the Revealed*."

31. de Man, "Conclusions," 86.

32. Cassin, "Introduction," xvii.

33. Benjamin, "The Task of the Translator," in *Illuminations*, 70.

34. Benjamin, "The Task of the Translator," in *Illuminations*, 70.

35. Benjamin, "The Task of the Translator," in *Illuminations*, 71.

36. Benjamin, "The Task of the Translator," in *Illuminations*, 70.

37. Johnson, "Correctional Facilities," 169.

38. Johnson, "Correctional Facilities," 169.

39. Johnson, "Correctional Facilities," 168.

40. Hartman, *Scenes of Subjection*, and Lyotard, *Libidinal Economy*.

41. Zupančič, *Ethics of the Real*, 3.

42. Zupančič, *Ethics of the Real*, 4.

43. Harris, "Whiteness as Property."

44. Harris, "Whiteness as Property," 1714.

45. Harris, "Whiteness as Property," 1714.

46. Harris, "Whiteness as Property," 1731.

47. Harris, "Whiteness as Property," 1734.

48. Harris, "Whiteness as Property," 1729.

49. Bhandar, "Property, Law, and Race," 208–211. Bhandar offers an incisive elaboration and critique of Harris's canonical essay. For Bhandar, "Harris' theorization of how whiteness becomes property maps the transition from real forms of property to abstract forms of property rooted in expectation; however, she does not identify this transition as in part, a

consequence of the radical changes occurring in modes of propertization" (211). Bhandar considers these changes in the modes of propertization to be part and parcel of financialization. She explains further, "Abstraction functions in such a way so as to create legal forms of property and racial ontologies coterminously" (211). Bhandar's critique is informative in articulating the relationship between finance capital and what she understands as the racial. As much as I agree with Bhandar's critique of Harris, I depart from her positioning of ontology here as coterminous with the creation of legal forms of property and its permutations, including money. On this note, see Chapters 1 and 6.

50. Harris, "Whiteness as Property," 1727.

51. Harris, "Whiteness as Property," 1726.

52. Harris, "Whiteness as Property," 1727.

53. Weheliye, *Habeas Viscus*, 78.

54. Weheliye, *Habeas Viscus*, 78.

55. Harris, "Whiteness as Property," 1725.

56. Benjamin, "Critique of Violence."

57. Zupančič, *Ethics of the Real*, 18.

58. Sexton, "Affirmation in the Dark," 105.

59. Sexton, "Affirmation in the Dark," 104.

60. Sexton citing Calvin Warren, "Affirmation in the Dark," 104.

61. Sexton, "Affirmation in the Dark," 105.

62. Marriott, *Whither Fanon?*, 373n3. See also Marriott, *Lacan Noir*, for a definitive exposition on the distinction between Fanon's and Lacan's conceptions of the *real*.

63. Lacan, *Seminar III: The Psychoses*, 193.

64. Lacan, *Seminar III: The Psychoses*, 193.

65. da Silva, *Toward a Global Idea of Race*, 20.

66. Lacan, *Seminar III: The Psychoses*, 193.

67. Lacan, *Seminar III: The Psychoses*, 194.

68. Lacan, *Seminar III: The Psychoses*, 194.

69. Lacan, *Seminar III: The Psychoses*, 194.

70. Here, I have added the translation of *l'être qui fuit*.

71. Karera, "Paraontology," 167.

72. Lacan, *Seminar III: The Psychoses*, 217.

73. Copjec, *Read My Desire*, 176.

74. Copjec, *Read My Desire*, 176.

75. Goldsby, "The High and Low Tech of It."

76. Marriott, *Whither Fanon?*, 64.

77. Weigel, *Walter Benjamin*, 170.

Chapter 4

1. Marriott, *Whither Fanon?*, 161.

2. Morrison, "Friday on the Potomac," xvi.

3. Elving, "A Refresher on Anita Hill and Clarence Thomas."

4. Video stills of Anita Hill's testimony before the Senate Judiciary Committee, October 11, 1991. Source: C-SPAN Archive.

5. Goldsby, "The High and Low Tech of It," 246.

6. Bradley, "Living in the Absence of a Body."

7. Wilderson, "Gramsci's Black Marx," 231.

8. Freud, "Repression," 146.

9. Freud, "Repression," 146.

10. Freud, "Repression," 146.

11. Freud, "Repression," 147.

12. Freud, "Repression," 148.

13. Lacan, *Four Fundamental Concepts*, 60.

14. Freud, "The Unconscious," 181. Of course, Freud's use of the term *metapsychology* can be seen much earlier than in "Repression" and "The Unconscious," which I refer to and lean on in this chapter. Freud's use of the term can be tracked back to his correspondence with Wilhelm Fleiss. See, for example, his letter to Fleiss on March 10, 1898, where he writes, "I am going to ask you seriously, by the way, whether I may use the name metapsychology for my psychology that leads behind consciousness." Freud, "The Complete Letters," 301–302.

15. Douglass and Wilderson, "Violence of Presence."

16. Video still of Clarence Thomas's opening statement before the Senate Judiciary Committee, October 11, 1991. Source: C-SPAN Archives.

17. My transcription. "October 11, 1991: Clarence Thomas Full Opening Statement (C-SPAN)." https://www.youtube.com/watch?vZPNkkUJtjo8, 38:15–39:43.

18. Goldsby, "The High and Low Tech of It," 1996.

19. Goldsby, "The High and Low Tech of It," 1996.

20. Bradley, *Anteaesthetics*, 63.

21. As mentioned in the acknowledgments, the reflections in this particular paragraph, as well as the chapter in general, have greatly benefited from the works-in-progress group Tall Trees Society, in particular the insights of those present: Amal Ali, Rizvana Bradley, Scholastique Iradukunda, Jaeden Johnson, David Marriott, Gabriela Puche, and Sara-Maria Sorentino.

22. Morrison, *Race-ing Justice, En-gendering Power*.

23. Lacan, *The Psychoses*, 218.

24. Lacan, *The Psychoses*, 218.

25. Lacan, *The Psychoses*, 221.

26. Morrison, "Friday on the Potomac," xviii–xix.

27. Fenves, "The Genesis of Judgment," 87.

28. Fenves, "The Genesis of Judgment," 88.

29. See, for example, Kant's discussion of the copula and schema in the *Critique of Pure Reason* (A 68 / B 93) where *judgment* is defined as the faculty of thinking the particular under the universal, thus tying it intrinsically to the process of representation (*Vorstellung*). Similarly, in Hegel's *Science of Logic*, judgment (*Urteil*) is the initial determinate distinction within the Notion (*Begriff*). My argument here defines constitutive foreclosure as a structural violence that operates *antecedent* to these conditions, foreclosing the possibility of the subject/predicate relation necessary for judgment/representation to even begin in the anti-black world.

30. See Park, "Can Feminism Think Black Incapacity?," 57.

31. Morrison, "Friday on the Potomac," xvi–xvii.
32. Williams, "A Rare Case Study of Muleheadedness and Men," 170.
33. Marriott, *Whither Fanon?*, 164.
34. Here, I cite from Rodolphe Gasché's "'Setzung' and 'Übersetzung,'" 42, which draws from Paul de Man's "Semiology and Rhetoric."
35. Gasché, "'Setzung' and 'Übersetzung,'" 42.
36. de Man, "The Epistemology of Metaphor," 27–28.
37. de Man, "The Epistemology of Metaphor," 24.
38. Wilderson, *Red, White, and Black*, 48.
39. See de Man, "The Concept of Irony."
40. Marriott, *Whither Fanon?*, 162.
41. Marriott, *Whither Fanon?*, 162.
42. Sexton, *Amalgamation Schemes*, 188.
43. Lacan, "L'étourdit," 46.
44. Lacan, "On Feminine Sexuality," 9.
45. Sexton, *Amalgamation Schemes*, 182.
46. Jackson, *Becoming Human*, 8–9.
47. Zupančič, *Why Psychoanalysis?*, 26.
48. Morrison, "Friday on the Potomac," xxiv.
49. Morrison, "Friday on the Potomac," xxv.
50. Morrison, "Friday on the Potomac," xxv–xxvi.
51. Morrison, "Friday on the Potomac," xxxvi–xxxvii.
52. Morrison, "Friday on the Potomac," xxv.
53. Nyquist, *Arbitrary Rule*, 219.
54. Nyquist, *Arbitrary Rule*, 219–220.
55. Nyquist, *Arbitrary Rule*, 220.
56. Morrison, "Friday on the Potomac," xxviii.
57. See Marriott, *Of Effacement*.
58. I borrow this line directly from James, *The Book of Night Women*, 20.

Chapter 5

1. In an earlier version of this chapter, entitled "The Eternal Captive," I explored similar themes of uncanniness and perversion. While I draw here on the same event (the arrests) and similar themes, this chapter is a significant revision of the earlier publication. See Park, "The Eternal Captive."
2. Massie, "What Activist Jasmine Richards's 'Lynching' Conviction Means for the Black Lives Matter Movement."
3. See Massie, "What Activist Jasmine Richards's 'Lynching' Conviction Means for the Black Lives Matter Movement" and Rivera, "Black Lives Matter Pasadena Organizer Convicted of Felony 'Lynching' Charge."
4. Massie, "What Activist Jasmine Richards's 'Lynching' Conviction Means for the Black Lives Matter Movement."
5. Rivera, "Black Lives Matter Pasadena Organizer Convicted of Felony 'Lynching' Charge."

6. "California 'Lynching' Conviction Is a Threat to All!"
7. Sexton, "People-of-Color-Blindness," 48.
8. Benjamin, "Critique of Violence," in *Toward the Critique of Violence*, 41.
9. Benjmain, "Critique of Violence," in *Toward the Critique of Violence*, 41.
10. Hamacher, "Afformative, Strike," 1135.
11. Hamacher, "Afformative, Strike," 1146.
12. Hamacher, "Afformative, Strike," 1146.
13. Hamacher, "Afformative, Strike," 1136.
14. Sexton, *Amalgamation Schemes*, 193.
15. Wilderson, "Gramsci's Black Marx," 229.
16. Wilderson, "Gramsci's Black Marx," 226.
17. Wilderson, "Gramsci's Black Marx," 226.
18. See Hartman and Wilderson, "The Position of the Unthought." Also see Marriott, "The Crisis of Truth."
19. Wang, *Carceral Capitalism*, 85.
20. Wang, *Carceral Capitalism*, 89.
21. Wang, *Carceral Capitalism*, 340n38.
22. Wang, *Carceral Capitalism*, 122.
23. Sorentino, "Impossible Labour History," 62.
24. Sorentino, "Impossible Labour History," 62.
25. Campbell, "A Critique of the Occupy Movement from a Black Occupier," 49.
26. Campbell, "A Critique of the Occupy Movement from a Black Occupier," 49.
27. Sorentino, "Impossible Labour History," 52.
28. See Gramsci, "State and Civil Society" in *Selections from the Prison Notebooks*.
29. Wilderson, "Gramsci's Black Marx," 230.
30. Her emphasis. Wang, *Carceral Capitalism*, 297–298.
31. Chandler, *X—The Problem of the Negro as a Problem for Thought*.
32. Chandler, *X—The Problem of the Negro as a Problem for Thought*, 2–3.
33. Douglass, *Engendering Blackness*, 267.
34. Patton, "Why Blacks Aren't Embracing O.W.S."
35. Jefferson, "Policing, Whiteness, and the Death-Wage."
36. Jefferson, "Policing, Whiteness, and the Death-Wage."
37. ross, "Call It What It Is: Anti-Blackness."
38. Warren, "Barred Objects," 31.
39. Sexton, "Proprieties of Coalition," 90.
40. See, to name only a few examples, Ancheto, "Neither Black Nor White"; Kim, *Asian Americans in an Anti-Black World*; and Matsuda, "Beyond, and Not Beyond."
41. See Terada, *Metaracial*.
42. Mulvey, "Visual Pleasure and Narrative Cinema," 807.
43. See Kim's critique in *Asian Americans in an Anti-Black World*.
44. Sexton, *Amalgamation Schemes*, 35–36.
45. Sexton, *Amalgamation Schemes*, 35.
46. My use of the words "liberal" and "neoliberal" follows the broader arguments that Sexton develops in his *Amalgamation Schemes*. He explains: "Antiracist politics is challenged

to devise responses to the obsessive structure of racialization if it is to mount a more effective intervention in the post-civil rights era. Liberal models of multicultural 'unity-in-diversity' and conservative prescriptions of colorblindness have proved themselves to be as damaging to movements for radical social change as they are intractable as elements of contemporary political discourse. Critics on the Left seem unsatisfied with the bleakness of these options yet at a loss for an alternative framework" (32).

47. Lacan specifically characterizes this disappearance as *aphanisis,* following Ernest Jones's work on the concept. Lacan expands upon Jones's focus on *aphanisis* as disappearance by conceiving of it as a movement that underscores "the *fading* of the subject." Lacan, *The Four Fundamental Concepts,* 208.

48. Lacan, *The Four Fundamental Concepts,* 211.

49. Fanon, *Black Skin, White Masks,* 113.

50. See Freud, "Instincts and Their Vicissitudes."

51. See Freud, "Instincts and Their Vicissitudes."

52. Freud, "Instincts and Their Vicissitudes."

53. Lacan explains, "The real may be represented by the accident, the noise, the small element of reality, which is evidence that we are not dreaming. But, on the other hand, this reality is not so small, for what wakes us is the other reality hidden behind the lack of that which takes the place of representation—this says, Freud is the *Trieb.*" Lacan, *The Four Fundamental Concepts,* 60. Also see Marriott, "Bastard Allegories," 188.

54. Marriott, "Bastard Allegories," 188. For a further detailed elaboration on the Fanonian real, see Marriott, *Whither Fanon?.*

55. On similar explorations, namely those of real-fantasy, perversion, and policing, see Warren's insightful article, "Barred Objects."

56. Marriott, *Haunted Life,* xxi.

57. Freud, "The Uncanny," 132.

58. Freud, "The Uncanny," 132.

59. Freud, "The Uncanny," 124.

60. Freud, "The Uncanny," 124.

61. Freud, "The Uncanny," 125.

62. Freud writes, "*Heimlich* thus becomes increasingly ambivalent, until it finally merges with its antonym *unheimlich.* The uncanny (*das Unheimliche,* 'the unhomely') is in some way a species of the familiar (*das Heimliche*), 'the homely.'" Freud, *The Uncanny,* 134.

63. Freud, *The Uncanny,* 143.

64. Freud, *The Uncanny,* 142.

65. Freud, *The Uncanny,* 143.

66. Wilderson, "The Vengeance of Vertigo," 3.

67. Wilderson in Ball's "Irreconcilable Anti-Blackness and Police Violence."

68. Wilderson, "Afro-Pessimism and the End of Redemption."

69. Sexton, "Unbearable Blackness," 160.

70. For further meditations and critiques on the notions of world and worlding in relation to (anti)blackness, see Bradley's *Anteaesthetics* and Palmer's "Otherwise than Blackness."

71. Bradley, *Anteaesthetics,* 314–315. For an exceptional elaboration of blackness that con-

stitutes relations to the world and un-worlding, see Bradley, *Anteaesthetics*, in particular her chapter "Unworlding, or the Involution of Value."

72. Wilderson, "Afro-Pessimism and the End of Redemption."

73. Derrida, *Writing and Difference*, 4.

74. Weigel, *Grammatology of Images*, 107.

75. Zupančič, *Ethics of the Real*, 17.

76. Marriott, *Whither Fanon?*, 68.

77. Fanon, *Black Skin, White Masks*, 133.

78. Abdullah, Goodman, and Gyamfi, "Black Lives Matter Activist Convicted of 'Felony Lynching.'"

79. Fanon, *Wretched of the Earth*, 15.

80. Park, "The Eternal Captive."

81. My emphasis. Marriott, "The Crisis of Truth."

82. Abdullah, Goodman, and Gyamfi, "Black Lives Matter Activist Convicted of 'Felony Lynching.'"

83. Bass, "Primary Perversion and Universal Law," 1301.

84. Spillers, "Mama's Baby, Papa's Maybe," in *Red, White, and in Color*, 225.

85. Spillers, "Mama's Baby, Papa's Maybe," in *Red, White, and in Color*, 224.

86. Spillers, "Mama's Baby, Papa's Maybe," in *Red, White, and in Color*, 225.

87. Spillers, "Mama's Baby, Papa's Maybe," in *Red, White, and in Color*, 225.

88. Fishzon, "What Are Perversions?"

89. Marriott, "On Decadence."

90. Marriott, "On Decadence."

91. Spillers, "Mama's Baby, Papa's Maybe," in *Feminisms*, 446.

92. Sexton, "People-of-Color-Blindness," 35–36.

93. Marriott, "On Decadence."

94. Sexton, "All Black Everything."

95. To name only a few examples, see Han's "Slavery as Contract," Moten's *Stolen Life*, Harney and Moten's *The Undercommons*, Nyong'o's *Afro-Fabulations*, and Halberstam's *Wildness*.

96. Park, "Can Feminism Think Black Incapacity?," 67–68.

97. Hartman, *Scenes of Subjection*, 40.

98. Hartman, *Scenes of Subjection*, 41.

99. Moten, "The Case of Blackness," 179.

100. Moten, "The Case of Blackness," 179.

101. Marriott writes extensively about how the distinction between *casus* and case shapes Moten's reading of Fanon and his use of the term *para-ontology*. See Marriott, "Judging Fanon" and "The Condemned," in his *Whither Fanon?*, 190–231.

102. Benjamin, "The Task of the Translator," in *Walter Benjamin: Selected Writings*, 262.

103. Moten, "The Case of Blackness," 179.

104. Axelle Karera's pathbreaking intervention is crucial here as she traces a philosophical genealogy of the term *para-ontology* and places pressure on it. See Karera, "Paraontology."

105. Hamacher, "95 Theses on Philology," xi.

106. See Fanon, *Black Skin, White Masks,* specifically "The Fact of Blackness," where Fanon discusses the denial of ontological explanation and resistance.

107. Karera offers an astute critique on the terms "fugitivity" as well as "flight" in regard to the question of being in the works of Moten and Ronald Judy, respectively. See Karera, "Indebtedness." Her critique echoes interrogations of Moten's conceptualization of fugitivity previously made by Sexton and Marriott. See Sexton, "The Social Life of Social Death," and Marriott, "Judging Fanon" and *Whither Fanon?*, 190–231.

108. See Marriott, "Judging Fanon" and *Whither Fanon?*, 190–231.

109. In this sense, Marriott's reading of Fanon's *n'est pas* as a type of abyss radically departs from Moten, since he conceptualizes blackness, in my view, less as an absence and more as a zero. As a zero, blackness is not only unthinkable but also singular.

110. Park, "Unhomeliness." See also Wilderson, "The Vengeance of Vertigo."

111. Moten, "Knowledge of Freedom," 273–274.

112. Copjec, *Read My Desire*, 18.

113. Johnson, "Correctional Facilities," 162.

114. Moten draws the term "non-performance" from Sora Han's "Slavery as Contract." See in particular his chapter "Erotics of Fugitivity." There is something concerning about this peculiar disconnect, where Moten's discussion of fugitivity as exemplary of the non-performance of blackness is placed under the title, "Erotics of Fugitivity," in a chapter that hardly mentions the role or function of racial-sexual relations, sexuality, desire, intimacy, and so forth. On this view, it is unclear what qualifies fugitivity as erotic or what elicits the erotics of fugitivity. Of course, per our discussion above, any qualification or elicitation in its representation of erotics would necessarily be a misrepresentation, misidentification, and misrecognition of sorts. Moreover, what remains as a question is not just what is conceived here as the "erotics of fugitivity," but what libidinally tethers blackness to a politics of representation or a representation of politics. How might the elision of a libidinal investment to represent blackness in a particular way give rise to the political demand to represent blackness as an erotics of fugitivity? Further, how can one discuss the laws of contract or what performance might re-signify under the auspices of erotics without any attention to desire as law?

115. Nancy, "*Lapsus judicii*," 152.

116. See Spillers, "Mama's Baby, Papa's Maybe," on the flesh; and Marriott's *Whither Fanon?*, namely his chapter, "The Abyssal," on impersonation and corpsing.

117. Sorentino, "Natural Slavery, Real Abstraction," 655.

118. Sorentino, "Natural Slavery, Real Abstraction," 655.

Chapter 6

1. Marriott, *Before Whiteness*, 4–5.

2. Derrida, *Before the Law*, 36.

3. Bradley, *Anteaesthetics*, 31.

4. Bradley, *Anteaesthetics*, 290.

5. Bradley, *Anteaesthetics*, 290.

6. Bradley, *Anteaesthetics*, 89.

7. Bhandar and Toscano, "Race, Real Estate and Abstraction."

8. Rose, *Hegel Contra Sociology.*

9. See Derrida, *Memoirs of the Blind*, 121.

10. "Melvin Edwards," Alexander Gray Associates; Edwards, "America"; and "Melvin Edwards," Smithsonian American Art Museum.

11. "*Lynch Fragments*: 1960s–present."

12. "Melvin Edwards. 4 works from the *Lynch* Fragments series. 1968."

13. See Johnson, "Poetry and Syntax," 32.

14. Elsewhere, Rei Terada has proposed something similar by examining the imposition on modern individuals to imagine and experience relations "as anything but given," while nonetheless avowing them "to be a product of contingencies" that simultaneously "allows that relation . . . as an impermeant abstraction." Terada, *Metaracial*, 69.

15. Césaire, *Discourse on Colonialism*, 86.

16. For an incisive reading on poetry, blackness, and abstraction, see Bhandar's "Property, Law, and Race." While much of my argument in this chapter aims to trouble tenets of what Bhandar presents, including her conception of ontology that places race as a shared difference across racial lines, and her stress on forwarding the term *racial* as a rhetorical and analytic device, I greatly appreciate her astute reading of Amiri Baraka's poem that "captures in a few words the conflation of race, the money form, and its impossible contradictions for the subject who bears the legacy of this monstrous hybridization wrought by chattel slavery and finance capital, the former being indispensable to the growth of the latter" (217).

17. Hamacher, *On the Brink*, 63.

18. Žižek, *Violence*, 154.

19. Marriott, "On Racial Etiquette," n.p.

20. De'Ath, "Hidden Abodes and Inner Bonds," 236.

21. De'Ath, "Hidden Abodes and Inner Bonds," 236.

22. De'Ath, "Hidden Abodes and Inner Bonds," 232.

23. I adopt the term and conceptual framework of "underdetermination" from Sara-Maria Sorentino's "Abstraction." Her work is pivotal here for its refusal to subordinate the ontological singularity of slavery to the dialectics of labor and value-form.

24. In this sense, my argument is in critical tension with works such as Leigh Raiford's *Burning All Illusion*. Raiford posits that abstraction—by moving away from the figurative—might offer a "critical visuality" that "moves toward a more just vision" and an "ethics of seeing." By contrast, I contend that abstraction, such as in the work of Dyson, does not offer a reconciliatory path toward a "just vision" or a more "thinkable" justice, but rather serves as an impossible register that marks the representational collapse part and parcel with any attempt to capture the foundational violence of antiblackness.

25. Meier, "Creating a Spatial History of Slavery Through Abstraction."

26. "Torkwase Dyson."

27. Sexton, "All Black Everything."

28. Here, I am significantly influenced by and lean on Louis Althusser's interpretation of Leonardo Cremonini as a painter. Though my argument about Dyson departs from his reading of Cremonini, I find useful Althusser's assertion of "Cremonini [as] *a painter of abstraction*" (his emphasis, "Cremonini, Painter of Abstraction," 158). Althusser writes of

Cremonini, "Not an abstract painter, 'painting' an absent, pure possibility in a new form and matter, but a painter of the real *abstract*, 'painting' in a sense we have to define, real relations (as relations they are necessarily *abstract*) between 'men' and their 'things', or rather, to give the term its stronger sense, between 'things' and *their* 'men'" (Althusser, "Cremonini, Painter of Abstraction," 158).

29. Bhandar and Toscano, "Race, Real Estate and Real Abstraction."

30. See Sorentino, "Money, Slavery, Myth."

31. Sorentino, "Money, Slavery, Myth," 2.

32. Sorentino, "Money, Slavery, Myth," 12. Sorentino's work has been indispensable for centralizing antiblackness as a core abstraction and analytic to conceive structural violence, and for unsettling the prevailing circuits of capitalist abstraction. The enduring challenge remains, however, that these critical elaborations might be tethered to a Marxian mode of abstraction. This conceptual framing, which retains the grammar of value and commodity form—even while theoretically basing itself on the underdetermination of slavery—maintains a very narrow margin in critically assessing the appearance of contradictions not just between antiblackness and capitalism but also between antiblackness and abstraction.

33. Fanon, *Wretched of the Earth*, 37.

34. Lebeau, "Psycho-Politics," 114.

35. Fanon, *Wretched of the Earth*, 5.

36. Fanon, *Wretched of the Earth*, 5.

37. For more on the work of transformation, see Marriott, "Racial Fetishism" in *Whither Fanon?* and Lebeau, "Psycho-Politics," 114. See Park, "Decolonization and the Question of Transformation."

38. Lebeau, "Psycho-Politics," 114.

39. Fanon, *Wretched of the Earth*, 5.

40. Meier, "Creating a Spatial History of Slavery Through Abstraction."

41. Meier, "Creating a Spatial History of Slavery Through Abstraction."

42. Dyson, "Black Interiority."

43. Mansoor, "Dyson's Black Composition Contra Abstraction."

44. Mansoor, "Dyson's Black Composition Contra Abstraction."

45. El-Shakry, "Psychoanalysis and the Imaginary," 332.

46. Mansoor, "Dyson's Black Composition Contra Abstraction."

47. Kim, *The Politics of Collecting*, 110–111.

48. Kim, *The Politics of Collecting*, 111.

49. Kim, *The Politics of Collecting*, 110.

50. Kim, *The Politics of Collecting*, 110.

51. Kim, *The Politics of Collecting*, 112.

52. Žižek, *The Sublime Object of Ideology*, 19.

53. De'Ath, "Hidden Abodes and Inner Bonds," 236.

54. Fanon, *Wretched of the Earth*, 4.

55. Bhandar, "Property, Law, and Race," 207. Bhandar's elaboration and critique of the now well-known concept of whiteness as property is yet again instructive here—especially in her attention to the question of ontology and Lockean and Benthamian justifications of

private property ownership (211). Bhandar incisively delineates the influence of Jeremy Bentham and John Locke on Harris's notion of "whiteness as property," yet uses in particular Locke to show that abstraction "functions in such a way so as to create legal forms of property and racial ontologies coterminously" (211). It is all the more peculiar then that Kim misses Bhandar's very open critique of Harris—which has spanned across several publications—and her criticism of Ian Baucom's *Specters of the Atlantics,* specifically "the utter absence in Baucom's text of any serious or sustained treatment of race" (216). Thus, when Kim refers to Bhandar, albeit in passing, as "[taking] up Bentham's notion to situate why property scholars such as Cheryl Harris and Ian Baucom begin with chattel slavery in order to discuss property," her misreading risks reproducing the limitations outlined in Harris's and Baucom's frameworks. The risk of uncritically referring to Baucom at least is the deracialization of slavery.

56. On this latter point, also see the Introduction and Chapter 1 in this book.

57. I am reminded of Axelle Karera's incisive critique of new materialism that is in conversation with Dianne Leong. Both astutely observe the disavowal of race as "a structural necessity for the new materialisms" (44 in Karera's "Blackness and the Pitfalls of Anthropocene Ethics," citing Leong's "The Mattering of Black Lives").

58. Dyson, "Black Interiority."

59. Wilderson, *Red, White, and Black*, 55.

60. Here, I rely on Sara-Maria Sorentino's citation of Sohn-Rethel. Sorentino, "Abstraction."

61. The pathbreaking work of Rizvana Bradley's *Anteaesthetic* is crucial here.

62. Harris, "Whiteness as Property," 1725.

63. Warren, *Ontological Terror*, 6.

64. Warren, *Ontological Terror*, 72.

65. Warren, *Ontological Terror*, 74.

66. Sorentino, "Abstraction."

67. Bhandar, "Property, Law, and Race," 212. Bhandar explains further, "Abstraction functions in such a way so as to create legal forms of property and racial ontologies coterminously. Emergent forms of property ownership were constituted with racial ontologies of settler and native, master and slave" (211).

68. Sorentino, "Money, Slavery, Myth," 2.

69. Sexton, *Amalgamation Schemes*, 27.

70. My translation. Lacan, "La Troisième," 190.

71. Lacan, *The Ethics of Psychoanalysis*, 68.

72. Sexton, "The *Vel* of Slavery," 593.

73. Marriott, *Lacan Noir*, 86.

Bibliography

Abdullah, Melina, Amy Goodman, and Nana Gyamfi. "Black Lives Matter Activist Convicted of 'Felony Lynching.'" *Democracy Now!*, June 2, 2016. https://www.democracynow.org/2016/6/2/black_lives_matter_activist_convicted_of.

Althusser, Louis. "Cremonini, Painter of the Abstract." In *Lenin and Philosophy and Other Essays*, translated by Ben Brewster, 157–166. New York: Monthly Review Press, 2001.

Ancheto, Angelo N. "Neither Black nor White." In *Asian American Studies Now: A Critical Reader*, edited by Jean Yu-Wen Shen Wu and Thomas C. Chen, 21–34. New Brunswick, NJ: Rutgers University Press, 2012.

Anderson, Carol. *The Second: Race and Guns in a Fatally Unequal America*. New York: Bloomsbury Publishing, 2021.

Apel, Dora. *Imagery of Lynching: Black Men, White Women, and the Mob*. New Brunswick, NJ: Rutgers University Press, 2004.

Apter, Emily. "Armed Response: Translation as Judicial Hearing." *e-flux Journal* 84 (2017). https://www.e-flux.com/journal/84/149339/armed-response-translation-as-judicial-hearing/.

Bahti, Timothy. *Allegories of History: Literary Historiography After Hegel*. Baltimore: Johns Hopkins University Press, 1992.

Ball, Jared. "Irreconcilable Anti-Blackness and Police Violence with Dr. Frank Wilderson." *I Mix What I Like*, October 1, 2004, podcast, 1 hour 15 minutes [approx]. https://imixwhatilike.org/2014/10/01/frankwildersonandantiblackness-2/.

Barthes, Roland. *Image-Music-Text*. New York: Farrar, Straus and Giroux, 1977.

Bass, Alan. "Primary Perversion and Universal Law." *Cardozo Law Review* 16, no. 3/4 (1994/1995): 1293–1302.

Baucom, Ian. *Specters of the Atlantic: Finance Capital, Slavery, and the Philosophy of History*. Durham, NC: Duke University Press, 2005.

Beasley, Delilah. *The Negro Trail Blazers of California*. Los Angeles: unknown publisher, 1919.

Benjamin, Ruha. *Race After Technology: Abolitionist Tools for the New Jim Code*. Medford, MA: Polity, 2019.

Benjamin, Walter. "Critique of Violence." In *Reflections: Essays, Aphorisms, Autobiographical*

Writings, translated by Edmund Jephcott and edited by Peter Demetz, 277–300. New York: Schocken Books, 1978.

———. "Critique of Violence." In *Walter Benjamin: Selected Writings, Volume 1, 1913–1926*, edited by Marcus Bullock and Michael W. Jennings, 236–252. Cambridge, MA: The Belknap Press of Harvard University Press, 1996.

———. "Critique of Violence." In *Toward the Critique of Violence: A Critical Edition*, edited by Peter Fenves and Julia Ng, 39–60. Stanford, CA: Stanford University Press, 2021.

———. "The Task of the Translator." In *Illuminations*, translated by Harry Zohn, 69–82. New York: Schocken Books, 1968.

———. "The Task of the Translator." In *Walter Benjamin: Selected Writings, Volume 1 1913–1926*, edited by Marcus Bullock and Michael W. Jennings, 253–263. Cambridge, MA: The Belknap Press of Harvard University Press, 1996.

———. "Zur Kritik der Gewalt." In *Angelus Novus: Ausgewählte Schriften 2*, 42–66. Frankfurt: Suhrkamp, 1966.

Bentham, Jeremy. *Theory of Legislation*. Translated by R. Hildreth, 6th ed. London: Kegan Paul, Trench, Trübner & Co., 1890. First published 1802.

Bhandar, Brenna. *Colonial Lives of Property: Law, Land, and Racial Regimes of Ownership*. Durham, NC: Duke University Press, 2018.

———. "Property, Law, and Race: Modes of Abstraction." *UC Irvine Law Review* 4, no. 1 (March 2014): 203–218.

Bhandar, Brenna, and Alberto Toscano. "Race, Real Estate and Abstraction." *Radical Philosophy* 194 (Nov./Dec. 2015): 8–17.

"Black Lives Matter Activist Convicted of 'Felony Lynching: 'It's More Than Ironic, It's Disgusting.'" *Democracy Now: Independent Global News*, last modified June 2, 2016. https://www.democracynow.org/2016/6/2/black_lives_matter_activist_convicted_of.

Bradley, Rizvana. *Anteaesthetics: Black Aesthesis and the Critique of Form*. Stanford, CA: Stanford University Press, 2023.

———. "Living in the Absence of a Body: The (Sus)Stain of Black Female (W)holeness." *Rhizomes* 29 (2016): 1–13. http://www.rhizomes.net/issue29/bradley/index.html.

———. "On Black Aesthesis." *Diacritics: A Review of Contemporary Criticism* 49, no. 4 (2021): 21–53.

Butler, Daniel G. "Blackout." *Psychoanalytic Dialogues* 34, no. 5 (2024): 614–617.

"California 'Lynching' Conviction Is a Threat to All!," *The Internationalist*, June 2016. https://www.internationalist.org/freedomforjasmineabdullah.html.

Campbell, Emahunn Raheem Ali. "A Critique of the Occupy Movement from a Black Occupier." *The Black Scholar* 41, no. 4 (Winter 2011): 42–51.

Carby, Hazel. *Reconstructing Womanhood: The Emergence of the Afro-American Woman Novelist*. New York: Oxford University Press, 1989.

Cassin, Barbara. Introduction to *Dictionary of Untranslatables: A Philosophical Lexicon*, translated by Michael Wood, xvii–xx. Edited by Emily Apter, Jacques Lexra, and Michael Wood. Translated by Steven Rendall Christian Hubert, Jeffrey Mehlman, Nathanael Stein, and Michael Syrotinski. Princeton, NJ: Princeton University Press, 2014.

Césaire, Aimé. *Discourse on Colonialism: A Poetics of Anticolonialism*. Translated by Joan Pinkham. New York: Monthly Review Press, 1972.

Chabria, Anita. "Black Woman's 'Lynching' Charges: An Unsettling Tactic to Punish Activism?" *The Guardian*, April 5, 2015. https://www.theguardian.com/us-news/2015/apr/05/maile-hampton-woman-lynching-charge-california-law.

Chandler, Nahum. *X—The Problem of the Negro as a Problem for Thought.* New York: Fordham University Press, 2013.

Chimurenga, Thandisizwe. "In Strange Twist of History, Black Activist Charged with 'Lynching.'" *Truthout*. April 5, 2015. https://truthout.org/articles/in-strange-twist-of-history-black-activist-charged-with-lynching/.

Coleman, Kenneth. *Dangerous Subjects: James D. Saules and the Rise of Black Exclusion in Oregon*. Corvallis: Oregon State University Press, 2017.

Collins, Patricia. *Black Feminist Thought: Knowledge, Consciousness, and the Politics of Empowerment.* New York: Routledge, 2009.

Copjec, Joan. *Read My Desire: Lacan Against the Historicists.* London: Verso, 2015.

Cornell, Drucilla. *Beyond Accommodation: Ethical Feminism, Deconstruction, and the Law.* New York: Routledge, 1991.

Cornell, Sarah. "Citizens of Nowhere: Fugitive Slaves and Free African Americans in Mexico, 1833–1857." *Journal of American History* 100, no. 2 (September 2013): 351–374.

Cover, Robert. "Nomos and Narrative." In *Narrative, Violence, and the Law: The Essays of Robert Cover*, edited by Martha Minow, Michael Ryan, and Austin Sarat, 95–172. Ann Arbor: University of Michigan Press, 1992.

da Silva, Denise Ferreira. "No-Bodies: Law, Raciality and Violence." *Griffith Law Review* 18, no. 2 (2009): 212–236.

———. *Toward a Global Idea of Race*. Minneapolis: University of Minnesota Press, 2007.

David-Ménard, Monique. "Kant, the Law, and Desire." Translated by Leslie Lykes de Galbert. In *Feminist Interpretations of Immanuel Kant*, edited by Robin May Schott, 341–354. University Park: Pennsylvania State University Press, 1997.

Davis, Angela. "Reflections on the Black Woman's Role in the Community of Slaves." *The Black Scholar* 3, no. 4 (1971): 2–15.

Dayan, Colin. *The Law Is a White Dog.* Princeton, NJ: Princeton University Press, 2011.

de Man, Paul. "The Concept of Irony." In *Aesthetic Ideology*, 163–184. Minneapolis: University of Minnesota Press, 1996.

———. "'Conclusions': Walter Benjamin's 'The Task of the Translator.'" 1986. In *The Resistance to Theory*, 73–105. Minneapolis: University of Minnesota Press, 2002.

———. "The Epistemology of Metaphor." *Critical Inquiry* 5, no. 1 (Autum 1978): 13–30.

———. "Semiology and Rhetoric." In *Allegories of Reading: Figural Language in Rousseau, Nietzsche, Rilke, and Proust*, 3–19. New Haven, CT: Yale University Press, 1979.

De'Ath, Amy. "Hidden Abodes and Inner Bonds: Literary Study and Marxism-Feminism. In *After Marx: Literature, Theory, and Value in the Twenty-First Century*, edited by Colleen Lye and Chritopher Nealon, 225–239. Cambridge: Cambridge University Press, 2022.

Derrida, Jacques. *Before the Law: The Complete Text of Préjugés.* Translated by Sandra van Reenen and Jacques de Ville. Minneapolis: University of Minnesota Press, 2018.

———. "Justices." Translated by Peggy Kamuf. *Critical Inquiry* 31, no. 3 (Spring 2005): 689–721.

. *Memoirs of the Blind*. Translated by Pascale-Anne Brault and Michael Naas. Chicago: University of Chicago Press, 1990.

———. *Of Grammatology*. Translated by Gayatri Spivak. Baltimore: Johns Hopkins University Press, 1976.

———. *Writing and Difference*. Translated by Alan Bass. Chicago: University of Chicago Press, 1978.

Didi-Huberman, Georges. *Confronting Images: Questioning the Ends of a Certain History of Art*. University Park: Pennsylvania State University Press, 2004.

———. *Images in Spite of All: Four Photographs from Auschwitz*. Translated by Shane B. Lillis. Chicago: University of Chicago Press, 2012.

Douglass, Patrice. *Engendering Blackness: Slavery and the Ontology of Sexual Violence*. Stanford, CA: Stanford University Press, 2025.

Douglass, Patrice, and Frank B. Wilderson III. "The Violence of Presence: Metaphysics in a Blackened World." *The Black Scholar* 43, no. 4 (Winter 2013): 117–123.

Dyson, Torkwase. "Black Interiority: Notes on Architecture, Infrastructure, and Environmental Justice and Abstract Draw." Pace Gallery, February 1, 2023. https://www.pacegallery.com/journal/black-interiority-by-torkwase-dyson/

Edwards, Melvin. *America*. 1978. Steel. Cleveland Museum of Art, Cleveland (2021.164). Accessed November 25, 2025. https://www.clevelandart.org/art/2021.164.

El-Shakry, Omnia. "Psychoanalysis and the Imaginary: Translating Freud in Postcolonial Egypt." *Psychoanalysis and History* 20, no. 3 (2018): 313–335.

Elving, Ron. "A Refresher on Anita Hill and Clarence Thomas." *NPR*, December 10, 2017. https://www.npr.org/2017/12/10/569716802/a-refresher-on-anita-hill-and-clarence-thomas.

Fanon, Frantz. *Black Skin, White Mask*. Translated by Richard Philcox. New York: Grove Press, 1952.

———. *Wretched of the Earth*. Translated by Richard Philcox. New York: Grove Press 1963.

Farley, Anthony Paul. "Perfect Slavery." *Loyal University Chicago Law Journal* 36, no. 10 (2004): 225–237.

Farrell, Harry. *Swift Justice: Murder and Vengeance in a California Town*. New York: St. Martin's Press, 1992.

Fishzon, Anna. "What Are Perversions?" *European Journal of Psychoanalysis* 3, no.1 (2017). https://www.journal-psychoanalysis.eu/articles/what-are-perversions.

Freud, Sigmund. *Briefe an Wilhelm Fließ 1887–1904*. Edited by Jeffrey Moussaieff Masson. Frankfurt am Main: Fischer, 1986.

———. *The Complete Letters of Sigmund Freud to Wilhelm Fliess: 1887–1904*. Translated and edited by Jeffrey Moussaieff Masson. Cambridge, MA: Belknap Press, 1985.

———. "The Dream-Work." In *The Norton Anthology of Theory and Criticism*, edited by Vincent B. Lietch, 497–514. New York: W.W. Norton & Company, 2001.

———. "Instincts and Their Vicissitudes" (1915). In *Standard Edition, Volume 14: On the History of the Psychoanalytic Movement: Papers on Metapsychology and Other Works*, edited and translated by James Strachey, 111–140. London: Vintage Books, 2001.

———. "Repression" (1915). In *The Standard Edition of the Complete Psychological Works of Sigmund Freud, Volume 14: On the History of the Psychoanalytic Movement: Papers on Metapsychology and Other Works*, edited and translated by James Strachey, 141–58. London: Hogarth Press, 1957.

———. *The Uncanny*. New York: Penguin Classics, 2003.

———. "The Unconscious" (1915). In *The Standard Edition of the Complete Psychological Works of Sigmund Freud, Volume 14: On the History of the Psychoanalytic Movement: Papers on Metapsychology and Other Works*, edited and translated by James Strachey, 159–215. London: Hogarth Press, 1957.

Fenves, Peter. "The Genesis of Judgment: Spatiality, Analogy, and Metaphor in Benjamin's 'On Language as Such and on Human Language.'" In *Walter Benjamin: Theoretical Questions*, edited by David. S. Ferris, 75–93. Stanford, CA: Stanford University Press, 1996.

Fischer, Sibylle. *Modernity Disavowed: Haiti and the Cultures of Slavery in the Age of Revolution*. Durham, NC: Duke University Press, 2004.

Forbes, Jack D. "The Early African Heritage of California." In *Seeking El Dorado: African Americans in California*, edited by Lawrence B. De Graaf, Kevin Mulroy, and Quintard Taylor, 73–97. Seattle and London: University of Washington Press in association with Autry Museum of Western Heritage (Los Angeles), 2001.

Gasché, Rodolphe. "'Setzung' and 'Übersetzung': Notes on Paul de Man." *Diacritics* 11, no. 4 (Winter 1981): 36–57.

Goldsby, Jacqueline. "The High and Low Tech of It: The Meaning of Lynching and the Death of Emmett Till." *Yale Journal of Criticism* 9, no. 2 (1996): 245–283.

———. *A Spectacular Secret: Lynching in American Life and Literature*. Chicago: University of Chicago Press, 2006.

Gonzales-Day, Ken. *Erased Lynchings*. kengonzalesday.com/projects/erased-lynchings/.

———. *Lynching in the West: 1850–1935*. Durham, NC: Duke University Press, 2006.

Graaf, Lawrence B., Kevin Mulroy, and Quintard Taylor, eds. *Seeking El Dorado: African Americans in California*. Seattle: University of Washington Press in association with Autry Museum of Western Heritage (Los Angeles), 2001.

Gramsci, Antonio. "State and Civil Society." In *Selections from Prison Notebooks*, edited and translated by Quentin Hoare and Geoffrey Nowell Smith, 445–557. London: Lawrence and Wishart, 1971.

Gray, Erin. "Anti-Lynching Laws Were Never Meant to Defend Black Lives: The Case of Jasmine Abdullah." *Truthout*, June 15, 2016. https://truthout.org/articles/anti-lynching-laws-were-never-meant-to-defend-black-lives-the-case-of-jasmine-abdullah/.

———. "Necrophagy at the Lynching Block." *GLQ: A Journal of Lesbian and Gay Studies* 21, no. 1 (January 2015) 13–15.

Halberstam, Jack. *Wild Things: The Disorder of Desire*. Durham, NC: Duke University Press, 2020.

Haley, Sarah. *No Mercy Here: Gender, Punishment, and the Making of Jim Crow Modernity*. Chapel Hill: University of North Carolina Press, 2016.

Hamacher, Werner. "95 Theses on Philology." *Diacritics: A Review of Contemporary Criticism* 49, no. 1 (2009): 25–44.

———. "Afformative, Strike." Translated by Dana Hollander. *Cardoza Law Review* 13 (1991): 1133–57.

———. *On the Brink: Language, Time, History, and Politics*. Edited by Jan Plug. London: Rowman & Littlefield, 2020.

Han, Sora. *Letters of the Law: Race and the Fantasy of Colorblindness in American Law*. Stanford, CA: Stanford University Press, 2015.

———. "Slavery as Contract: *Betty's Case* and the Question of Freedom." *Law and Literature* 27, no. 3 (Fall 2015): 395–416.

Harney, Stefano, and Fred Moten. *The Undercommons: Fugitive Planning and Black Study.* New York: Autonomedia, 2013.

Harris, Cheryl. "Whiteness as Property." *Harvard Law Review* 106, no. 8 (1993): 1707–1791.

Hartman, Saidiya. *Scenes of Subjection: Terror, Slavery, and Self-Making in Nineteenth-Century America*. Oxford: Oxford University Press, 1997.

———. "Seduction and the Ruses of Power." *Callaloo* 19, no. 2 (Spring 1996): 537–560.

Hartman, Saidiya, and Frank B. Wilderson. "The Position of the Unthought." *Qui Parle: Critical Humanities and Social Sciences* 13, no. 2 (Spring/Summer 2003): 183–201.

Hegel, Georg Wilhelm Friedrich. *Hegel's Philosophy of Mind: Being Part Three of the Encyclopedia of the Philosophical Sciences* (1830). Translated by William Wallace, together with the *Zusätze* in Boumann's text (1845), translated by A. V. Miller. Revised with an Introduction by M. J. Inwood. Oxford: Oxford University Press, 1977.

———. *Phenomenology of Spirit*. Translated by A. V. Miller. Oxford: Oxford University Press, 1977.

———. *The Science of Logic*. Translated by George di Giovanni. Cambridge: Cambridge University Press, 2010.

Higginbotham, Evelyn. "African-American Women's History and the Metalanguage of Race." *Signs* 17, no. 2 (Winter 1992): 251–274.

Hooker, Juliet. *Theorizing Race in the Americas: Douglass, Sarmiento, Du Bois, and Vasconcelos*. Oxford: Oxford University Press, 2017.

Jackson, George. *Blood in My Eye*. Baltimore: Black Classic Press, 1990.

———. *Soledad Brother: The Prison Letters of George Jackson*. New York: Bantam Books, 1972.

Jackson, Zaikyyah Iman. *Becoming Human: Matter and Meaning in an Antiblack World*. New York: New York University Press, 2020.

James, Marlon. *The Book of Night Women*. New York: Penguin Books, 2010.

Jefferson, Brian Jordan. "Policing, Whiteness, and the Death Wage." *Society and Space* (2016). https://www.societyandspace.org/articles/policing-whiteness-and-the-death-wage.

Johnson, Barbara. "Anthropomorphism in Lyric and Law." In *Persons and Things*, 188–207. Cambridge, MA: Harvard University Press, 2008.

———. "Correctional Facilities." In *The Barbara Johnson Reader: The Surprise of Otherness*, edited by Melissa Feuerstein, Bill Johnson González, Lili Porten, and Keja Valens, 155–178. Durham, NC: Duke University Press, 2014.

———. *The Critical Difference: Essays in the Contemporary Rhetoric of Reading.* Baltimore: Johns Hopkins University Press, 1985.

———. "Ego Sum Game." In *The Barbara Johnson Reader: The Surprise of Otherness*, edited by Melissa Feuerstein, Bill Johnson González, Lili Porten, and Keja Valens, 275–288. Durham, NC: Duke University Press, 2014.

———. *The Feminist Difference*. Cambridge, MA: Harvard University Press, 1998.

———. "Moses and Intertexuality." In *The Barbara Johnson Reader: The Surprise of Otherness*, edited by Melissa Feurstein, Bill Johnson González, Lili Porten, and Keja Valens, 126–140. Durham, NC: Duke University Press, 2014.

———. "Poetry and Syntax: What the Gypsy Knew." In *The Barbara Johnson Reader: The Surprise of Otherness*, edited by Melissa Feuerstein, Bill Johnson González, Lili Porten, and Keja Valens, 26–35. Durham, NC: Duke University Press, 2014.

———. "The Task of the Translator." In *The Barbara Johnson Reader: The Surprise of Otherness*, edited by Melissa Feuerstein, Bill Johnson González, Lili Porten, and Keja Valens, 377–400. Durham, NC: Duke University Press, 2014.

———. "Using People." In *The Barbara Johnson Reader: The Surprise of Otherness*, edited by Melissa Feuerstein, Bill Johnson González, Lili Porten, and Keja Valens, 262–274. Durham, NC: Duke University Press, 2014.

Johnson, David A. "Vigilance and the Law: The Moral Authority of Popular Justice in the Far West." *American Culture and the American Frontier*, special issue of *American Quarterly* 33, no. 5 (Winter 1981): 558–586.

Jones, Jennifer A., Tianna S. Paschel, and Petra R. Rivera-Rideau. "Introduction: Theorizing Afrolatinidades." In *Afro-Latin@s in Movement: Critical Approaches to Blackness and Transnationalism in the Americas (Afro-Latin@ Diasporas)*, 1–30. New York: Palgrave Macmillan, 2016.

Kant, Immanuel. *Critique of Pure Reason*. Translated and edited by Paul Guyer and Allen W. Wood. Cambridge: Cambridge University Press, 1998.

Karera, Axelle. "Blackness and the Pitfalls of Anthropocene Ethics." *Critical Philosophy of Race* 7, no. 1 (2019): 32–56.

———. "Paraontology: Interruption, Inheritance, or a Debt One Often Regrets." *Critical Philosophy of Race* 10, no. 2 (2022): 168–197.

Kaufman-Osborn, Timothy V. "Capital Punishment as Legal Lynching?" In *From Lynch Mobs to the Killing State*, edited by Charles J. Ogletree, Jr. and Austin Sarat, 21–54. New York: New York University Press, 2006.

Kim, Claire. *Asian Americans in an Anti-Black World*. Cambridge: Cambridge University Press, 2023.

Kim, Eunsong. *The Politics of Collecting: Race and the Aestheticization of Property*. Durham, NC: Duke University Press, 2024.

Kiser, William S. *Borderlands of Slavery: The Struggle over Captivity and Peonage in the American Southwest*. Philadelphia: University of Pennsylvania Press, 2017.

———. *Coast-to-Coast Empire: Manifest Destiny and the New Mexico Borderlands*. Norman: University of Oklahoma Press, 2018.

Lacan, Jacques. *Écrits: The First Complete Edition*. Translated by Bruce Fink in collaboration with Héloïse Fink and Russell Grigg. New York: W. W. Norton & Company, 2006.

———. *The Ethics of Psychoanalysis, 1959–1960: The Seminar of Jacques Lacan, Book VII*. Edited by Jacques-Alain Miller, translated by Dennis Porter. New York: W. W. Norton & Company, 1992.

———. *The Four Fundamental Concepts of Psychoanalysis, the Seminar of Jacques Lacan, Book XI*. Edited by Jacques-Alain Miller, translated by Alan Sheridan. New York: W. W. Norton & Company, 1991, 1998.

———. "La Troisième." *Lettres de l'École Freudienne* 16 (1975): 177–211.

———. "L'étourdit." *The Letter* 41 (2009): 31–80.

———. "The Mirror Stage as Formative of the *I* Function as Revealed in Psychoanalytic Experience." In *Écrits: The First Complete Edition in English*, translated by Bruce Fink, 75–81. New York: W. W. Norton & Company, 2006.

———. *The Object Relation: The Seminar of Jacques Lacan, Book IV (Seminar of Jacques Lacan, 4)*. Edited by Jacques-Alain Miller and translated by Adrian Price. Medford, MA: Polity, 2021.

———. *On Feminine Sexuality, The Limits of Love and Knowledge, 1972–1973, Encore: The Seminar of Jacques Lacan Book XX*. Edited by Jacques-Alain Miller, translated by Bruce Fink. New York: W. W. Norton & Company, 1999.

———. *The Psychoses, 1955–1956: The Seminar of Jacques Lacan, Book III*. Edited by Jacques-Alain Miller. Translated by Russell Grigg. New York: W. W. Norton & Company, 1997.

Lapp, Rudolph M. *Blacks in Gold Rush California*. New Haven, CT: Yale University Press, 1977.

Lear, Jonathan. *Freud*. New York: Routledge, 2005.

Lebeau, Vicky. *Psychoanalysis and Cinema: The Play of Shadows*. London: Wallflower, 2001.

———. "Psycho-Politics: Frantz Fanon's *Black Skin, White Masks*." In *Psycho-Politics and Cultural Desires*, edited by Janet Harbord and Jan Campbell, 107–117. First published London: Routledge, 1998. Taylor and Francis Group e-Library version, 2005.

LeMenager, Stephanie. *Manifest and Other Destinies: Territorial Fictions of the Nineteenth Century United States*. Lincoln: University of Nebraska Press, 2004.

Leong, Dianne. "The Mattering of Black Lives." *Nothing/More: Black Studies & Feminist Technoscience*, special issue of *Catalyst: Feminism, Theory, Technoscience* 2, no. 2 (2016): 1–35.

Locke, John. *Two Treatises of Government (1689)*. Edited by Peter Laslett. Cambridge: Cambridge University Press, 1988.

"*Lynch Fragments*: 1960s–Present." Alexander Gray Associates. https://www.alexandergray.com/series/melvin-edwards/melvin-edwards-lynch-fragments/.

Lyotard, Jean-François. *Libidinal Economy*. New York: Bloomsbury, 2015.

Mansoor, Jaleh. "Dyson's Black Composition Contra Abstraction." Pace Gallery, November 10, 2022. https://www.pacegallery.com/journal/dysons-black-composition-contra-abstraction/.

Marriott, David. "Bastard Allegories: Black British Independent Cinema." *Black Camera* 7, no. 1 (2015): 179–198.

———. *Before Whiteness*. San Francisco: City Lights, 2022.

———. "The Crisis of Truth." *Oxford Literary Review* 46, no. 1 (2024): 75–112.

———. *Haunted Life: Visual Culture and Black Modernity*. New Brunswick, NJ: Rutgers University Press, 2007.

———. "Judging Fanon." *Rhizomes* 29 (2016). http://www.rhizomes.net/issue29/marriott.html.

———. *Lacan Noir: Lacan and Afro-Pessimism*. Cham, Switzerland: Palgrave Macmillan, 2021.

———. *Of Effacement: Blackness and Non-Being*. Stanford, CA: Stanford University Press, 2023.

———. *On Black Men*. New York: Columbia University Press, 2000.

———. "On Decadence: *Bling Bling*." *e-flux Journal* 79 (2017). https://www.eflux.com/journal/79/94430/on-decadence-bling-bling/.

———. "On Racial Etiquette: Adrian Piper's My Calling (Cards)." *Postmodern Culture* 24, no.

1 (2013). https://www.pomoculture.org/2016/09/25/on-racial-etiquette-adrian-pipers-mycalling-cards/.

———. "On Revolutionary Suicide." *Diacritics: A Review of Contemporary Criticism* 49, no. 4 (2021): 101–131.

———. "The Perfect Beauty of Black Death." *The Philosophical Salon* (2017). https://thephilosophicalsalon.com/the-perfect-beauty-of-black-death/.

———. *Whither Fanon? Studies in the Blackness of Being.* Stanford, CA: Stanford University Press, 2018.

Martinot, Steven, and Jared Sexton. "The Avante-Garde of White Supremacy." *Social Identities* 9, no. 2 (2003): 169–181.

Marx, Karl. "Economic and Philosophical Manuscripts." In *The Marx-Engels Reader,* 2nd ed., edited by Robert C. Tucker, 66–125. New York: W. W. Norton & Company, 1978.

———. "Grundrisse." In *The Marx-Engels Reader,* 2nd ed., edited by Robert C. Tucker, 221–293. New York: W. W. Norton & Company, 1978.

Mason, Melanie. "Gov. Brown Signs Measure Striking 'Lynching' Charge from California Law." *Los Angeles Times,* July 2, 2015. https://www.latimes.com/local/political/la-me-pc-california-code-lynching-20150702-story.html.

Massie, Victoria M. "What Activist Jasmine Richards's 'Lynching' Conviction Means for the Black Lives Matter Movement." *Vox,* June 21, 2016. https://www.vox.com/2016/6/6/11839620/jasmine-richards-black-lives-matter-lynching.

Matsuda, Mari. "Beyond, and Not Beyond, Black and White: Deconstruction Has a Politics." In *Crossroads, Directions and A New Critical Race Theory,* edited by Jerome McCristal Culp, Angela P. Harris, and Fracisco Valdes, 393–398. Philadelphia: Temple University Press, 2002.

Meier, Allison. "Creating a Spatial History of Slavery Through Abstraction." *Hyperallergic,* 4 April 2016. https://hyperallergic.com/287833/creating-a-spatial-history-of-slavery-through-abstraction/.

"Melvin Edwards." Alexander Gray Associates. Accessed November 25, 2025, https://www.alexandergray.com/artists/melvin-edwards/.

"Melvin Edwards. 4 Works from the *Lynch* Fragments Series. 1968." Museum of Modern Art, https://www.moma.org/audio/playlist/290/3802.

"Melvin Edwards." Smithsonian American Art Museum. Accessed November 25, 2025, https://americanart.si.edu/artist/melvin-edwards-6598.

Miles, Tiya. *The Dawn of Detroit: A Chronicle of Slavery and Freedom in the City of the Straits.* New York: The New Press, 2017.

Mills, Charles. *The Racial Contract.* Ithaca, NY: Cornell University Press, 1997.

Morrison, Toni. "Introduction: Friday on the Potomac." In *Race-ing Justice, En-gendering Power: Essays on Anita Hill, Clarence Thomas, and the Construction of Social Reality,* edited by Toni Morrison, vii–xxx. New York: Pantheon Books, 1992.

———. *Playing in the Dark: Whiteness and the Literary Imagination.* New York: Vintage Books, 1992.

Moten, Fred. "The Case of Blackness." *Criticism* 50, no. 2 (Spring 2008): 177–218.

———. "Erotics of Fugitivity." In *Stolen Life,* 241–267. Durham, NC: Duke University Press, 2018.

———. "Knowledge of Freedom." *CR: The New Centennial Review* 4, no. 2 (Fall 2004): 269–310.

———. *Stolen Life*. Durham, NC: Duke University Press, 2018.

Mulvey, Laura. "Visual Pleasure and Narrative Cinema." *Screen* 16, no. 3 (Autumn 1975): 6–18.

Nancy, Jean-Luc. "*Lapsus judicii*." In *A Finite Thinking: Jean-Luc Nancy*, edited by Simon Sparks, 152–171. Stanford, CA: Stanford University Press, 2003.

Ng, Julia. "Benjamin on Law." Leibniz-Zentrum für Literatur- und Kulturforschung (Zfl), July 9, 2021. youtube.com/watch?v=DnGaTvvJU-Q.

Nokes, R. Gregory. *Breaking Chains: Slavery on Trial in the Oregon Territory*. Corvallis: Oregon State University Press, 2013.

Nolan, Michael J. "Defendant, Lynch Thyself: A California Appellate Court Goes from the Sublime to the Ridiculous in People v. Anthony J." *Howard Scroll: The Social Justice Law Review* 4, no. 2 (2001): 53–96.

Nyong'o Tavia. *Afro-Fabulations: The Queer Drama of Black Life*. New York: New York University Press, 2018.

Nyquist, Mary. *Arbitrary Rule: Slavery, Tyranny, and the Power of Life and Death*. Chicago: University of Chicago Press, 2013.

Palmer, Tyrone. "Otherwise Than Blackness: Feeling, World, Sublimation." *Qui Parle: Critical Humanities* 29, no. 2 (2020): 247–283.

Park, Linette. "Can Feminism Think Black Incapacity?: On Resistance, Ambivalence, and the Ungendered Reading of Blackness and Sexuality: Revisiting Judith Butler and Hortense Spillers." *Cultural Critique* 124 (Summer 2024): 54–99.

———. "Decolonization and the Question of Transformation: On Fanon's 'Stretching' of Marx and Lacan." In *Fanon and Lacan: Decolonial Psychoanalysis*, edited by Derek Hook and Sinan Richards. In *Fanon and Psychoanalysis*. London and New York: Routledge, forthcoming.

———. "The Eternal Captive in Contemporary 'Lynching' Arrests: On the Uncanny and the Complex of Law's Perversion." *Theory & Event* 22, no. 3 (July 2019): 674–698.

———. "A Real Black Aesthetic." In *The Routledge International Handbook of Psychoanalysis and Gender*, edited by Patricia Gherovici and Manya Steinkoler. New York: Routledge, forthcoming.

———. "Unhomeliness—Afterlife and Testimony." *Political Theology* (2022): 1–17.

———. "Whence Disinheritance Holds: On Ida B. Wells and America's 'Unwritten Law.'" *Souls: A Critical Journal of Black Politics, Culture, and Society* 22, no. 1 (2020): 11–23.

Pasadena Now. "Gather After Black Lives Matter March Clashes with Pasadena Police Effecting an Unrelated Arrest in Incident Near La Pintoresca Park." September 2, 2015. https://pasadenanow.com/main/breaking-police-arrest-black-lives-matter-pasadena-organizer-jasmine-richards.

Patton, Stacy. "Why Blacks Aren't Embracing O.W.S." *New York Times*, October 24, 2011. https://archive.nytimes.com/opinionator.blogs.nytimes.com/2011/10/24/why-blacks-arent-embracing-o-w-s/.

People v. Anthony J., 85 Cal. 2d 783 (App. 4th 1999).

People v. Jones, 19 Cal. App. 3d 437 (Cal. App. 4th 1971).

Pfeifer, Michael J., ed. *Lynching Beyond Dixie: American Mob Violence Outside the South*. Champaign: University of Illinois Press, 2013.

Raiford, Leigh. "*Burning All Illusion*: Abstraction, Black Life, and the Unmaking of White Supremacy." *Art Journal* 79, no. 4 (Winter 2020): 76–91.

Reiter, Keramet. "The Pelican Bay Hunger Strike: Resistance Within the Structural Constraints of a US Supermax Prison." *South Atlantic Quarterly* 113, no. 3 (2014): 579–611.

Rivera, Eddie. "Black Lives Matter Pasadena Organizer Convicted of Felony 'Lynching Charge.'" *Pasadena Now*, June 1, 2016. https://www.pasadenanow.com/main/black-lives matter-pasadena-organizer-convicted-of-felony-lynching-charge#.V1BE_5MrJTY.

Roberts, Sylvia Alden. *Mining for Freedom: Black History Meets the California Gold Rush*. Bloomington, IL: iUniverse, 2008.

Rose, Gillian. *The Broken Middle: Out of Philosophical Fragments*. Oxford: Blackwell Publishers, 1992.

Rose, Jacqueline. *Sexuality in the Field of Vision*. New York: Verso, 2006.

———. *States of Fantasy*. Oxford: Clarendon Press, 1998.

ross, kihana miraya. "Call It What It Is: Anti-Blackness." *New York Times*, June 4, 2020. https://www.nytimes.com/2020/06/04/opinion/george-floyd-anti-blackness.html

Sexton, Jared. "Affirmation in the Dark: Racial Slavery and Philosophical Pessimism." *The Comparatist* 42 (October 2019): 90–111.

———. "Afro-Pessimism: The Unclear Word." *rhizomes: Cultural Studies in Emerging Knowledge* 29 (2016). https://rhizomes.net/issue29/sexton.html.

———. "All Black Everything." *e-flux Journal* 79 (2017). https://www.eflux.com/journal/79/94158/all-black-everything/.

———. *Amalgamation Schemes: Antiblackness and the Critique of Multiracialism*. Minneapolis: University of Minnesota Press, 2008.

———. "People-of-Color-Blindness: Notes on the Afterlife of Slavery." *Social Text* 28, no. 2 (2010): 31–56.

———. "Proprieties of Coalition: Blacks, Asians, and the Politics of Policing." *Critical Sociology* 36, no. 1: 87–108.

——— "The Rage: Some Closing Comments on 'Open Casket.'" *Contemporary* (2017).

———. "The Social Life of Social Death." *InTensions Journal* 5 (Fall/Winter 2011): 1–47. https://contemptorary.org/the-rage-sexton/.

———. "The *Vel* of Slavery: Tracking the Figure of the Unsovereign." *Critical Sociology* 42, no. 45 (2016): 583–597.

———. "Unbearable Blackness." *Cultural Critique* 90 (Spring 2015): 159–178.

Siders, David. "Jerry Brown Signs 'Lynching' Law Bill." July 2, 2015. https://www.sacbee.com/news/politics-government/capitol-alert/article26105974.html.

Smith, Stacey. "Pacific Bound: California's 1852 Fugitive Slave Law." January 7, 2014. https://blackpast.org/african-american-history/pacific-bound-california-s-1852-fugitive-slave-law/.

Sohn-Rethel, Alfred. *Intellectual and Manual Labor: A Critique of Epistemology*. Translated by Martin Sohn-Rethel. Chicago: Haymarket Books, 2020.

Sorentino, Sara-Maria. "Abstraction." *Political Theology*. https://politicaltheology.com/abstraction/.

———. "Impossible Labour History: Solidarity Dreams and Antiblack Subsumption." *The Oxford Literary Review* 46, no. 1 (2024): 49–74.

———. "Money, Slavery, Myth." *Environment and Planning D: Society and Space* 42, no. 3 (2023): 1–20.

———. "Natural Slavery, Real Abstraction, and the Virtuality of Anti-Blackness." *Theory & Event* 22, no. 3 (2019): 630–673.

Spillers, Hortense. "Mama's Baby, Papa's Maybe: An American Grammar Book." In *Feminisms: An Anthology of Literary Theory and Criticism*, edited by Robyn R. Warhol and Diane Price Herndl, 451–69. New Brunswick, NJ: Rutgers University Press, 1997.

———. "Mama's Baby, Papa's Maybe: An American Grammar Book." In *Red, White, and in Color*, 203–229. Chicago: University of Chicago Press, 2003.

Teo, Tze-Yin. "Non-Event." *New Centennial Review* 17, no. 1 (Spring 2017): 73–92.

Terada, Rei. *Looking Away: Phenomenality and Dissatisfaction, Kant to Adorno*. Cambridge, MA: Harvard University Press.

———. *Metaracial: Hegel, Antiblackness, & Political Identity*. Chicago: University of Chicago Press, 2023.

Tomlins, Christopher. *Freedom Bound*. Cambridge: Cambridge University Press, 2010.

Tomšič, Samo. *The Capitalist Unconscious: Marx and Lacan*. London: Verso, 2015.

"Torkwase Dyson." Pace Gallery. Accessed November 25, 2025. https://www.pacegallery.com/artists/torkwase-dyson/.

Toscano, Alberto. "The Open Secret of Real Abstraction." In *In the Mind but Not from There: Real Abstraction and Contemporary Art*, edited by Gene Moreno, 17–41. London: Verso, 2019.

Vásquez, Delio. "Illegalist Foucault, Criminal Foucault." *Theory & Event* 23, no. 4 (2020): 935–972.

Vismann, Cornelia. *Files: Law and Media Technology*. Translated by Geoffrey Winthrop-Young. Stanford, CA: Stanford University Press, 2008.

Waldrep, Christopher. *The Many Faces of Judge Lynch: Extralegal Violence and Punishment in America*. New York: Palgrave Macmillan, 2002.

———. "Word and Deed: The Language of Lynching, 1820–1953." In *Lethal Imagination: Violence and Brutality in American History*, edited by Michael A. Bellesiles, 229–258. New York: New York University Press, 1999.

Wang, Jackie. *Carceral Capitalism*. South Pasadena, CA: Semiotext(e), 2018.

Warren, Calvin. "Barred Objects: Police Brutality, Black Fetishes, and Perverse Demonstrations." *The Comparatist* 45 (October 2021): 29–40.

———. *Ontological Terror: Blackness, Nihilism, and Emancipation*. Durham, NC: Duke University Press, 2018.

Weheliye, Alexander. *Habeas Viscus: Racializing Assemblages, Biopolitics, and Black Feminist Theories of the Human*. Durham, NC: Duke University Press, 2014.

Weigel, Sigrid. *Grammatology of Images: A History of the A-Visible*. Translated by Chadwick Truscott Smith. New York: Fordham University Press, 2022.

———. *Walter Benjamin: Images, the Creaturely, and the Holy*. Translated by Chadwick Truscott Smith. Stanford, CA: Stanford University Press, 2013.

Wells-Barnett, Ida B. "Lynch Law in America." In *The Light of Truth: Writings of an Anti-Lynching Crusader*, edited by Mia Bay, 394–403. New York: Penguin Books, 2014.

Wheeler, B. Gordon. *Black California: The History of African-Americans in the Golden State*. New York: Hippocrene Books, 1992.

White, Hayden. *The Content of the Form: Narrative Discourse and Historical Representation*. Baltimore: Johns Hopkins University Press, 1987.

———. "History as Fulfillment." In *Philosophy of History After Hayden White*, edited by Robert Doran, 35–45. London: Bloomsbury Press, 2013.

Wilderson III, Frank B. "Afro-Pessimism and the End of Redemption." *The Occupied Times* (2016). https://theoccupiedtimes.org/?p14236.

———. "Gramsci's Black Marx: Whither the Slave in Civil Society?" *Social Identities* 9, no. 2, 2003.

———. *Red, White, and Black: Cinema and the Structure of U.S. Antagonism*. Durham, NC: Duke University Press, 2010.

———. "The Vengeance of Vertigo: Aphasia and Abjection in the Political Trials of Black Insurgents." *InTensions Journal* 5 (2011): 1–41.

Williams, Patricia. "A Rare Case Study of Muleheadedness and Men." In *Race-ing Justice, En-gendering Power: Essays on Anita Hill, Clarence Thomas, and the Construction of Social Reality*, edited by Toni Morrison, 159–205. New York: Pantheon Books, 1992.

Winnicott, D. W. "Psycho-Analysis and the Sense of Guilt." In *The Maturational Processes and the Facilitation Environment: Studies in the Theory of Emotional Development*, edited by M. Msaud and R. Khan, 15–28. London: Hogarth Press and the Institute of Psycho-Analysis, 1965.

Wood, Amy. *Lynching and Spectacle: Witnessing Racial Violence in America, 1890–1940*. Chapel Hill: University of North Carolina Press, 2009.

Woodward, Vincent. *The Delectable Negro: Human Consumption and Homoeroticism within US Slave Culture*. Edited by Justin A. Joyce and Dwight A. McBride. New York: New York University Press, 2014.

Žižek, Slavoj. *Incontinence of the Void: Economico-Philosophical Spandrels*. Cambridge, MA: MIT Press, 2017.

———. *The Sublime Object of Ideology*. London: Verso, 1989.

———. *Violence*. New York: Picador, 2008.

Zupančič, Alenka. *Ethics of the Real: Kant and Lacan*. London: Verso, 2001, 2011.

———. *Why Psychoanalysis?: Three Interventions*. Aarhus, Denmark: NSU Summertalk, 2008.

Index

Inventions Black Philosophy, Politics, Aesthetics

Edited by David Marriott

Le véritable saut consiste à introduire l'invention dans l'existence—the real leap consists in introducing invention into existence. Among this and other demands for a thought, a blackness of thought that is itself an act of liberation, for Frantz Fanon, the critical task of any aspirational black philosophy is its ability to tell apart blackness from its mirages and impossibilities in science, art, and European history and philosophy. Is it still possible to pursue this goal today, within the ongoing reaches of anti-blackness? And what could this "leap" be, given the undecidability of blackness as a concept, feeling, or figure? The premise of the series is that blackness cannot be subsumed under the prevailing forms of philosophy, politics, or aesthetics without putting into question what this leap could be, or mistaking invention for their presuppositions, and so losing sight of what this invention could be *in its very difference*. To that end, *Inventions* seeks to publish works that set the agenda for what this leap would look like or be.

Engendering Blackness Slavery and the Ontology of Sexual Violence
Patrice D. Douglass

Anteaesthetics Black Aesthesis and the Critique of Form
Rizvana Bradley

Of Effacement Blackness and Non-Being
David Marriott

Printed and bound by CPI Group (UK) Ltd, Croydon, CR0 4YY
16/09/2026
14963946-0004